HOLLYWOOD GOTHIC

BOOKS BY DAVID J. SKAL

Novels

SCAVENGERS

WHEN WE WERE GOOD

ANTIBODIES

Non-Fiction

HOLLYWOOD GOTHIC

*Frontispiece: the three weird sisters stand
guard at the castle in Universal's 1931
film version of* Dracula. *(Photofest)*

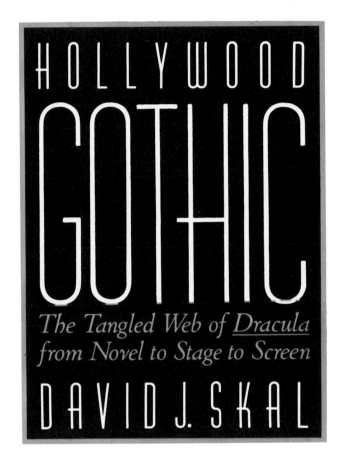

HOLLYWOOD
GOTHIC

*The Tangled Web of Dracula
from Novel to Stage to Screen*

DAVID J. SKAL

W.W. NORTON & COMPANY

NEW YORK · LONDON

The text of this book is composed in Cloister Roman with the display set in Huxley Vertical Bold.

Composition by the Sarabande Press, New York, and Solotype, Oakland, California.

Manufactured by Murray Printing Company, Westford, Massachusetts.

Designed by the author.

FIRST EDITION

Library of Congress cataloging-in-Publication Data

Skal, David J.
Hollywood gothic: the tangled web of Dracula from novel to
stage to screen / by David J. Skal

p.   cm.
Includes bibliographical references and index.
1. Stoker, Bram, 1847–1912. Dracula. 2. Stoker, Bram, 1847–1912—Adaptations.
3. Stoker, Bram, 1847–1912—Film and video adaptations.
4. Horror tales, English—History and criticism. 5. Vampire films—history and criticism.
8. Dracula, Count (Fictitious character) 7. Vampires in literature. I. Title.
PR6037.T6170787 1990
823′.8—dc20

ISBN 0-393-02904-2

W.W. Norton & Company, Inc., 500 Fifth Avenue, New York, N.Y. 10110
W.W. Norton & Company, Ltd., 10 Coptic Street, London WC1A 1PU

1 2 3 4 5 6 7 8 9 0

CONTENTS

"Don't have any picture shows here, except Jesus ones in the courthouse sometimes," said Jem. "Ever seen anything good?"

Dill had seen *Dracula,* a revelation that moved Jem to eye him with the beginning of respect. "Tell it to us," he said.

Harper Lee, *To Kill a Mockingbird*

Introduction

CASTLES, COBWEBS AND CANDELABRA

◆

*In which the reader draws nearer to a modern myth,
shuddering in delicious anticipation, and discovers
the Count to be a closer relation than previously
imagined, not reflected in mirrors, but lurking in them
all the same.*

THE IMAGE, OF COURSE, IS IN BLACK AND WHITE.

A woman—blonde, platinum-bobbed, her face framed by a satin pillowcase—succumbs to sleep, and more. As her eyes close, looking inward upon a dream, a mist swirls outside her open window, and within its gray depths, like an obscene, winged metronome, a huge bat hovers, eyes blazing. The camera's gaze—our gaze—returns to the dreaming girl, then slowly pulls back to reveal the black-cloaked figure that has replaced the flapping bat at the window. It moves forward silently, with the cold deliberation of a panther . . . we have been here before, we know what this is . . . the lamp at the bedside throws the features into sharp relief. The talonlike fingers make indentations on the pillow. The dark lips part, revealing a deeper darkness still. The sleeper's neck is white as radium . . .

The scene is instantly recognizable to almost everyone in the late twentieth century as a pivotal scene from *Dracula.* We may not be able to identify the exact version of the film, or even the performers involved, but the primal image of the black-caped vampire has become an indelible fixture of the modern imagination. Its recognition factor probably rivals, in its own perverse way, the familiarity of Santa Claus.

Without knowing anything of the myth's origins, most of us can recite without prompting the salient characteristics of the vampire—how it sleeps by

"Children of the night — what music they make!" Bela Lugosi performs a disappearing act in this trick publicity shot from the 1931 Dracula. (Photofest)

day, rising from its coffin-bed at dusk to feed on the blood of the living; its ability to take the form of a bat, a wolf, or mist; how it can be destroyed by a stake driven through its heart, and effectively repelled by garlic, wolfbane, the crucifix, or the power of the Eucharist. We have received this information by a curious cultural transfusion, not by direct experience ... and yet on some psychological level it must reflect some kind of universal knowledge, however veiled or obscure.

Ever adaptable, Dracula has been a literary Victorian sex nightmare, a stock figure of theatrical melodrama, a movie icon, a trademark, cuddle toy, swizzle stick, and breakfast cereal. Complex, contradictory, and confounding, Dracula tantalizingly begs the question put to the ghost in *Hamlet:* "Be thou a spirit of health or goblin damned."[1]

The appeal of Dracula is decidedly ambiguous. The emphatic white tie and black cape, so striking at first glance, rapidly yield endless shades of gray. Most monsters take and trample. Dracula alone seduces, courting before he kills. Unlike other monsters, he is not always recognizable as such. Dracula looks too much like one of us. With patent-leather shoes and patent-leather hair, he mocks our concepts of civility and society, uses them as brazen camouflage, the better to stalk us, his readers, his film audiences, his prey.

Dracula didn't begin in Hollywood, but it traveled there with an inexorable momentum. The film medium itself had its origins in the trappings of the occult. The magic lantern salons of Paris in the late 1700s projected bat-winged demons on clouds of smoke to terrify and entertain the ancestors of the modern motion picture audience. Even today we still speak of the "magic" of the movies, as if despite our sophistication about special effects we cannot dismiss what we see on the screen as just a set of tricks. Maxim Gorky, writing on the introduction of Lumière's Cinematographe in Moscow in 1896, the year before *Dracula*'s publication, was deeply disturbed by what he beheld. To Gorky, cinema itself was a technological vampire that promised a kind of living death. "Your nerves are strained, imagination carries you to some unnaturally monotonous life, a life without color and without sound, but full of movement, the life of ghosts, or of people, *damned* to the damnation of eternal silence, people who have been deprived of all the colors of life."[2]

Bram Stoker himself seems to have had certain ambitions for *Dracula* as a theatrical entertainment, though a successful stage adaptation would not be realized until after his death. But *Dracula* and vampire stories in general have found their greatest expression in the popular media, be they penny-dreadful novels, stage melodramas, or movies. *Dracula* has been a hallmark of the motion picture from the early days of German expressionism. The character has been depicted in film more times than almost any fictional being, with the single possible exception of Sherlock Holmes, and has now so pervaded the

Frank Langella in the 1977 Broadway revival, with sets and costumes by Edward Gorey. (Photo courtesy of the estate of Kenn Duncan, ©1977)

Bat-winged demons were among the
earliest projected images to entertain the
public, forging a prototypical link between
film and the fantastic. Above, the
Fantasmagorie *as it was seen in Paris
circa 1797. (Collection of the
Cinémathèque Française)*

The vampire as movie usher: a
contemporary metaphor in a Cuban film
poster. (Courtesy of the Cinemateca de
Cuba)

world of communications and advertising that it is no longer necessary to read the novel or see one of its film adaptations to be thoroughly acquainted with the Count and his exploits.

This is not the first book written on the subject of *Dracula,* and it will not be the last. But most treatments to date have largely ignored the fascinating history, now nearly a century old, of the men and women whose lives have become entangled in the myth's peculiar power. *Dracula* has exerted an irresistible, and at times, Faustian attraction upon numerous individuals who used the ever-expanding dream-machinery of publishing, theatre, and film to exploit the story's power and expand its influence.

This book is also, without apology, eclectic and interdisciplinary, mixing the historical record with the author's own observations on culture and psychology. A completely straightforward academic history would simply not do the subject matter justice; the *Dracula* legend rudely refuses to observe conventional parameters of discussion, and touches upon areas as disparate as Romantic literature and modern marketing research, Victorian sexual mores and the politics of the Hollywood studio system.

Whatever else it might be, *Dracula* is certainly one of the most obsessional texts of all time, a black hole of the imagination. The story seems to get younger with age, drawing vitality from its longevity, and attracting an ever-widening public. Originally scorned by the critics, the book has nonetheless remained in print for nearly a hundred years, and in the last decade has begun to attract the serious notice of academics as a significant, if problematic, Victorian text. As the 1997 *Dracula* centenary approaches, there will no doubt be even more books, revivals, and reappraisals.

The Hollywood of *Hollywood Gothic* is less the geographical location than the psychic shadow-land we all inhabit to one extent or another, the private theatre to which we return again and again to watch the midnight movies of our minds.

For quite some time now, *Dracula* has been the perennial blockbuster attraction.

I felt doubts and fears crowding upon me. What sort of place
had I come to - and amongst what kind of people. What sort
of grim adventure was it on which I had embarked ? I began
to rub my eyes and prick myself to see if I were awake. It
all seemed like a horrible nightmare to me, and I expected
that I should suddenly awake, and find myself at home with
the dawn struggling in through the windows, as I had now and
again felt in the morning after a day of overwork. But my
flesh answered the pinching test and my eyes were not to be
deceived. I was indeed awake and among the Carpathians.
~~and~~ ~~as I knew~~ ~~miles away from any human being on~~
~~the man who had caught me here.~~ All I could do now was
to be patient, and to wait ~~if necessary~~ the coming of the morning.

Just as I had come to this conclusion I heard a heavy
step approaching beyond the great door, and saw through the
chinks the gleam of a coming light. ~~I do not think I was ever~~
~~startled to see anything in my life for the sense of loneli-~~
~~ness in few was sweeping irresistible.~~ Then there was the
sound of rattling chains and the clanking of massive bolts
drawn back. A key was turned with a loud grating noise of la
long disuse, and the great door swung back.

Within stood a tall old man, clean shaven save for a long
white moustache, and clad in black from head to foot without
a single speck of white about him anywhere. He held in his
hand an antique silver lamp in which the flame burned without
chimney or globe of any kind, and which threw long quivering

[left margin, handwritten:] Was this a customary incident in the life of a solicitor's clerk ? Sent out to explain the purchase an estate to a foreigner ? Solicitor's clerk ! Mina would not like it to a Solicitor, for just before leaving London I got word that my examination was successful. and I am now a full-blown solicitor !

Chapter One

MR. STOKER'S
BOOK OF BLOOD

—— ◆ ——

*In which a theatre manager pens a tale of surpassing terror,
reviving a Gothic tradition, while indirectly addressing
unspoken tensions between the sexes. An ambiguous
portrait, in the manner of Mr. Wilde, of a celebrated knight and
actor, who is not amused. The unexpected appearance of
Mr. Wilde himself, old rivalries and new revelations,
an inattentive wife, and a lingering malady.*

——————————— ———————————

IN THE RARE BOOKS ROOM OF A SMALL LIBRARY[1] ON A TREE-LINED street in Philadelphia is a leather slipcase containing a sheaf of mounted note cards, almost a century old but not yellowing—they are an exceptionally high grade of linen stock, the property of Henry Irving's prestigious Royal Lyceum Theatre in London. The notes contained on them do not pertain to the theatre, and are addressed to no one other than the writer himself. The culmination of years of obsessional research and rumination, the working notes of an author of fiction, they are written in a tiny, often nearly indecipherable pencil scrawl, as if the writer had miniaturized his hand to complement the dimensions of his paper. A psychiatrist, the visitor is told, has spent nearly ten years transcribing, annotating, and interpreting their contents. The frequent cross-outs and marginal additions, trailing-off sentences and one-word reminders vividly depict the fictional process—the writer intuitively steering his unconscious through the refinement of language, discovering the incantatory words and patterns of words that can best describe the troubling image and give it a form in the world.

The first page, headed *Historiae Personae*, lists seventeen embryonic fictional characters. Several names are unfamiliar: Kate Reed, a young English-

Manuscript page from The Undead, *later titled* Dracula, *introducing* The Count *and demonstrating Stoker's technique of composition. (Courtesy of John McLaughlin, The Book Sail, Orange, California)*

woman; Cotford, a detective; a "psychical research agent" known as Alfred Singleton; a German professor, Max Windshoeffel; an "American inventor from Texas" (discarded in favor of "A Texan—Brutus M. Marix"); a deaf-mute woman and "a silent man," servants to a mysterious Eastern European count. Other names and characters ring more familiar. Dr. Seward. Lucy Westenra. Wilhelmina Murray. Jonathan Harker. A mad patient ("theory of getting life," one entry says). And very nearly at the center of the page, the author has scrawled the name of his pivotal character: *Count Wampyr.* He let it stand for an indeterminate period of time. Somehow, it didn't work. Perhaps it was too . . . obvious? He consulted his typewritten notes. He had recorded the Rumanian words for Satan and hell, and perhaps considered the possibilities there. Count *Ordog*? Count *Pokol*? No, there had to be better. Yes, elsewhere in his notes—something. He struck out the old name and inked in a Wallachian diminutive for "devil," till then unheard in England:

Dracula.

Did it sound right?

He wrote the name again at the top of the page, twice, flanking the original heading. *Dracula. Dracula.*

Yes.

One final time, then, in the top left corner, boldly underscored:

COUNT DRACULA.

Bram Stoker's 1897 novel *Dracula* presents one of the most intriguing puzzles in literary history, a book that has attained the status of a minor classic on the basis of its stubborn longevity and disturbing psychological resonance more than on technical or narrative achievement. Stoker was not an innovator or a stylist of any distinction—even his most partisan critics cannot avoid the word "hack" in connection with his minor works—and yet *Dracula* remains among the most widely read novels of the late nineteenth century. It has never been out of print. Its theatrical and film adaptations are among the most indelible and influential of the twentieth century, and the *Dracula* legacy will no doubt continue into the twenty-first.

A span of centuries is no mean feat for an icon of popular culture, especially for one consistently ignored or denigrated by the "respectable" critical authorities. Stoker's name does not appear in most textbooks of Victorian literature, the stage version is almost never mentioned in theatre surveys (although it enjoyed a popularity in the 1920s rivaling *Uncle Tom's Cabin* and *Abie's Irish Rose*), and the landmark 1931 film version is usually sidestepped in most film histories. Only through the pirated German silent *Nosferatu* has *Dracula* achieved a quasi-respectable niche in modern art circles, and that only in retrospect.

Yet *Dracula* persists. In the words of Dr. Abraham Van Helsing in the

Bram Stoker. (Billy Rose Theatre Collection, New York Public Library at Lincoln Center, Astor, Lenox and Tilden Foundations)

Count Dracula.

Dracula **Historiae Personae** Dracula

- Doctor of mad house ~~Ash~~ y Seward
  Girl engaged to him Lucy Westenra Schoolfellow of Miss Murray
- Mad Patient (theory of getting life – instinctively goes for count & follows up idea with mad cunning.
- Lawer ~~Arthur Abbott John~~ Peter Hawkins Exeter.
- His clerk ——— Jonathan Harker
- Fiancee of above pupil teacher Wilhelmina Murray (called Mina)
  ~~lawyer Ding-ray~~
  ~~advocate~~
- ~~Undertaker's man~~ Kate Reed
  Friend of schoolfellow of above ———
  The Count ——— Count ~~Wampyr~~ Dracula
  A Deaf Mute woman ⎫ servants of
  A Silent Man ⎭ the Count
- A Detective ———————— Cotford
- A Psychical Research agent ——— Alfred Singleton
- ~~An American inventor from Texas~~
- A German Professor ——— Max Windshoeffel
- A Painter ——— Francis Aytown
- a Texan ——— Brutus M. Maris

notes diner of 13   new
    secret room ———

Bram Stoker's working notes for Dracula *reveal a plot and characters quite different than those that emerged in the finished book. (The Rosenbach Museum & Library, Philadelphia)*

stage and movie versions, "The strength of the vampire is that people will not believe in him." In the words of Dracula himself, in Stoker's novel, "You think to baffle me, you—with your pale faces all in a row, like sheep in a butcher's. You shall be sorry yet, each one of you! You think you have left me without a place to rest; but I have more. My revenge has just begun! I spread it over centuries, and time is on my side."[2]

He might as well have been addressing his critics as any fictional enemies.

Superstitions about the restless dead who return to drink the blood of the living are as old as recorded civilization. At its most primitive level, the vampire myth is connected to cannibalism, and to the corollary belief that the devouring of body and blood also imparts a transference of the victim's strength, courage, or other attributes. Mysterious wasting plagues, catalepsy, and premature burial also contributed to the myth, fostering prescientific explanations for frightening biological phenomena. Modern psychoanalytic theory on the subject, as classically argued by Ernest Jones in *On the Nightmare*,[3] finds the genesis of vampire legend in the universal experience of the nightmare, and its interpretation by early man as a literal visitation by a life-draining demon. From the psychoanalytic viewpoint, the suppression of sexual feeling by social or institutional strictures gave rise to the popular belief in the incubus or succubus, male and female spirits believed to have sexual relations with sleeping victims. Outbreaks of incubation, reported as matter-of-factly as if they were medical plagues rather than psychosexual delusions, were widespread in cloisters from the Middle Ages onward.[4]

Like the incubus, the vampire is a spectre that frequently rises at the boundaries of social, religious, and sexual conformity. Excommunicants, it was long believed, could expect to return from death with a terrible thirst. Illegitimacy, incest, and homosexuality have long had implicit and explicit links to the vampire in legend and literature. The Rumanian *Nosferat* was believed to be the result of an illegitimate birth to parents who were themselves illegitimate.[5] Legends involving the return of dead relatives have been observed to contain distinct undertones of incestuous guilt.[6] And the bisexuality and homosexuality of vampires has, by the late twentieth century, become a virtual *donnée;* the modern image of the female vampire especially is almost always tinted by lesbianism (the concept is so accepted and ingrained that, at the time of this writing, the longest-running comedy on the New York stage is entitled *Vampire Lesbians of Sodom*). It is probably significant that the diatribes of modern-day crusaders against sexual minorities, with their fearful fantasies of seduction, transformation, and unholy corruption, find a distinct parallel in antique tracts on the exorcism of vampires. When the definitive anthropological history of the AIDS epidemic is finally written, the irrational, vampire-related undercurrents of scapegoating, blood superstition, and plague panic

George Gordon, Lord Byron.
(The Bettmann Archive)

will no doubt be prominent considerations.

Prior to the Romantic revolution of the early 1800s, the popular image of the vampire was that of walking, predatory carrion. Byron, whose mystique would leave an indelible, transforming mark on the evolution of the vampire image, first dealt with the subject in a curse contained in his poem "The Giaour" (1813):

> But first on earth, as Vampyre sent,
> Thy corse shall from its tomb be rent;
> Then ghastly haunt thy native place,
> And suck the blood of all thy race;
> There from thy daughter, sister, wife,
> At midnight drain the stream of life;
> Yet loathe the banquet, which perforce
> Must feed thy livid, living corse,
> Thy victims, ere they yet expire,
> Shall know the demon for their sire;
> As cursing thee, thou cursing them,
> Thy flowers are withered on the stem.

Byron implies a tragic, ambivalent dimension to vampirism that was hitherto unknown, but which would exert a major influence on future writers. The author himself was the model for an autobiographical novel by Lady Caroline Lamb, *Glenarvon* (1816), in which she depicted Byron as a libertine, Ruthven Glenarvon, fatal to women, who is finally carried away by supernatural forces.[7]

A close friend of Byron's, Dr. John Polidori, did Lamb one better by borrowing the *nom de clef* for his own Romantic thriller. In 1819, Polidori's novella *The Vampyre* first introduced many of the now-familiar Byronic trappings—on its first publication, in fact, authorship was mistakenly attributed to Byron (Goethe, who had dealt with Illyrian vampire legends in his *Bride of Corinth* in 1797, was completely taken in, and called *The Vampyre* Byron's finest work.)[8] The story concerns Lord Ruthven, a libertine in the Byronic mode. Killed in Greece and returned to London as a vampire, he relentlessly stalks the sister of his former friend, Aubrey. The friend is restrained by a solemn oath made to Ruthven before his death not to reveal his preternatural state, and watches horrified as Ruthven pursues, seduces, marries, and kills his sister. While the blood-drinking is more metaphorical than explicit, the story provided a narrative blueprint for all the major vampire sagas that were to follow. Significantly, the story was a product of the celebrated literary house party that also inspired Mary Shelley to write *Frankenstein*; as we will see, the Frankenstein and Dracula images have been linked in imagination and commerce ever since.

Dr. John Polidori. Under Byron's influence, he created the first Romantic vampire in literature. (Courtesy of Philip J. Riley)

While it was well-known in literary circles that Polidori was the author, Byron's was the bankable name (his scandalous love affairs were then the sensation of Europe), and the story was attributed to him in numerous editions and translations and even in collections of his work.[9]

In Paris, where the projected magic lantern demons of the *Fantasmagorie* had thrilled the public at the turn of the previous century, the theatrical possibilities of Polidori's tale were quickly grasped. Charles Nodier, under whose aegis an unauthorized sequel, *Lord Ruthwen ou les Vampires,*[10] by Cyprien Bérard, had been published in February 1820, collaborated with Achille Jouffroy and Carmouche on the first vampire stage melodrama, *Le Vampire,* presented at the Théâtre Porte-Saint-Martin in June of the same year. The production was reportedly thrilling, controversial—and an immense success.[11] The public appetite for vampire dramas prompted a veritable stampede of imitations. According to Montague Summers, vampire chronicler extraordinaire, "Immediately upon the furore [*sic*] created by Nodier's *Le Vampire* . . . vampire plays of every kind from the most luridly sensational to the most farcically ridiculous pressed on to the boards. A contemporary critic cries: 'There is not a theatre in Paris without its Vampire! At the Porte-Saint-Martin we have *Le Vampire*; at the Vaudeville *Le Vampire* again; at the Varietes *Les trois Vampires ou le clair de la lune.*'"[12] Other Parisian stage vampires of 1820 were seen in *Encore un Vampire, Les Étrennes d'un Vampire,* and *Cadet Buteux, vampire* (the published libretto carried the motto: "*Vivent les morts!*").[13]

Readers of Anne Rice's recent best-seller *The Vampire Lestat*[14] will no doubt recognize in this real-life vampire fever Rice's inspiration for her Théâtre des Vampires of the same period (Rice's actors, however, are true vampires, who share a Romantic sensibility that could put Byron to shame). *The Vampire Lestat,* steeped in French art and culture, illustrates the major contribution of the French sensibility, and the city of Paris in particular, to the development of the modern vampire image. Paris in the days before the grand boulevards and gaslight was a dangerous place full of narrow streets, menace, and shadows. At night, fearful pedestrians carried torches. After sunset, even the open expanses of the Champs Élysées and the Luxembourg Gardens "were concealed by an almost impenetrable darkness."[15] Such was the Paris whose citizenry would respond en masse to the new, consummate theatre of shadows, the vampire melodrama.

Alexandre Dumas *père*, on his first night as a citizen of Paris in 1823, decided to attend a revival of *Le Vampire* at the Porte-Saint-Martin. Obtaining admission was not a simple matter, but the young Dumas, fresh from the provinces, was determined; seeing *Le Vampire* became a ritual of cosmopolitan validation. On his first attempt he was ejected from the raucous pit in an altercation with Frenchmen who took exception to the mulatto curl of his hair.

Cover illustration for Varney the Vampyre. *Note the variant spelling of the word, which was used interchangeably throughout the nineteenth century, and eventually became standardized.*

Nonetheless, *Le Vampire* intrigued Dumas, and he tried again, this time buying an orchestra ticket. He was seated without incident, and enthralled by the play. However, a certain strange gentleman beside him was vocally and unremittingly critical of the proceedings. According to Dumas' biographer Herbert Gorman, "He groaned, made audible remarks of the most caustic nature, was angrily hissed by his neighbors." In time the gentleman created a scene and was ejected from the theatre. Dumas learned later that the gentleman was one of the play's authors, Charles Nodier himself.[16]

Dumas' life and adventures in Paris were to be framed by the story of the vampire Lord Ruthven; nearly thirty years later, his own elaborate adaptation of the Polidori tale would be his final offering under his own name to the Paris stage.[17]

Meanwhile, the French play had been adapted into English by James Robinson Planché as *The Vampire, or, The Bride of the Isles* and presented to packed houses in August 1820 at the English Opera House, later to be called the Lyceum. To please the management, the author adapted the story to a Scottish setting, with bagpipes and kilts, though the vampire legend was not indigenous to Scotland. Planché would have preferred an Eastern European setting, but the management had a full complement of Scottish costumes in stock and was determined to use them. The production employed a special trapdoor to permit the sudden disappearance of the vampire in plain view of the audience; this innovative device—actually called a "vampire" in theatrical parlance—was destined for an appropriate revival a century later in dramatizations of *Dracula*.[18]

On March 28, 1828, an operatic adaptation of the Nodier play, entitled *Der Vampyr* and setting the story in Hungary, was produced at Leipzig, with libretto by Wilhelm August Wohlbruck and music by Heinrich August Marschner. (A record of an earlier, unrelated opera, *il vampiri* by Neapolitan composer Silvestro di Palma, notes its production in Italy in 1800.) James Robinson Planche made a free English adaptation of the Marschner work in 1829, which was produced at the Lyceum. Ruthven's nationality had changed yet again; this time he was a Wallachian boyard.[19]

Dion Boucicault's *The Vampire* (1852), another Polidori-inspired drama, had three acts set in three centuries, including the future, and so must qualify as an early attempt at science fiction as well as horror. One notably harsh London critic savaged the effort, stating that he had no objection to "an honest ghost" but "an animated corpse which goes about in Christian attire, and although never known to eat, or drink, or shake hands, is allowed to sit at good men's feasts; which renews its odious life every hundred years by sucking a young lady's blood, after fascinating her by motions which resemble mesmerism burlesqued . . . such a ghost as this passes all bounds of toleration."[20] *The*

Lord Varney prepares for his hideous repast. Illustration from Varney the Vampyre *(1847).*

Vampire was nonetheless successful and, revived under the title *The Phantom*, had the distinction of being the first vampire play exported from England to America, with Boucicault reprising the lead role.[21]

The vampire in prose received a tranfusion of energy with the appearance in 1847 of James Malcolm Rymer's *Varney the Vampyre: or, The Feast of Blood*. Subtitled "A Romance of Exciting Interest," this overheated 900-page "penny dreadful," originally sold in installments, is almost the definition of hack writing. Stuffed with rambling purple prose and weirdly shifting tenses (the present-tense passages oddly anticipate the diction of a screenplay treatment), even today it retains an odd, campy fascination. The plot is endlessly convoluted, the scenes and dialogue padded for length, as Sir Francis Varney leaves a trail of blood and verbiage in his wake, only to call off the proceedings abruptly by leaping into the cauldron of Mount Vesuvius. A far cry from literature, the work served to reinforce the popular image of the bloodsucking fiend who scrabbled at the bedroom windows of virtuous Victorian virgins. And its major motifs, notably the plot element of a vampiric Eastern European nobleman arriving in England by way of a shipwreck in a storm, foreshadowed much that was to come.

The publication of *Varney the Vampyre* coincided with another milestone in vampire literature: the birth in Dublin of Abraham Stoker.

Born in Dublin in November 1847, Bram Stoker began life as a sickly child and persisted in an invalid state, never walking until the age of seven.[22] Psychoanalytic commentators have made much of the possible effect of this prolonged illness on his imagination and his writing, but only a few have questioned whether the illness itself was psychological. Considering the robust athleticism of Stoker's later years, recorded in his own memoirs and in the accounts of others, the sudden disappearance of a crippling congenital condition with no lasting effects seems odd indeed. The episode brings to mind case histories of children who, for traumatic reasons, refuse to speak, or of "hysterical" paralysis and blindness in adults. Could Bram the boy have acted out a conflict in a dramatic, psychosomatic fashion? A child barely out of infancy, after all, cannot write horror novels to sublimate his terrors. It may be worth noting that as Bram reached school age and discovered books, his "paralysis" vanished. "I was naturally thoughtful," he wrote in 1906, "and the leisure of long illness gave opportunity for many thoughts which were fruitful according to their kind in later years."[23]

One piece of writing that captured his imagination as a young man was Joseph Sheridan Le Fanu's elegant novella *Carmilla* (1871), in which tasteful lesbianism became part of the literary vampire stew. Le Fanu, another Dubliner whose highly crafted ghost stories would likely also have been well-known by Stoker, tells a dreamlike story in which childhood memories, vampirism, and same-sex love unfold with the surreal logic of a fairy tale. Laura, a young woman living in a kind of storybook castle in a land called Styria, narrates the story. She has a strange memory from early childhood of a night visitation by a beautiful girl, carrying a distinct flavor of vampirism to the reader if not the teller. Years later, the girl appears to her again in the form of Carmilla, a mysterious young lady who joins her household under a cloud of secrecy and intrigue. Carmilla remembers the same dream. The two young women form a powerful bond: "Sometimes after an hour of apathy, my strange and beautiful companion would take my hand and hold it with a fond pressure, renewed again and again; blushing softly, gazing in my face with languid and burning eyes, and breathing so fast that her dress rose and fell with the tumultuous respiration. It was like the ardor of a lover; it embarrassed me; it was hateful and yet overpowering; and with gloating eyes she drew me to her, and her hot lips travelled along my cheek in kisses; and she would whisper, almost in sobs, 'You are mine, you *shall* be mine, and you and I are one for ever.'"[24]

Le Fanu's hypnotic cadences elevate *Carmilla* to something approaching a prose poem, and it is without question one of the most distinguished and influential pieces of vampire literature in English. The narrator gradually discovers Carmilla Karnstein's identity as a vampire in a narrative in which identity itself becomes blurred and ambiguous. There is a strong undercurrent of the doppelgänger in the story, and the poignant irony that Carmilla (who, we learn, is also known variously as Marcilla and Millarca) is herself victim as well as predator.

It is not known precisely when Stoker encountered *Carmilla*; his biographers and critics alike seem to take the matter on faith, based on the story's eventual echoes in *Dracula*. His initial attempts at writing weird fiction must have roughly coincided with Le Fanu's popularity in the early 1870s; Stoker's first horror story, a four-part serial called "The Chain of Destiny," was published in 1875. The young man's interests and activities were wide; at Trinity he excelled athletically and academically. From an early age, Stoker was drawn to the exaggerated reality of the debating team and the theatre, to

J. Sheridan Le Fanu.
(Courtesy of Philip J. Riley)

The vampire at the window:
archetypal penny-dreadful dread.
From Varney the Vampyre.

literature and to individuals who embodied dramatic, archetypal qualities. He positively worshipped Walt Whitman, defending the poet at the height of the controversy over *Leaves of Grass* and writing him long, emotionally revealing letters. At the age of twenty-four, Stoker articulated to his American hero a radical yearning for fusion transcending convention and gender: "How sweet a thing it is for a strong healthy man," Stoker wrote, describing himself, "with a woman's eyes and a child's wishes to feel that he can speak so to a man who can be if he wishes father and brother and wife to his soul." At the same time, Stoker assured Whitman—or perhaps reassured himself—that he was basically "conservative."[25] Whitman responded, and they eventually met.[26]

But the most significant relationship of Stoker's life—indeed, most commentators agree that it eclipsed even his marriage—was his friendship with the celebrated actor Henry Irving, whom he served as manager and confidante for nearly thirty years. In 1876 Stoker was working as a civil servant in Dublin, but also contributing unpaid theatre reviews to the *Dublin Mail*. His glowing appraisals of the Shakespearean actor Henry Irving, who felt he was unappreciated in Ireland, finally prompted the celebrated thespian to request an introduction. After their second dinner together, Irving recited a grisly dramatic monologue, "The Dream of Eugene Aram," in which a murderer is overcome by guilt and the fear of God. Following the recitation, Irving himself collapsed into a chair. "Art can do much," Stoker wrote in retrospect, "but in all things even in art there is a summit somewhere. That night for a brief time in which the rest of the world seemed to sit still, Irving's genius floated in blazing triumph above the summit of art."[27] As for Stoker himself, "I burst into something like hysterics."[28]

Irving was deeply impressed ("Soul had looked into soul!" wrote Stoker. "From that hour began a friendship as profound, as close, as lasting as can be between two men"[29]) and a few seasons thereafter claimed the young man as his own, at least professionally. Stoker assumed the acting managership of Irving's new venture, London's Lyceum Theatre, in December 1878, to the dismay of his practical family, who disapproved of his theatrical interests and of theatrical people. But to Stoker, Irving and the Lyceum became a passion—so much so that his appointment actually preempted his honeymoon.[30] Later, it would become almost a cliché among his chroniclers that Stoker's "real" marriage was to Irving and not to his bride, the beautiful Florence Balcombe from Dublin's seaside suburb, Clontarf, where Stoker himself was born.

Stoker's responsibilities at the Lyceum were both heady and overwhelming. He oversaw the artistic and administrative aspects of the new theatre, and acted as Irving's buffer, goodwill ambassador, and hatchet man. He learned the pleasures of snobbery. Author Horace Wyndham, one of Stoker's few acquaintances who later published his impressions, recalled in 1923, "To see Stoker in his element was to see him standing at the top of the theatre's stairs, surveying a 'first night' crowd trooping up them. There was no mistake about it—a Lyceum *première* did draw an audience that really was representative of the best of that period in the realms of art, literature and society. Admittance was a very jealously guarded privilege. Stoker, indeed, looked upon the stalls, dress circle and boxes as if they were annexes to the Royal Enclosure at Ascot, and one almost had to be proposed and seconded before the coveted ticket would be issued."[31]

Stoker accompanied Irving on his many tours to America and made scouting expeditions to plan the same. It should be noted that his dedication to Irving was not without compensation; Stoker was paid rather handsomely out of the Lyceum coffers. Records of the 1893–94 American tour showed that he drew a weekly salary of $1,694, or approximately £350, a more than comfortable wage for the time.[32]

The Stokers acquired a fashionable house on one of the most fashionable streets in Chelsea, Cheyne Walk, where their neighbors and guests included the likes of James McNeill Whistler, John Singer Sargent, Dante Gabriel Rossetti, W. S. Gilbert, Mark Twain, and Alfred, Lord Tennyson (to whom he would in time inscribe a copy of *Dracula*).

To an outside observer like Horace Wyndham, Stoker's working relation-

BRAM STOKER

A rare photograph of Bram Stoker at work, used to publicize his memoirs of Henry Irving in 1906. (The Billy Rose Theatre Collection, New York Public Library at Lincoln Center, Astor, Lenox and Tilden Foundations)

Bram Stoker created the prototype of Castle Dracula in his book of children's stories, Under the Sunset *(1882). (Courtesy of Jeanne Youngson)*

ship with Henry Irving was less a Whitmanesque union of souls than an unending exercise in institutional politics. According to Wyndham, "Irving — who, despite his general astuteness, was a pretty poor judge of character, and would believe anyone who flattered him sufficiently — surrounded himself with a greedy host of third-rate parasites at the expense of the theatre's not inexhaustible revenues . . .

"Stoker, who had more brains than the entire pack put together, hated the sight of them. He once told me that if he could have made a clean sweep of the lot, the Lyceum treasury would have been saved some thousands a year. Irving, however, would not listen. . . . He thought it enhanced his dignity to be surrounded by a courtier-like crowd of sycophants. As a matter of fact, it merely made people laugh at him."[33]

Almost unbelievably, during this period of relentless professional stress and pressure, Stoker's literary output did not suffer, but increased markedly.

Before *Dracula,* in addition to his short stories, Stoker had already published three books, including the 1879 government handbook *The Duties of the Clerks of Petty Sessions in Ireland,* an Irish adventure novel called *The Snake's Pass* (1890), and, perhaps most prophetically, a disturbing collection of "children's stories" called *Under the Sunset* which appeared in 1882, subsidized, at least in part, by Stoker himself.[34] The writer's decidedly morbid turn of mind is intimated in the dedication of the volume to his three-year-old son, Noel, "whose Angel doth behold the face of THE KING."

The king, as we soon learn from the stories, is the King of Death.

Under the Sunset is full of death and shadows, images of infanticide and plague, and anticipates many of Stoker's later preoccupations in his "adult" novels of horror. One of the collection's strongest stories, "The Castle of the King," concerns the mythic journey of a poet to rescue his wife from a skull-shaped castle in the kingdom of death; love and fatality merge in a single, dreamlike vision.

The theme of the divided self, which would play a prominent role in Stoker's later work, was presented with a vengeance in one of the author's least-known and most bizarre stories, "The Dualitists; or, the Death Doom of the Double Born," published in 1887. Two malicious little boys, Harry and Tommy, find in each other a malignant soul mate and together play an escalating game called "Hack" which begins with the terrorizing of neighborhood girls. "It was a thing of daily occurrence for the little girls to state that when going to bed at night they had laid their dear dollies in their beds with tender care, but . . . when again seeking them in the period of recess they had found them with all their beauty gone, with arms and legs amputated and faces beaten from all semblance of human form."[35]

The boys spend considerable time comparing, rubbing together, and brooding over their respective knives. "So like were the knives that but for the initials scratched in the handles neither boy could not have been sure which was his own."[36] Soon they tire of vandalism and grow bloodthirsty, and take to murdering all the neighborhood's pets, using rabbits and other small bound animals as bludgeons. When all the available fauna have been sacrificed, they turn their interest toward a pair of baby twins, Zachariah and Zerubbabel Bubb ("They are exactly equal! This is the very apotheosis of our art!"[37]). They lure the twins into a fatal game on a stable roof, bloodily beating each with the other. That Stoker's manner of narration is clearly intended to be comic adds another level of horror to the proceedings. When the Bubb parents take a shot at the young killers, they miss and blow the heads off their own children instead. Tommy and Harry gleefully play catch with the headless trunks of the twins and finally hurl them down to their parents, who are killed by the falling corpses. On the boys' testimony, the Bubbs themselves are charged posthumously with infanticide and suicide, and are buried with stakes driven through their bodies. Tommy and Harry, we learn, are precociously knighted.

"The Dualitists" is sadistic and shocking, all the more so for its author's snickeringly evident pleasure in its telling. The story blends raging infantile aggression with highly controlled prose, and implies volumes about the paradoxical dynamics of Stoker's literary imagination on the eve of his magnum opus.

Bram Stoker, as sketched by a newspaper artist during one of Henry Irving's American tours. (Billy Rose Theatre Collection, New York Public Library at Lincoln Center, Astor, Lenox and Tilden Foundations)

Just how early the vampire theme attracted Stoker is not known; the working notes that survive date from 1890. Years later, when *Dracula* would be dramatized in London, press stories stated that Stoker had had the story in mind while still a young man in County Dublin, and discussed its possibilities with one of his "great friends," the young daughter of Colonel Deane, owner of an adjoining estate. Her son, Hamilton, would eventually be responsible for the play's popularization in the theatre.[38]

The story, of course, could be something of an exaggeration, but Stoker was still a Dublin resident at the time of *Carmilla*'s publication in 1871, and *Carmilla* was without question a major influence on *Dracula*. One direct tribute to Le Fanu was Stoker's plan to use the name "Styria" for Dracula's homeland, although he would later drop the name in favor of the more geographically plausible Transylvania. Stoker was also inspired to an extent (and only to an extent) by accounts of the fifteenth-century Wallachian prince Vlad "The Impaler" Tepes, whose ferocious father had earned the sobriquet of *Dracul* or devil. The son, even more bloodthirsty than his progenitor, came to be known as the son of the devil—*Dracula*. But trappings of historicity were only atmosphere in an otherwise completely fictive invention.

Stoker's early working notes for *Dracula* outline a messy potboiler with far too many characters and an overcomplicated plot; at just what point these crystalized into tight, archetypal drama is not precisely known. The *Dracula* notes, with their abundance of overlapping characters, offer one of the few tangible insights into Stoker's working methods and suggest a connection between theme and process: just as his finished work deals time and again with doubles and dualities, so too does his working imagination seem to spontaneously clone, merge, and shuffle fictional identities, as if testing the possibilities. Given Stoker's amazing output—eighteen books in all, most completed during a period of all-consuming professional commitment to the Lyceum Theatre—it is not unreasonable to assume that he worked rapidly, with more feverish inspiration than careful design.

Rumanian postage stamp bearing the portrait of Vlad "The Impaler" Tepes, the "historical" Dracula. (Courtesy of Jeanne Youngson)

Whatever his methods, Stoker finished the manuscript and submitted it to his publisher, Constable, as *The Un-Dead* (his working notes indicate three possible working titles—*Count Dracula*, *The Un-Dead*, and *The Dead Un-Dead*). At some point the title was changed to *Dracula*. It is not known whether this was at Stoker's insistence or the publisher's, but the decision was fortuitous—the one-word title itself, the three sinister syllables that crack and undulate on the tongue, ambiguous, foreign, and somehow alluring, was certainly a component of the book's initial and continued mystique.

The 1984 reappearance on the collector's market of the book's manuscript (long thought to have been lost) proved without question that the book was heavily edited and reworked by the author by typewriter (the invention had

The Stoker residence at the time of Dracula's first publication, St. Leonard's Terrace, Chelsea. (Photographs by the author)

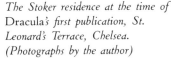

just been introduced), by hand, and by extensive cut-and-paste additions and transpositions. Though none of Stoker's prose could be called undying, the care with which he prepared and polished his chronicle of the un-dead no doubt contributed to its effectiveness and wide popular appeal. Unlike his later, inferior novels, *Dracula* coincided with Stoker's most prosperous years at the Lyceum and he was presumably under no undue financial pressure to finish it. In later years, he would not have such a luxury.

The novel unfolds as a series of diaries and letters. Jonathan Harker, a young English solicitor, travels to the wilds of Transylvania to conduct a real estate transaction for one Count Dracula, who desires to relocate to England. Harker's firm has secured for the Count an abandoned estate called Carfax, near Whitby. But once received at Dracula's castle, Harker finds himself pulled into a waking nightmare, held captive by the Count and his harem of vampires. A living-dead creature who sleeps in an earth-box by day and scales the walls of his castle like a monstrous lizard by night, Dracula intends to use Harker to increase his knowledge of England (and English), then abandon him to his bloodthirsty wives upon his departure. Harker attempts to kill Dracula with a spade as he rests in his earth-box, but suffers a failure of will. Dracula leaves for England with crates of the native burial earth necessary for his survival abroad, and Harker's journal ends as he plans a dangerous escape from the castle.

The scene switches to England, where the story is taken up by the letters of Harker's fiancée, Mina Murray, a "New Woman" of independent mind and aspirations. Her best friend, Lucy Westenra, is of opposite temperament, an ideal of Victorian passivity. Soon after a derelict sailing ship drifts into Whitby harbor during a storm, Lucy is taken by nightmares, sleepwalking, and anemia. Although cared for by a physician (Dr. Seward, who runs a local sanitarium adjacent to the Carfax estate) and despite a series of blood transfusions from her friends and fiancé, she succumbs to the mysterious blood loss and dies. Jonathan, suffering from a severe brain fever, is returned to England, where he slowly recovers. Mina, however, falls prey to Lucy's symptoms, including what she believes are visitations by the dead friend herself. As young children in the vicinity are molested by a "lady in white," Dr. Seward, in consultation with Dr. Abraham Van Helsing, a specialist in obscure diseases, concludes that a vampire is at work. In a bloodcurdling scene, the vampire Lucy is chased to her tomb, staked, and decapitated. Harker regains strength and assists them in the search for Dracula, who has made use of Renfield, a fly-eating lunatic in Seward's care, to gain access to Mina. When Renfield begins to resist the vampire's demands, Dracula kills him. Several of the Count's earth-boxes are located and destroyed, but the vampire safeguards one and flees back to the continent. A suspenseful chase back to Transylvania ensues, Dracula is destroyed just short of reaching his lair, and Mina is released from her thrall.

Program for the marathon staged reading of Dracula *at the Lyceum, 1897. (Courtesy of Jeanne Youngson)*

Dracula is a radically different book in the 1990s than it was a century ago; though the text has not been altered, its context has been transformed—and transformed substantially. Attempts to make sense of its author's intentions are particularly difficult since the notes and manuscript are unaccompanied by journals, diaries, or letters that might reveal Stoker's state of mind, and there is a relative dearth of biographical information.* In all likelihood he considered the book no more than an entertainment, a page-turning thriller. Stoker's serious critics are virtually unanimous in their conclusion that Dracula was in large part the product of unconscious influences, and not a totally controlled work. Stoker's voluminous correspondence on behalf of Henry Irving (he said that he wrote as many as fifty letters a day, and as many as half a million during the twenty-six years of his employment[39]) as well as his own prolific fictional output suggests that he could produce prose with a facility approaching automatic writing.

The interpretive conundrums thus raised are nearly overwhelming. If

---

*Stoker's life has been the subject of two full-length books, Harry Ludlam's *A Biography of Dracula: The Life Story of Bram Stoker* in 1962, and *The Man Who Wrote Dracula* by Daniel Farson in 1975. The Ludlam book, while breezily readable, was authorized by Stoker's son Noel, and has some of the distracting gloss one expects from family-sanctioned biographies. Farson, Stoker's great-nephew, apparently had a freer hand with family documents and is considerably more candid in his assessments and speculations.

Stoker didn't intend a larger meaning, can such a meaning be legitimately imposed? *Dracula* has, for instance, come to be regarded in many quarters as a tantalizing Rosetta Stone of the darker aspects of the Victorian psyche, and indeed serves the function admirably, as dozens of scholarly articles and studies will attest. But *Dracula* can also be read fruitfully as a Christian allegory (or parody), as a parable of cultural xenophobia, as an occult text, or as a thinly veiled Darwinian or even Marxist tract. The inescapable conclusion is that Bram Stoker, working in a largely intuitive manner, and no doubt propelled by more than a few personal demons, managed to tap a well of archetypal motifs so deep and persistent that they can assume the shape of almost any critical container.

Dracula was published in late spring of 1897—the month has been variously given as May or June—with no literary theorists in sight. Stoker arranged a marathon staged reading of the book at the Lyceum on the morning of May 18, ostensibly to protect his interest in a dramatic copyright, but quite possibly as an exercise in vanity. The date, curiously enough, is two days before Stoker signed a memorandum of agreement for the book's publication, and may in fact have preceded the novel's release. The Lyceum, in any event, briefly became Stoker's own macabre toy theatre, though brevity may have seemed like an eternity; the reading was stupefyingly long—five acts and forty-seven scenes. Any hopes Stoker may have had of impressing his employer with his dramaturgical skills came to naught in a scene recounted by his biographer and great-nephew Daniel Farson: "Legend has it that Sir Henry entered the theatre during the reading and listened for a few moments with a warning glint of amusement. 'What do you think of it?' someone asked him unwisely, as he left for his dressing room. '*Dreadful!*' came the devastating reply, projected with such resonance that it filled the theatre."[40]

Whatever the merits of this particular event, Stoker was correct in anticipating the theatrical possibilities of his story, though they would not be realized in his lifetime. Had motion pictures been sufficiently developed at the time, he would quite likely have seen *Dracula*'s cinematic potential as well. At the time of *Dracula*'s publication it was possible to view in London proto-nickelodeons (the very cinematographs that Gorky saw as harbingers of living death). Stoker never published his thoughts on the motion picture or its possible future, though his work often makes use of up-to-date inventions; *Dracula,* for instance, includes references to the Kodak camera, the telephone, the portable typewriter, and updates the epistolary form with transcriptions of Dr. Seward's phonograph diary. It is reasonable to assume that the creator of Dracula would have been as intrigued by the possibilities of film as film would later become intrigued with *Dracula*. The book is a work positioned uniquely between the ages of Gutenberg and McLuhan, filled with and fueled by images

TUESDAY, MAY 18, 1897, AT A QUARTER-PAST TEN O'CLOCK A.M.,

WILL BE PRESENTED, FOR THE FIRST TIME,

DRACULA
OR
THE UN-DEAD
IN A PROLOGUE AND FIVE ACTS
BY
BRAM STOKER.

Count Dracula	Mr. JONES.
Jonathan Harker	Mr. PASSMORE.
John Seward, M.D.	Mr. RIVINGTON.
Professor Van Helsing	Mr. T. REYNOLDS.
Quincey P. Morris	Mr. WIDDICOMBE.
Hon. Arthur Holmwood (*afterwards Lord Godalming*)	Mr. INNES.
M. F. Renfield	Mr. HOWARD.
Captain Swales	Mr. GURNEY.
Coastguard	Mr. SIMPSON.
Attendant at Asylum	Mr. PORTER.
Mrs. Westenra	Miss GURNEY.
Lucy Westenra	Miss FOSTER.
Mina Murray (*afterwards Mrs. Harker*)	Miss CRAIG.
Servant	Miss CORNFORD.
Vampire Woman	Mrs. DALY.

almost tailor-made for a dreamy new medium unfettered by language.

For the moment, however, the popular dramatic medium was the theatre, and it was inevitable that readers would envision Dracula in the trappings of a popular theatrical equivalent, the most obvious being Henry Irving in his celebrated role of Mephistopheles.

In her biography of actress Ellen Terry, Irving's celebrated partner (as well as an intimate of Stoker), Nina Auerbach calls Dracula "an unforgettable Irving caricature,"[41] the portrait of an actor who "possessed others' minds so intensely that he linked the theatrical to the supernatural."[42]

Certainly, Stoker's own language in describing his first encounter with Irving supports this view, using words like "commanding force," "the magnetism of his genius," "so profound was the sense of his dominance that I sat spellbound . . . The surroundings became non-existent . . . recurring thoughts of self-existence were not at all."[43] "For Stoker," writes Auerbach, "Irving's portrayals of great men were triumphs of witchcraft as well as mesmerism."[44] Ellen Terry, too, was caught in a web of possession: "Believers knew that Ellen Terry's 'marriage' to this magus empowered her as well, just as in *Dracula*, Lucy and Mina, the vampire's brides, acquire metaphoric powers that are at once infernal and celestial. . . . Later, when Ellen Terry acted without Irving, the legend of her charm would cloy and cripple her performances. . . . Irving's holy circle made her less an actress than an object of belief. . . . Like Mina in *Dracula*'s final scene, Ellen Terry froze into her magic circle, immobilized and adored."[45] (Terry's daughter, Edith Craig, took the part of Mina in Stoker's staged reading.)

Stoker's great-nephew and biographer Daniel Farson recalls a story told him by Orson Welles in 1950. " 'Stoker,' [Welles] declared expansively, 'told me this extraordinary story—that he had written this play about a vampire especially for his friend Henry Irving, who threw it aside contemptuously. But—you know . . . Stoker had his revenge! He turned the play into a novel and if you read the description of the Count you will find it identical to Irving!' " Farson reports being intially impressed by this story—until he realized that Stoker had died three years before Welles was born.[46] However, the account does demonstrate how deeply rooted was the perception of Irving-as-Dracula among theatrical people.

Another descendent, Ivan Stoker Dixon, has taken to the lecture circuit in recent years, claiming that *Dracula* was inspired by Stoker's deep resentment of Irving's control and influence, which had drained his energies and crippled his literary aspirations. In Dixon's view, Irving became an almost literal vampire in Stoker's life.[47] Stoker may have been a frustrated, or at least highly sublimated, playwright; his eager thrusting of *Dracula* onto the Lyceum stage suggests that his theatrical aspirations, or illusions, were strong indeed.

Henry Irving, Bram Stoker's probable inspiration for the Dracula persona, seen here as Mephistopheles in the Lyceum Theatre's celebrated production of Faust. *(Courtesy of the Board of Trustees of the Victoria and Albert Museum)*

References to *Macbeth,* Irving's favorite role, recur throughout *Dracula* (the cursed warrior-king in a desolate castle, the three weird sisters, the somnabulism and blood imagery). Given Sir Henry's response to the Lyceum reading, however, any salutory influences of *Macbeth* must have been lost on him entirely.

It is not surprising that readers sought a real-life explanation or counterpart for a character who is drawn so vividly and yet so vaguely, a central player who is offstage for most of the play and who does not interact with the other characters in a conventional fashion, and yet is the source of our continuing fascination. Like an optical illusion only partially drawn, the portrait of Dracula demands completion in the mind of the beholder.

First-time readers of *Dracula,* or readers who return to the novel after many years, are often surprised at what a repellent, unattractive character the Count truly is, more literal wolf than literary Lothario. Stoker broke sharply with the Byronic tradition in his delineation of Dracula as a cadaverous ancient with pointed ears, bad breath, and hairy palms. He also took pains to establish a physiognomy for his villain consistent with the Victorian age's concept of the "criminal type"; as a young man he had professed his belief in the "science" of physiognomy in one of his letters to Walt Whitman.[48] Stoker's first description of Dracula (aquiline profile, bushy hair, massive eyebrows that meet over the nose, the pointed ears, etc.) is almost a verbatim reiteration of characteristics that could be found in criminology textbooks.[49] Stereotyping of this sort also begat bigotry; according to cultural historian Bram Dijkstra, "Dracula may not officially have been one of those horrid inbred Jews everyone was worrying about at the time Stoker wrote his novel, but he came close, for he was very emphatically Eastern European . . . like [George] du Maurier's 'filthy black Hebrew,' Svengali."[50] Stoker's physical creation finally goes beyond racist notions of degeneracy into outright atavism: Count Dracula, with his satyr ears and animal appetites, is a vivid evocation, in part, of the phallic goat-god Pan, the nightmare-demon of antiquity.[51]

Stoker's vampire, in short, is no seducer alighting from the *Orient Express,* but rather a rapist leaping unceremoniously from the animal brain. At this point, the horror of Dracula becomes almost indistinguishable from a generalized horror of nature itself, with vampirism representing hypercivilized man's revulsion for the basic interdependency of living things.

Dracula leaves it to women to carry on the fatal Byronic traditions, and they do so with relish. If an alluring, malignant sexuality, previously a sine qua non of the genre, is denied the vampire king, the female figures in the novel more than compensate. The sexual politics of *Dracula* were not remarked upon at all at the time of its publication, though today they seem all too obvious and dominate most discussions of the book.

Irving's Mephistopheles in Draculean attire, as interpreted by the artist Sir Bernard Partridge. (Courtesy of the Board of Trustees of the Victoria and Albert Museum)

To enter the castle of Dracula is to enter the Victorian mind, upstairs and downstairs, with all its sexual contradictions and complexities, hidden rooms, and closeted skeletons. Almost nowhere in history do we find a society in which the public face and the private behavior are so divorced. Although other interpretations are possible, *Dracula* read today is first and foremost the sexual fever-dream of a middle-class Victorian man, a frightened dialogue between demonism and desire. Much more is at issue than the role of women; then, as today, women who break the traditional sexual molds challenge the male's sexual identity as well. And this may be what is really at stake in *Dracula*—not the rescue of a woman by a man but the rescue of an embattled male's deepest sense of himself as a male.

The Darwinian economic and social currents of the late Industrial Revolution placed an unprecedented competitive pressure on middle-class men, while opening new possibilities for women. The same period saw the image of the Fatal Man in literature and art rapidly overtaken by the Fatal Woman, *la belle dame sans merci.* "Man's fear of woman is as old as time," writes Peter Gay in *Education of the Senses,* "but it was only in the bourgeois century that it became a prominent theme in popular novels and medical treatises."[52] As males grew anxious over their socioeconomic prowess, a cultural reaction-formation desexualized women. "To deny woman native erotic desires was to safeguard man's sexual adequacy. However he performed, it would be good enough."[53] (As one of the influential medical commentators of the day, Dr. William Acton, wrote, "The majority of women (happily for them) are not very much troubled with sexual feelings of any kind. . . . No nervous or feeble young man need, therefore, be deterred from marriage by an exaggerated notion of the duties required of him."[54]) Women who did expect more, both in and out of bed, were widely believed to be life-draining killers, castrators . . . and vampires.

To read much of the medical literature on sex at the time of Dracula is to discover another kind of Victorian horror fiction. As Steven Marcus points out in *The Other Victorians,* many authorities thought of sex as "a universal and virtually incurable scourge" that served as a kind of "metaphor for death, as cancer does today."[55] All sex was suspected to contain the seeds of insanity and physical degeneration, and men and boys alike were frequently terrorized by the spectre of an imaginary, catchall condition called "spermatorrhea" that could be the cause or result of almost anything.[56] The loss of semen was tantamount to the loss of blood. In *Dracula* the link was metaphorical; to the Victorian medical establishment, sexual vampirism was almost a tenet of faith. Philip Burne-Jones' scandalous fin de siècle painting *The Vampire,* which inspired Kipling's poem of the same title, illustrates the anxiety at its apex. Burne-Jones, incidentally, was the son of Sir Edward Burne-Jones and a friend

The victim on a pedestal: George du Maurier's Svengali orchestrates evil in Trilby *(1894).*

The actress Mrs. Patrick Campbell as depicted by painter Philip Burne-Jones in his fin de siècle scandal, The Vampire. The painting inspired the artist's cousin Rudyard Kipling to write his poem of the same title:

A Fool there was and he made his prayer
(Even as you and I!)
To a rag and a bone and a hank of hair
(We called her the woman who did not care)
But the fool he called her his lady fair—
(Even as you and I!)

Oh, the years we waste and the tears we waste
And the work of our head and hand,
Belong to the woman who did not know
(And now we know that she never could know)
And did not understand!

A fool there was and his goods he spent
(Even as you and I!)
Honour and faith and a sure intent
(And it wasn't the least what the lady meant)
But a fool must follow his natural bent
(Even as you and I!)

Oh, the toil we lost and the spoil we lost
And the excellent things we planned
Belong to the woman who didn't know why
(And now we know that she never knew why)
And did not understand!

The fool was stripped to his foolish hide
(Even as you and I!)
Which she might have seen when she threw him aside—
(But it isn't on record the lady tried)
So some of him lived but the most of him died—
(Even as you and I!)

And it isn't the shame and it isn't the blame
That stings like a white hot brand.
It's coming to know that she never knew why
(Seeing at last she could never know why)
And never could understand.

of the Stokers; *The Vampire* was first exhibited in 1897, the year *Dracula* was published. (The scandal of the painting derived not from its misogyny but from the gossip surrounding its female model, the actress Mrs. Patrick Campbell, and her relationship with the painter.)

The late Industrial Revolution was a time of dualism and polarity in science and society; men were obsessed with controlling an untamed nature through the application of science, and woman-as-nature became a wholesale target for male projections (it was near this time that Freud boasted of controlling his patients' menstrual bleeding through hypnosis). It was an age that eroticized the consumptive, corpselike woman in literature and art, corseted the female body, and held in general horror anything that might be construed as animated—or animal—in the female of the species.

Read as an unconscious parable of the sexual contradictions of its time rather than as a supernatural thriller, *Dracula* is a profoundly disturbing book. In *Idols of Perversity: Fantasies of Feminine Evil in Fin-de-Siècle Culture,* Bram Dijkstra cuts to the heart of the matter: "In Stoker's novel . . . all aspects of the period's suspicions about the degenerative tendencies in women have been brought together in such an effortless fashion that it is clear that for the author these were not so much a part of the symbolic structures of fantasy as the conditions of universal truth. Stoker's work demonstrates how thoroughly the war waged by the nineteenth-century male culture against the dignity and self-respect of women had been fought. . . . Stoker clearly was a man of limited intelligence, typical of the fairly well-educated, fairly well-off, middle-minded middle class. But he had a remarkably coherent socio-logical imagination and a brilliant talent for fluid, natural-sounding, visually descriptive prose. Together these qualities made it possible for him to write, perhaps without ever completely realizing what he had done, a narrative destined to become the twentieth century's basic commonplace book of the antifeminine obsession."[57]

The feminist critic Andrea Dworkin goes even further. "The women are transformed into predators, great foul parasites. . . . As humans, they begin to learn sex in dying. And the men, the human suitors and husbands . . . are given a new kind of sex, too . . . watching the women die." The story "goes beyond metaphor in its intuitive rendering of an oncoming century filled with sexual horror: the throat as a female genital; sex and death as synonyms; killing as a sex act; slow dying as sensuality; men watching the slow dying, and the *watching* is sexual; mutilation of the female body as male heroism and adventure; callous, ruthless, predatory lust as the one-note meaning of sexual desire; intercourse itself needing blood, someone's, somewhere, to count as a sex act in a world excited by sadomasochism, bored by the dull thud thud of the literal fuck."[58]

Clearly, such appraisals are colored as much by the sexual politics of our own time as by those of the Victorians . . . but it is a rare book indeed that can still incite such passionate responses almost a century after its publication. To be fair—and to illustrate the amazing elasticity of *Dracula*'s subtexts—the book has also been read as a veiled feminist myth. In *Woman and the Demon,* Ellen Terry's biographer Nina Auerbach points out that between the lines of *Dracula* is a story of female transformation and empowerment. The women grow stronger and are more vividly portrayed as the novel progresses, while "the Count is reduced to an increasingly immobilized catalyst. . . . The power of Dracula himself narrows to the dimensions of his vulnerable coffin, for

"The Vampire," a lithograph by Edvard Munch.

despite his ambitious designs on the human race, he seems to be the world's last surviving male vampire."[59]

No doubt, Bram Stoker would also resist the suggestion that his novel was a misogynistic diatribe—did not, after all, his story concern above all else the *protection* of innocent women by chivalrous men? (As Peter Gay points out, "Anti-feminism was not solely a symptom of castration fears. It was a display of ignorance, of misplaced chivalry, or of a timid clinging to tradition—other kinds of fear."[60]) There is nothing to suggest that Stoker had any comprehension of the larger irony of this attitude, or of a society that had made a fetish, even a requirement, of women's subservient helplessness. *Dracula* can be read—in our time, at least—as an almost transparent metaphor for the Victorian confusion, guilt, and anger over the "proper" role of women. The attack of the vampire—a male's act of oral, infantile rage—succeeds in sexualizing women, who, according to the double standard of the time, must then be punished and purified through more sex and violence (penetrated by stakes, etc.). The whole notion of "the un-dead" also seems an obvious representation of the life force or libido in suspended animation, a state of sexual limbo, change, or indecision.

Fin de siecle feminine evil: painter Albert Pénot's 1890 concept of a bat-woman.

What, then, of the woman who had the most intimate knowledge of all concerning Bram Stoker's imagination and sexuality?

Stoker had been married since 1878 to the former Florence Anne Lemon Balcombe, a celebrated beauty whom George du Maurier (the aforementioned author of *Trilby,* the source of the Svengali legend) considered to be one of the three most beautiful women he had ever seen. Her former suitor having been none other than Oscar Wilde, Florence had effectively captured the imaginations of the creators of Svengali, Dracula, and Dorian Gray. Florence certainly attained a unique position in Victorian arts and letters. Rarely, if ever, has a woman been the focus of quite so much literary demonism.

She had apparently made the Cinderella transition from penniless Irish girl to London society hostess with great relish. Horace Wyndam remembered that "Mrs. Bram," as she was known, "was a charming woman and brim full of Irish wit and impulsiveness."[61] The striking, nearly Pre-Raphaelite features of Florence Stoker had graced even the sketch pad of Sir Edward Burne-Jones (the artist who designed for the Lyceum), and one fashionable artist executed a oil portrait notable for its link to the femme fatale iconography so prevalent in the art of the period. Walter Frederick Osborne, a well-known Dublin landscape artist and portraitist, created a likeness that was accepted for exhibition by the Royal Academy of Arts in 1895. Osborne's portrait, judging from a magazine reproduction of the time, was a good likeness but one with a subtle air of languorous decadence. The subject, with a sly, knowing expression, reclines against the skin of a dead animal, a visual motif that had become

a virtual cliché in popular depictions of *la belle dame sans merci*: fatal women were commonly presented as being surrounded, attended by, or even merged with predatory beasts. No doubt it was just fashion as well, but the ambiguous portrait has resonances with both *Dracula,* and, in a curious way, *The Picture of Dorian Gray.*

Stoker biographer Farson, in contrast to Wyndham, depicts Florence Stoker as a cold, vain beauty. "My family, speaking of her, gave me the impression of an elegant, aloof woman, more interested in her position in society than she was in her son [Noel Stoker, 1879–1961]."[62] A cartoon that appeared in *Punch* in 1886 reinforces this view: titled "A Filial Reproof," it depicts the unnamed, but recognizable Stoker family in the backyard of their Chelsea home. "Hush, Noel!" says "Mamma" to her son, who, the caption tells us, is inclined to be talkative. "Haven't I told you often that little boys should be *seen* and not *heard?*" The boy is caught in a classic double bind: "Yes, Mamma! But you don't *look* at me!"[63]

Farson recounts the description given him by Noel's daughter, Ann MacCaw: "She told me that she doubted if 'Granny Moo,' as Florence was called, was really capable of love. 'She was cursed by her great beauty and the need to maintain it. In my knowledge now, she was very anti-sex. After having my father in her early twenties, I think she was quite put off.'"[64]

Sexual ambivalence is bound up inextricably with self-ambivalence, and the theme of unstable, secret identities and alternate selves recurs throughout Stoker's published works.[65] The theme of the divided self and the paradoxes of sexual identity are dealt with openly on several occasions in his later books. In *Famous Imposters* (1910) Stoker examines the true histories of women who masqueraded as men, and the putative story of a man who became a woman (in this case, the strange, persistent conspiracy legend positing Elizabeth I as a male transvestite). In his novel *The Man* (1905) Stoker presents a female heroine named Stephen, born to parents who desired a boy. But however far Stoker's subjects stray from established social and sexual norms, the dominant social order is always reasserted. Drawn to Castle Dracula, fascinated by its threats and possibilities, Stoker always flees its ambiguous confines. Jonathan Harker writes in his diary as he prepares his escape, "God's mercy is better than that of these monsters, and the precipice is steep and high. At its foot a man may sleep—as a man."[66] Despite his admiration for *Macbeth,* Stoker the writer has no use for spirits who might unsex him, at least not permanently.

The vampire's mouth is an ambiguous orifice . . . engulfing yet penetrating, nightmarishly blurring the distinctions of gender. The three vampire women who approach Harker thus represent a hellish kind of "third sex" that needs to be vanquished with the help of Dr. Van Helsing, the patriarchal guardian of traditional dualities and distinctions.

In a lucid essay, Christopher Craft notes that the book's opening anxiety, from which the rest of the plot rises, "derives from Dracula's hovering interest in Jonathan Harker; the sexual threat that this novel first evokes, manipulates, sustains but never finally represents is that Dracula will seduce, penetrate, drain another male."[67] Throughout the story, in Craft's view, the homoerotic impulse "achieves representation as a monstrous heterosexuality."[68] The novel's climactic vampire attack, significantly, is a thinly veiled ménage à trois witnessed by Dr. Seward; Dracula crawls quite literally into the Harkers' marriage bed. Fluids comingle while the unconscious husband blocks out the implications:

"On the bed beside the window lay Jonathan Harker, his face flushed, and breathing heavily as though in a stupor. Kneeling on the near edge of the bed facing outwards was the white-clad figure of his wife. By her side stood a tall, thin man, clad in black. His face was turned from us, but the instant we saw it we all recognized the Count. . . . With his left hand he held both Mrs. Harker's hands, keeping them away with her arms at full tension; his right hand gripped her by the back of the neck, forcing her face down on his bosom. Her white nightdress was smeared with blood, and a thin stream trickled down the man's bare breast, which was shown by his torn-open dress. The attitude of the two had a terrible resemblance to a child forcing a kitten's nose into a saucer of milk to compel it to drink."[69]

Bloodletter and breastfeeder, the vampire rivals his three wives in gender-bending. The true horror of Dracula, to the Victorian mind, is his polymorphous perversity. More horrible still is the possibility that he is not merely an external threat, but something already lurking inside. Early in the book, Stoker suggests that the vampire may be a second self as Harker puzzles over Dracula's failure to reflect in his shaving mirror. "The whole room behind me was displayed; but there was no sign of a man in it, except myself."[70]

Doubling and splitting of identity is associated in clinical terms variously with the inability to escape extreme anxiety or physical violation, or to reconcile cruelly paradoxical circumstances, all of which have their thematic resonances in *Dracula*. Commentators have long sought explanations for the book's eruption of infantile rage in the known facts of Stoker's life. Dr. Joseph Bierman, in an influential if somewhat overheated psychoanalytical essay,[71] suggests that Stoker's imagination was under siege during the composition of *Dracula* by feelings of murderous envy and rivalry at the simultaneous knightings in 1895 of his brother, the successful physician William Thornley Stoker, and Henry Irving. But there was another dramatic public event in 1895 that could not have escaped Stoker's attention and touched upon his life, and which brought together themes of shifting sexuality and secret selves, Victorian hypocrisy, literary and marital rivalry.

The event was the trial of Oscar Wilde.

Wilde and Stoker present a fascinating set of Victorian bookends, shadow-mirrors in uneasy reciprocal orbits. Both were Dubliners, both attended Trinity College and were steeped in literature and theatre. At Trinity, Stoker sponsored Wilde's membership in the Philosophical Society. Wilde's parents were favorably impressed with Stoker, and once even entertained him at their home on Christmas day after Oscar had matriculated at Oxford. Both young men were devoted admirers of Henry Irving and at an early age both would approach him in the hopes of advancing their careers (only one would succeed). Both idealized Walt Whitman—and on separate occasions both make repeated pilgrimages in America to meet him. Both would write a masterwork of macabre fiction portraying archetypal title characters who

Bram Stoker, in a typically morose portrait. (Courtesy of the Dracula Society)

remain supernaturally young by draining the life force from Victorian inno-
cents. Both were attracted to literary themes of doubles, masks, and boundaries in general.

Most significantly, both loved the same woman.

The dowerless, but "exquisitely pretty"[72] Florence Balcombe became the
object of Wilde's affection in the summer of 1875. The sixteen-year-old
beauty from Clontarf was his first infatuation; he escorted her to church, drew
her portrait, wrote her poetry and by Christmas presented her with a small
gold cross inscribed with their names. (The presentation of a similar cross
would eventually become one of the most important talismanic rituals in
adaptations of *Dracula*.) The twenty-year-old Wilde, unfortunately, was as
penniless as his Florrie, and an engagement was never formalized.

Three years later, having turned down Dorian Gray, Florence Balcombe
married Dracula instead.

*Oscar Wilde, Stoker's ambiguous
doppelgänger in marriage and art. (Billy
Rose Theatre Collection, New York
Public Library at Lincoln Center, Astor,
Lenox and Tilden Foundations)*

*Florence Ann Lemon Balcombe, later
Mrs. Bram Stoker, as sketched by her first
suitor, Oscar Wilde. (Harry Ransom
Humanities Research Center Art
Collection, The University of Texas at
Austin)*

Whatever their similarities, the differences between the two men are equally striking. Wilde was a literary genius. Stoker was merely competent, and very uneven. Wilde was a wit. Irony is a quality noticeably lacking in Stoker. Wilde systematically demolished the bourgeois values and illusions that Stoker defended so strenuously. Nowhere is the difference in their outward temperaments more apparent than in their surviving photographic portraits. Wilde is languorous, epicene, posing with a flower, reclining voluptuously on a divan, an adrogynous insult to proper society. Stoker's portraits, by contrast, are stiff specimens of Victorian rectitude and restraint. His typical expression is pinched, uncomfortable. As both men moved in the same glittering social world, it is easy to imagine them circling each other uneasily, personally and professionally jealous, mutually fascinated and mutually repelled.

Stoker never mentions Wilde in his Irving reminiscences, published in 1906, despite Irving's public role in banning *Salome*—the impresario had denounced it before the Lord Chamberlain, though perhaps just for his own publicity; plays featuring Biblical characters were already forbidden as blasphemous in England. (After Irving's death, the *Evening Telegraph* lauded Irving's part in having rescued England from "the cult" of Oscar Wilde.[73]) Nonetheless, Florence and Wilde remained on friendly terms, and she received him at her Sunday salons. In June 1888, when *Under the Sunset* was still Stoker's only published volume of fiction, and a self-subsidized one at that, Wilde dispatched to Florence a copy of his own book of fairy tales, *The Happy Prince* ("I hope you will like them, simple though they are.... With kind regards to Bram"[74]). When *Salome* was published in French, he sent her an inscribed copy of the Paris first edition (with its "decadent" Aubrey Beardsley illustrations) adding his perfunctory regards to Stoker. (In retrospect, considering the artist's flair for the demonic, it is unfortunate indeed that Beardsley was never given the opportunity to illustrate *Dracula*.)

Dracula may contain a reference to Wilde's circle in the name of the vampire's English residence, Carfax. Wilde's first male lover and lifelong friend was Robert Ross, an art critic and codirector of a gallery in Ryder Street that was a focal point for artists, like Beardsley, who made no pretense of conventional sexuality. Ross' gallery, whose name alone, no doubt, connoted the variant sensibilities of its artists, also happened to be called Carfax.[75] Whether Carfax is a conscious allusion to the Ross/Wilde cenacle is a matter of speculation, but the gallery was certainly well-known, and Stoker was nothing if not well-connected in artistic circles.

In any event, as Bram Stoker was deep in the composition of *Dracula* his wife's former suitor was being branded a sexual monster in a collective social exorcism. Given the unmistakable sexual preoccupations of his work, is it possible Stoker was unaffected? Where were the feverish sentiments ex-

The 1916 Rider edition again featured the Count scaling the wall of his castle like a giant lizard, or bat. Note the esoteric symbol of a phoenix, concealed in the folds of the vampire's cloak. One of the most nightmarish images in the novel, it was not used in a stage or film adaptation until a television production in 1977. *(Courtesy of Robert James Leake)*

pressed to Walt Whitman now? Well in hiding, it would seem. Stoker himself would take up the censorious, antisex battle cry like a turn-of-the-century Senator Jesse Helms, proclaiming in a 1908 essay that "the only emotions which in the long run harm are those arising from sex impulses . . ."[76] This particular essay, attacking the "plague-spot" of decadence in fiction, reveals

Stoker as almost hysterically priggish—protesting too much, as a character in a Henry Irving production might observe.

Dracula's publication was marked by one final, and presumably unintentional, Wildean irony. *The Picture of Dorian Gray* had featured a notorious French novel with a yellow cover to which its hero is attracted; the literary magazine Aubrey Beardsley art-directed was called *The Yellow Book* in homage, and a great deal of comment was caused at the time of Oscar Wilde's arrest by the reports that he carried off to jail a book with a yellow wrapper (it turned out to be nothing special). *Dracula* would soon join this notorious company in jaundice; Constable issued the book in a bright yellow cover in May 1897.

Oddly, or perhaps all too predictably, the moral guardians of Victorian England found nothing objectionable in *Dracula*, reserving their brickbats of "loathsome . . . putrid indecorum . . . unwholesome and disgusting" for a work like Ibsen's *Ghosts*, which dared to deal openly with venereal disease.[77] *Dracula* received mixed reviews, typical of which was the *Athenaeum*'s appraisal, which faulted Stoker's characterizations while praising the book's "immense" energy: "his object, assuming it to be ghastliness, is fairly well fulfilled."[78]

It is remarkable, too, that *Dracula* has never been attacked as blasphemous, despite its perverse and complicated undermining and inversion of Christian symbols and motifs; the novel is a veritable black mass in book form. Curiously, an indirect connection may have also existed between Stoker and Oscar Wilde's wife, Constance, who (possibly as an escape from her deteriorating marriage) was an enthusiastic member of a secret occult society, the Hermetic Order of the Golden Dawn,[79] a magical offshoot of Rosicrucianism whose members included Yeats, Swinburne, and, briefly, the notorious Aleister Crowley. Though never substantiated, accounts would persistently name Stoker as a member as well.[80] The Golden Dawn attracted numerous men and women of accomplishment who would have been well-known to Stoker, and his supernatural fiction reveals more than a passing familiarity with esoteric lore. Hermetical symbols and iconography became associated with *Dracula* almost from its first publication, with or without Stoker's knowledge. The first paperback abridgment of the book, published by Constable, features a cover drawing in a dense symbolic style reminiscent of a Tarot card, and the illustrator of the Rider reissue painted a cover in which the classical shape of a phoenix has been superimposed into Dracula's flowing cape. A kind of secret visual handshake results, with special meanings to the initiated.

Dracula sold steadily but did not make Stoker a wealthy man. He and Florence were dogged by financial troubles: both the Lyceum's fiscal base and Irving's health were failing. The theatre suffered a devastating fire to its stock of scenery and costumes. Stoker wrote several more books, but none achieved

The Count, as depicted on the cover of the first French edition (1920).

Constable's first paperback edition featured a cover illustration in a dense symbolic style recalling the imagery of the Tarot, with distinctly Freudian overtones. (Courtesy of Robert James Leake)

the success of *Dracula,* the dynamics of which he apparently did not under-stand well enough to repeat; his attempts to duplicate the magic, as in 1903's resuscitated mummy melodrama *The Jewel of Seven Stars* or 1909's *The Lady of the Shroud* (in which a woman suffering from catalepsy is suspected of vampirism), rang largely hollow.

Shortly after Irving's death in 1905, Stoker suffered a stroke, as if in some sympathetic connection with his lost mentor and alter ego. The attack left him unconscious for twenty-four hours, and weakened and visually impaired there-after. Stoker was also ill with Bright's disease, a degenerative kidney disorder complicated by what his biographer Daniel Farson believes to have been tertiary syphilis, acquired outside of a sexless marriage, perhaps abroad (during at least one of his trips to America, he is known to have been elusive and secretive about his lodgings, which he kept oddly separate from those of the Lyceum company[81]).

With the aid of a magnifying glass to help him read and write, he completed his *Personal Reminiscences of Henry Irving*, a two-volume account of both men's years at the Lyceum. It was published in 1906. Other, unmemorable novels appeared, literal potboilers for the once-more struggling author, no longer young. Stoker's final novel, *The Lair of the White Worm* (1911), is a book distinguished—if that is the word—by imagery of an almost hallucinatory misogyny, focusing on the vampire-like Lady Arabella and her noxious and transparently emblematic "snake's hole," the smell of which Stoker compares to "the drainage of war hospitals, of slaughterhouses, the refuse of dissecting rooms ... the sourness of chemical waste and the poisonous effluvium of the bilge of a water-logged ship whereupon a multitude of rats had been drowned." The destroyed phallic worm of the novel's title is an image of physical corruption: "The whole surface of the fragments, once alive, was covered with insects, worms and vermin of all kinds. The sight was horrible enough, but, with the awful smell added, was simply unbearable. The Worm's hole appeared to breathe forth death in its most repulsive forms."[82]

If Farson's speculations are true, then Bram and Florence Stoker become doubly tragic figures, both for the burden of Stoker's untreatable physical suffering, and as victims of a social order that suppressed frank discussion of venereal disease, and thereby perpetuated tragedy. The ravages of syphilis on middle-class women were being well-documented, though not widely discussed in polite circles, by the "New Women" writers. As critic Carol F. Senf observes, the resulting caution of women in sexual matters is easily confused with frigidity. She offers an alternate view of the difficulty of the Stoker marriage: "Perhaps Florence Stoker was sensible, not frigid."[83]

Stoker's final illness was a long one and would have presented Florence with a constant, punishing reminder of the darker aspects of sex. (Her onetime suitor Oscar Wilde had also died a hideous syphilitic death in 1900— and had been infected at the time he had courted her.) Certainly, it is conceivable that they both denied to themselves the real nature of Stoker's illness—although Stoker's final literary imaginings are such disturbing evocations of sexual pestilence that it is difficult to believe he was not aware of his fate.

Then again, people have always believed what they needed to believe.

Bram Stoker died April 20th, 1912, the same week the *Titanic* went to the bottom of the Atlantic. Writer Hall Caine, one of Stoker's closest friends and the man behind the childhood nickname "Hommy-Beg"[84] to whom *Dracula* is dedicated, published an emotional eulogy in the *Telegraph* on the day of Stoker's

Dracula's Guest was to be the first of three story collections published posthumously by Stoker's widow, but no others followed. The title story would eventually serve as the basis for the film Dracula's Daughter. *(Courtesy of Jeanne Youngson)*

funeral. "Of the devotion of his wife during these last dark days, in which the whirlwind of his spirit had nothing left to it but the broken wreck of a strong man, I cannot trust myself to speak," wrote Caine. "That must always be a sacred memory to those who know what it was. If his was the genius of friendship, hers must have been the genius of love."[85]

The year following his death, Florence Stoker sold his working notes for *Dracula* at auction, presumably for need of money. They brought very little, scarcely over two pounds. In 1914, she published *Dracula's Guest,* a collection of her husband's short stories whose title piece was a chapter from *Dracula* deleted because of length, telling of Jonathan Harker's encounter with a female vampire on his way to Castle Dracula. Two other collections Stoker had been preparing at the time of his death were never to be realized.

A war was brewing in Europe. The new medium of motion pictures was making remarkable strides on both sides of the Atlantic. A new age of invention and apprehension had dawned.

It would be nearly a decade before the vampire would return to disturb the widow's sleep.

The burial urn containing the ashes of Bram Stoker and his son, Noel. (Courtesy of Jeanne Youngson)

Chapter Two

THE ENGLISH WIDOW AND THE GERMAN COUNT

In which the book is stolen, and made a rude spectacle of by Germans, who are not forgiven, and who are hounded into ruin by Florence and a pack of solicitors.

ON APRIL 27, 1922, G. HERBERT THRING DRAFTED A LETTER SIMILAR TO many he wrote as secretary of the British Incorporated Society of Authors. He had no idea of the convoluted affair that would arise from this particular missive, nor of the extraordinary intensity and determination of the person to whom it was addressed. "In accordance with my promise to you over the phone today, I am now sending you the papers of the Society. If, after perusal, you would like to join, would you kindly fill up and return the election form in order that your name may go before the Committee of Management at their next meeting, which will take place Monday next. The subscription, as you will see by the prospectus, is £1.10.0 a year.

"As I mentioned to you, we have many literary executors members of the Society, and if you are in need of help in regard to your husband's literary work, no doubt you will let me know when returning the election form."[1]

The letter's recipient, Mrs. Bram Stoker of William Street, Knightsbridge, returned the form with a cheque. Formalities dispensed with, she now left no doubt whatsoever about the kind of help she needed. Included with her letters were printed documents that had been sent her from Berlin — the program of a cinematographic event that had taken place the previous month at the Marble Hall of the Berlin Zoological Gardens, accompanied by advertisement drawings of one of the most grotesque creatures Thring had ever seen: a hideous face, more verminous than human, with a bald bulging cranium, pointed ears, and hooked nose. From the cruel slash of a mouth

Florence Stoker, the Victorian beauty who inspired the creators of Svengali, Dorian Gray, and Dracula, as sketched by Edward Burne-Jones. (Courtesy of Daniel Farson, from The Man Who Wrote Dracula*)*

Production designer Albin Grau's frightening conception of Max Schreck as Graf Orlok in Nosferatu. *(Courtesy of Goethe House)*

A symphony of terror and a rainbow of rats: one of Albin Grau's many striking advertising graphics for Nosferatu. *(Courtesy of Anthology Film Archives)*

sprouted two ratlike fangs. Whatever this monstrosity was, the Berlin Zoo was certainly the appropriate environment for it!

Thring read on, learning that the event in question was a German film adapation of Bram Stoker's *Dracula*—"freely adapted" according to the program—a point angrily confirmed by Stoker's widow, who had neither given permission nor received payment for *Nosferatu, Eine Symphonie des Grauens.* The "Symphony of Horror" seemed to be a rather elaborate, if relentlessly morbid affair, the first venture of a company called Prana-Film. The screening had, apparently, been quite lavish, with full orchestral accompaniment and generous coverage in the cinema press. Money was obviously being thrown around over this thing.

Florence Stoker was justifiably upset. Since her husband's death her financial situation had become increasingly precarious. She could depend to a certain extent upon her son, Noel, now an accountant, but their relationship had always been rather distant. Most of her husband's books had gone out of print, without much hope for reprints and royalties. Only *Dracula* provided a steady, if skimpy and unpredictable, income (the French rights, for example, had brought only 350 francs in 1920).[2] Publishing then was a prudent, conservative business—today's extravagant, speculative advances were unheard of—and *Dracula* was a steady backlist title, not a grand best-seller. Still, there had been several editions, from Constable and now Rider. She owned a certain number of paintings, with which she would never part—they were last memories of those distant days on Cheyne Walk, where the Stokers' lives had been entwined with the likes of Sargent, Whistler, and the Pre-Raphaelites. With the death of Henry Irving, the Stokers' connection to such glittering circles had grown tenuous, and after Stoker's death Florence found herself in the same penniless circumstances that prevented her marriage to Oscar Wilde. Wilde was dead. Her husband was dead. Irving, the Lyceum, the age. Was it possible that all that survived of her life was *Dracula*? Once, she remembered, she had attended the premiere of *Lady Windermere's Fan,* and had still drawn Wilde's eye with "a wonderful evening wrap of striped brocade."[3] Now she warmed herself by pawning the threadbare cloak of a moldering vampire—when takers could be found.

And in Germany, they were trying to steal this as well.

She was old, but still quite handsome, and though her own eyesight was failing badly, others could see very well the warrior-saint profile that had pleased Burne-Jones. At the age of sixty-four she was being called upon to live up to the faded image.

The makers of *Nosferatu* had no idea of the fierce adversary they were to have in Florence Stoker, and probably didn't even know that she existed. A general air of impracticality seems to have surrounded almost everything

Cinema as vampire: monstrous dreams, projected outward, transfix the spectator/victim. Production sketch by Albin Grau.

Shape-changing and beastly, Grau's graphic concepts for the vampire were even more hideous than the filmed result.

connected with Prana-Film and *Nosferatu.*

Prana-Film (the name derives from the Buddhist concept of *prana,* or breath-as-life) was founded in January 1921 on a capitalization of 20,000 marks, under the codirectorship of businessmen Enrico Dieckmann and the designer/painter/architect Albin Grau.[4] An ambitious prospectus of potential projects was unveiled, revealing a distinct predilection for the occult, the Romantic, and the bizarre. The films were to be produced according to "new principles."[5] In addition to *Nosferatu,* projects mentioned included such evocative titles as *Hollenträume* (*Dreams of Hell*) and *Der Sumpfteufel* (*The Devil of the Swamp*).[6] Only *Nosferatu* would be realized—Prana's first and last gasp.

Grau was an "ardent spiritualist"[7] with no apparent experience in motion picture production, and Dieckmann's credentials are sketchy. One thing is clear: *Dracula* was well-known to them, and Grau immediately understood the dreamlike story's powerful potential as cinema. One of his drawings for *Nosferatu,* reproduced here, almost explicitly evokes film itself as demonic magic. Standing over a woman's bed, the vampire illuminates his intended prey with beams of light projected from his eyes. The penetrating effect was, unfortunately, not used in the film.

The arts in Germany after the war were deep in the ferment of expressionism—a highly imprecise, but useful term, much like "postmodernism" today. Expressionism was a category sufficiently elastic to include "every kind of cultural commitment or posture of the first quarter of the twentieth century."[8] In theatre, film, and visual arts, it generally included distortion, exaggeration, and extreme metaphor. Images invariably represented inner landscapes, with an overriding emphasis on composition and shadow play. Expressionist filmmakers naturally gravitated toward the fantastic and occult, where many of these elements could be found ready-made, or begging to be shaped. Notable expressionist films and themes prior to *Nosferatu* included *The Golem* (1914, remade 1920) and *Homunculus* (1916), both dealing with the plight of artificially created beings; *The Student of Prague* (1913, remade 1926), spotlighting the doppelgänger legend, by way of Edgar Allan Poe; and, of course, *The Cabinet of Dr. Caligari* (1919), where somnambulism, murder, and madness play against some of the most deliriously off-kilter sets of all time. The films all have their distinct personalities, and draw eclectically from the materials of expressionism; *Caligari,* for instance, has been criticized for an overreliance on painted theatrical effects while ignoring the expressive possibilities of the camera. *Nosferatu,* conversely, would draw criticism—and praise—for its use of natural, rather than contrived settings. And Paul Wegener, director of both versions of *The Golem,* denied any expressionist intentions at all.[9] A major characteristic of the filmmakers of this period was an individualism that transcended labels and categories.

A sailor forced to share quarters with a vampire-in-transit makes no secret of his displeasure. Production sketch by Albin Grau.

A trick publicity shot of Nosferatu materializing above his tomb.

A close-up study of Max Schreck's prosthetic makeup.

As director for their premiere venture, Grau and Dieckmann engaged the thirty-two-year-old Friedrich Wilhelm Murnau, whose distinctly original vision would later earn him a place in the pantheon of world cinema, on the basis of such influential works as *The Last Laugh* (1924), *Faust* (1926), and *Sunrise* (1927). Murnau had worked with the legendary theatrical producer Max Reinhardt before the war and no doubt was influenced by Reinhardt's pictorial aesthetic of light, shadow, and spectacle. Murnau would soon pioneer the use of the mobile camera, and eventually create the cinematic equivalent of Reinhardt's theatre.

Another Reinhardt alumnus who contributed to *Nosferatu* was screenwriter Henrik Galeen, who, faced with adapting a lengthy, rather wordy Victorian novel as a silent film, deftly excised everything except the visual, metaphorical, and mythic. He changed all the characters' names—Count Dracula became Graf Orlok; Harker was now Hutter, Mina was called Ellen, Van Helsing renamed Bulwer, etc.—and simplified the plot while retaining the basic structure—the young man's journey to Transylvania to sell a house to a vampire, the creature's sea voyage to the young man's town and subsequent possession of his wife, and the intervention of a patriarchal scientist to reveal the nature of the vampire pestilence.

Murnau's copy of the shooting script, now in the possession of the Cinémathèque Française, shows that Galeen worked in an impressionistic, rhetorical style, suggesting rather than dictating the finished product. ("A rope is dangling from the deck. Is it swaying in the wind?"[10]) Since much of *Nosferatu* considerably deviates even from Murnau's personally annotated script, it is apparent that a good degree of improvisation occurred during the filming.

Murnau shot *Nosferatu* on location in the summer of 1921, with Fritz Arno Wagner as cameraman. Location shooting was a novel idea at the time, and in the case of *Nosferatu*, most likely a response to a limited budget. Thus, the heightened artificial settings so typical of expressionist films are absent, the director and photographer resorting instead to carefully plotted visual compositions, with the camera immobile. Night scenes were shot in broad daylight, then tinted deep blue for release.[11] Most prints in circulation today lack this key effect, and are in effect stripped-down skeletons of the original,* which also had an elaborate orchestral score by Hans Erdmann.[12]

Nosferatu opens with Hutter (Gustav von Wangenheim) taking leave of his wife Ellen (Greta Schroeder-Matray) at the behest of his strange employer, Knock (Alexander Granach). Knock, the Renfield character, directs Hutter to

---

*A major restoration of the film and its score was recently undertaken at the Film Museum of Munich under the direction of conservator Enno Patalas.

Nosferatu springs from his hiding place in the hold of the doomed ship, a startling, simultaneous evocation of erection, rigor mortis, and pestilence.

Upstairs/downstairs: the vampire rises from the ship's shadows into consciousness. Note the live rat on actor's elbow.

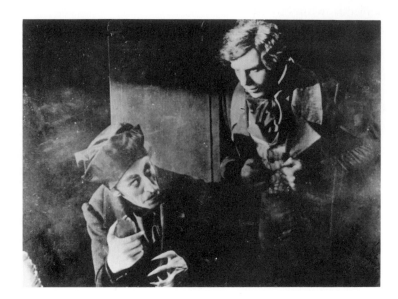

"What a lovely throat!" Graf Orlok examines the portrait miniature of his victim-to-be. (The British Film Institute)

The feast of life, the dance of death. Each creature finds its own sustenance in Nosferatu. (Collection of the Cinémathèque Française)

"Your precious blood!" Orlok's appetite is aroused at his guest's unfortunate mishap with a table knife. (Collection of the Cinémathèque Française)

travel to the castle of Graf Orlok; the mysterious nobleman wishes to buy a deserted house adjacent to Hutter's. Hutter travels by coach to Orlok's castle, stopping for one night at a gypsy inn where he reads a book of vampire superstitions. The next day he is driven to a bridge the gypsy drivers refuse to cross. Hutter traverses it by foot, and, having entered the land of phantoms by his own volition, is met by a coach that moves with a jerking, accelerated energy (a stop-motion effect meant to be frightening but which finally appears only comical). A muffled coachman with penetrating eyes directs Hutter into the coach, which returns the way it came, and this time the landscape of phantoms is projected in negative, another special effect that sounds more intriguing than it actually looks. It should be remembered, however, that Murnau and his crew were working with extremely limited technical resources.

F. W. Murnau, one of the cinema's most visionary pictorialists. Nosferatu *was among the director's fledgling efforts. (Free Library of Philadelphia Theatre Collection)*

At the castle, Hutter is greeted by Graf Orlok, a strange, secretive spectre of a man who becomes unaccountably excited at the sight of Hutter's blood when he accidentally cuts himself. He also admires a portrait of Ellen the young husband carries with him: "What a lovely throat!" he exclaims. Late that night, Hutter opens the door of his room, and is horrified to see Orlok approaching, his features exaggerated and hideous, a vampire as described in the gypsy book. Hutter hides in bed but the vampire enters the room and attacks him. Ellen, at home in the town of Wisborg, cries out her husband's name as she sleeps. The vampire, disturbed by the psychic warning, withdraws from the young man's bedchamber.

The next day, shaken by the vampire's midnight visit, Hutter discovers a rotting coffin in which Orlok is resting. He flees the crypt and watches helplessly as the awakened monster loads a wagon with coffin-boxes and departs for Hutter's town.

Murnau then crosscuts several sequences, including Hutter's escape, hospitalization, and recovery; Knock's madness and confinement to an asylum; and Professor Bulwer's experiments with carnivorous plants and other devouring organisms. Aboard the sailing ship carrying his earth-boxes, Orlok is now completely transformed into Nosferatu, even his fingers swollen into malignant, predatory hooks. One by one he stalks and kills the crew.

The derelict vessel glides into the Wisborg harbor, Nosferatu's arrival coinciding with the onset of plague. Hutter's wife Ellen reads the book about vampires he has brought with him from the land of phantoms; she learns that the vampire can be defeated only if a virtuous woman willingly lets him remain with her until dawn. Nosferatu, who has been watching her from his house across the street, gladly presents himself when she throws open her window. He fixes himself at her throat like a motionless leech, and never notices the onset of daybreak until it is too late. The sunlight reduces Nosferatu to a puff of smoke.[13] Ellen dies as well, sacrificing herself to banish the plague and to

The vampire as pestilence: an evocative poster design by Albin Grau. (Courtesy of Ronald V. Borst/Hollywood Movie Posters.)

restore a balance of nature.

The central, striking image of *Nosferatu* will forever and always be the cadaverous Max Schreck as the vampire, his appearance totally unlike the film vampires that were to follow. Schreck's characterization of Dracula as a kind of human vermin draws its energy in part from Stoker, but also from universal fears and collective obsessions. (How else is it possible for one character to be interpreted—as it has been—as "a Shylock of the Carpathians"[14] . . . as well as a pop culture anticipation of Hitler?[15] Ugliness, it seems, is in the mind of the beholder.) The inspired makeup was probably also Albin Grau's invention, building up the actor's features with putty, creating batlike ears and ratlike teeth, and gradually elongating the actor's fingers during the course of the film (John Barrymore had used the same kind of finger-effect in *Dr. Jekyll and Mr. Hyde,* though not quite so hideously). With his padded costume and stiff halting gait, Schreck is more a filmic precursor of Frankenstein's monster than the elegant, evening-clothed *blutsaugers* who were to come. Schreck—the name means "terror" in German—was the actor's actual name, and not

Vampires aren't supposed to throw shadows, but without them we would miss some of the great moments of German expressionism.

merely a pseudonym, as has been repeatedly suggested. Born in 1879 in Berlin, Schreck was also a former Reinhardt company member and went on to play character roles in German films until the time of his death in 1936.[16] None, of course, achieved the transcendent notoriety of *Nosferatu.*

Despite its technical limitations (one can only wonder at what Murnau could have achieved with the full studio resources later at his disposal for *Faust* or *Sunrise*) *Nosferatu* remains an impressive film. Its Dracula is genuinely, viscerally frightening. Conscious poetry and metaphor are everywhere, to a degree Stoker only hints at, or stumbles upon. In one famous scene aboard the doomed ship, the vampire springs from his rat-filled coffin like an obscene jack-in-the-box, an image simultaneously suggesting erection, pestilence, and death. In an influential essay, the French critic Roger Dadoun calls the character of Nosferatu "a walking phallus or 'phallambulist'." Nosferatu's rigidity is that of a corpse, "but the signs of an aggressive sexuality are abundant and spectacular. . . . Nosferatu might be called The Pointed One, bearing in mind all the simple and basic symbolism attached to pointedness. His face is pointed, so are his ears, his shoulders, his knees, his back and of course his nails and fangs. According to a primitive mental operation which prefers not to distinguish the structure of the parts from that of the whole, Nosferatu is an agglomeration of points."[17]

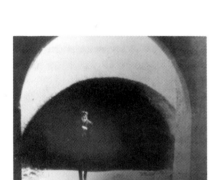

Arching shadows are a recurring visual motif in Nosferatu.

The more recent critics of *Nosferatu* have made much of Murnau's widely acknowledged homosexuality as being germane to the film; one much-quoted lecture-essay by the experimental filmmaker Stan Brakhage goes so far as to characterize *Nosferatu* as a deliberate exercise in "camp."[18] (After reading Brakhage, one is almost disappointed when Max Schreck fails to appear in garter belt and mascara.) While Stoker's novel is built on a complicated psychological foundation of sexual ambiguity, *Nosferatu* is starkly devoid of the consciously ambiguous or knowingly ironic. Modern culture and its complexities are banished; in sharp contrast to *Dracula*—a very up-to-date book for its time—Murnau's film is decidedly preindustrial, almost medieval in its preoccupations.

Nosferatu's continuing appeal lies in its formal elements. The pictorial compositions are frequently stunning: Nosferatu, for instance, clinging to a window grid like a spider in a Bauhaus web. The shadow of Nosferatu's extended talons glides up a victim's bedclothes, closing on his victim's heart. Arches and shadows repeatedly unify and bisect the images, often simultaneously. The sails and rigging of the death-ship divide the screen into nearly abstract patterns of light and shadow, austere and almost oriental in their minimalism—an aesthetic worthy of Beardsley.

The extent of Albin Grau's visual commitment to the material—as well as his fascination with the occult—can be seen in the extraordinary effort he spent in the creation of a single prop, the letter, or lease, filled with strange symbols that Hutter brings to Nosferatu from his mad employer. The document, front and back, is on screen only for a few moments. But a close analysis of frame blowups, published in the French film magazine *Positif* in 1980, shows that Grau utilized a complex synthesis of cabbalistic and astrological symbols that Nosferatu would take as favorable auguries for his purchase of the house.[19] The letter recalls the earlier use of hermetic symbols by Stoker's illustrators, and the widespread practice by members of secret magical societies of including alchemical or mystical signs in their signatures—a variation on the secret handshake, signaling others who know the code.

It is also possible that Grau was simply indulging his own interests in a manner wholly out of proportion to the requirements of the film. Certainly, the financial aspects of the production as a whole were totally out of balance and indicate unmistakable lapses in judgment; following the premiere, it would be revealed that *Nosferatu*'s publicity expenses had actually exceeded the cost of producing the film.[20] And it seems to have occurred to no one that there were any copyright problems involved in an unauthorized adaptation of *Dracula*. They had changed the names, after all. They had acknowledged the source, hadn't they?

An elaborate premiere was held at the Berlin Zoo on Saturday, March 4, 1922. The publicity material struck forbidding chords:

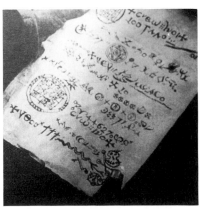

> Nosferatu—who cannot die!
> A million fancies strike you when you hear the name: Nosferatu!
> N O S F E
> R A T U
> does not die!
> What do you expect of the first showing of this great work? Aren't you afraid? Men must die. But legend has it that a vampire, Nosferatu, "the undead," lives on men's blood! You want to see a symphony of horror? You may expect more. Be careful. Nosferatu is not just fun, not something to be taken lightly. Once more: beware.[21]

Though glimpsed only briefly, the letter Orlok peruses is filled with arcane symbols and complicated patterns of esoteric meaning. The film's production designer, Albin Grau, was a devoted spiritualist.

The initial critical reaction in Germany was generally favorable. Profound metaphors were perceived, with Nosferatu and his accompanying plague representing aspects of human malaise (and, by extension, the German soul itself in the wrenching years during and immediately following World War I, providing for Germany a cathartic image roughly analogous to the one Godzilla provided for Japan after World War II). But artistic appreciation was soon overwhelmed by another kind of press coverage. Prana-Film, it seemed, could not pay its bills. The "new principles" of film production cited by Grau were unique indeed, in that they apparently included the mystical transmigration of funds. Inquiries by the press followed, and then attacks.

And then it was Florence Stoker's turn.

The Society of Authors proceeded cautiously in the matter. Florence was advised that her sale of the German translation rights had had no bearing whatsoever on German film rights. The fact that she had sought membership only in a crisis also caused a few eyebrows to be raised as to the sincerity of her interest in the Society's work as a whole.[22] By the middle of May, the committee chairman had reached a compromise decision: the Society was willing to place the matter in the hands of its German lawyer, a Dr. Wronker-Flatow of Berlin, "on the understanding that if the film company gives in, all well and good, but if they show a disposition to fight that we cannot take the case further on your behalf."[23] Thus, the Society was able to offer at least the appearance of chivalry without really having to make an open-ended commitment. It was far less than Florence would have wished, but at least she now had representation.

By June, Prana's precarious finances had driven it into receivership. Thring wrote Stoker that "the film company had put up some foolish points as a defence. If the company has gone into liquidation it is quite clear that we shall not obtain any money out of them, but it might be possible to obtain the film, or an injunction against anyone who purchases it."[24]

An extremely rare photo of actor Max Schreck sans vampire makeup, although he seems to have his upcoming role in Nosferatu *distinctly in mind. From* Der Richter von Zalamea *(1920). (Collection of the Cinémathèque Française)*

Florence Stoker's early letters over the *Nosferatu* affair are missing from the Society of Authors archives (now owned by the British Library), but judging from Thring's patient—if slightly exasperated—responses to them, her correspondence was frequent and insistent. She had been wronged. She wanted justice. Above all, she wanted money.

By early August, the Society's patience showed definite signs of thinning. The case had not turned out to be so straightforward, after all. Thring to Stoker, August 3, 1922: "I am sending you a copy of a letter I have received from our German lawyer. You will remember that this case was originally taken up in the hope that our Lawyer might be able to settle out of court. The question has now become so complicated, and the legal point so difficult, that I doubt whether the Society could afford to carry the matter any further. . . . Perhaps you would let me know whether you yourself would be willing to meet any expenses . . ."

It was but the first of many times Thring extended his regrets that the Society could no longer pursue her case, only to reverse himself a few days or weeks later. Evidently the widow still had a number of close acquaintances in publishing with ties to the Society, and knew how to extract favors or apply pressure as needed. The specific deliberations of the committee are not recorded, but presumably another reason for the Society's willingness to

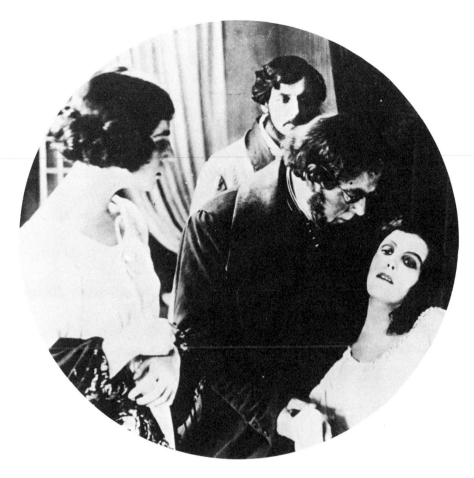

*The heroine's wasting malady
mystifies her household. (Collection
of the Cinémathèque Française)*

persevere was the unique and legitimate nature of Stoker's case and its
implications for literary contracts in the burgeoning age of cinema. It would
be far from the last legal battle involving film versions of *Dracula*.

On August 22 a power of attorney was forwarded to the German lawyer,
who had quoted probable fees of 24,000 marks. Thring asked for an equivalent guarantee of £20 (not an inconsiderable sum for Stoker, something like
$100 in 1922 terms) to cover the expenses.

Meanwhile, Florence Stoker had learned of showings of *Nosferatu* in
Budapest. The company had dared to claim bankruptcy while the film was still
being shown and making money as far east as the Danube!

The strategy, now, was to pursue the receiver of Prana's assets and
liabilities rather than the offending officers of Prana itself. But the action
threatened to become mind-bogglingly complicated: not only would the Society have to incur costs in Germany, but in every country where the receiver
might attempt to sell *Nosferatu*. "If the receiver is an unscrupulous man of
business," Thring wrote Stoker, "he will know it won't be worth our while to
take action, and most probably trade upon this." Obtaining injunctions in

*As usual, the forces of science are
mystified by the powers of the supernatural.
(Collection of the Cinémathèque Française)*

other countries could be "a very expensive and dangerous experiment."[25]

The Germans showed some small signs of yielding, and through the German lawyer made a small offer of financial participation, provided Stoker would allow them to use the title *Dracula* openly in England and America. Thring advised her against this line of negotiation, unless the Germans were willing to make her a substantial advance (they weren't) and was generally pessimistic about any settlement paid in marks because of the huge difference in exchange rates. The German economy was on shaky economic footing since the war, and its currency fluctuated wildly. If she won German money, she very well might have to invest it in Germany for it to have any worth.[26]

The case had now dragged on for a year. Florence Stoker continued to state her position, insisting that the Society take the matter seriously. There was a principle. Of fairness and of law. Was the British Society of Authors really willing to let the work of a British writer be stolen simply because his widow had no money to fight the case? The issue was larger than Bram Stoker.

Thring's exasperation shows through in a letter of March 17, 1923: "I am in receipt of your letter. I can but refer the whole matter to the Committee again. You might remember, however, the case would cost the Society a considerable amount of money and that you joined the Society only when you were in difficulties. The Committee of the Society are bound to consider themselves as Trustees for the subscription of those members who have subscribed to the Society for many years, and whose cases as it is cost the Society very large sums of money. Whether the Committee will take the view you take of the case is entirely for them to decide."

So skillful, however, was Florence Stoker's behind-the-scenes lobbying that she was able to transform the Society's original request for a £20 guarantee into an offer of £20 in advance of any damages the Society might recover for her. On April 12, 1923, Thring told Stoker that "I am instructed, however, to inform you, that this payment does not imply that the Society will—or bind the Society in any way—to take action on your behalf." Such an exceedingly strange arrangement could only be construed in one way: as a payoff. The old lady was getting tiresome. Thring hinted again that it might be better for her to deal through the German lawyer herself.

Once more, in June 1923, the committee concluded that it could not embroil itself in the messy *Nosferatu* matter any longer, and that it was the longstanding membership of the Society that was more deserving of support. "Further," Thring wrote, "it is most probable that the Prana Film Company, judging from their present methods, would refuse to pay any monies whatever even if judgement was secured against them, and would use every possible legal method to avoid such payment."[27]

This was not what the widow wanted to hear, so she ignored it, and again appealed to the committee. By this point it had to have been more than obvious to all parties that they were dealing with a ferociously determined woman, who was not going away. As she would not accept the "advance" of £20 and allow the Society to quietly drop the case, it was difficult to know just what to do with her. It would be unseemly indeed to just cut her off. The whole matter required a certain tactful . . . closure. She still had certain connections, with Heinemann, for instance, one of her husband's last publishers and one of the most prestigious houses. One of Heinemann's former right-hand men, C. A. Bang, was now advising her about stage rights, it appeared.

Between Florence Stoker's steely determination and the seeming inability of the Society's committee to deal decisively with her, the matter dragged on long enough for a development to occur in Berlin. Prana's bankruptcy files had been subpoenaed and the case had finally been fixed for a hearing on March 31, 1924.

The end, however, was not in sight. In July, the German court ruled against Prana. Florence Stoker was asking for payment of £5,000 from the receivers, the Deutsch-Amerikanisch Film Union, to give them title to the film. In August, the receivers refused the proposal and decided to appeal.[28] It was not until February 1925 that the appelate court ruled again in Stoker's favor, but apparently this, too, was subject to appeal.

Realizing that there was no possibility of obtaining money, the widow began to press for the outright destruction of all extant copies of the film, in negative and positive (she had considered taking possession of the negative herself, but seems to have been advised against it).

A window at Florence Stoker's former home in William Street, Knightsbridge, where she waged her relentless campaign against Nosferatu. *(Photograph by the author)*

No doubt at this juncture the story will begin to horrify film conservators and historians, as Florence Stoker attempts the obliteration of a classic film that she herself has never seen, or asked to see. Most "lost" films have vanished through neglect. But in the case of *Nosferatu* we have one of the few instances in film history, and perhaps the only one, in which an obliterating capital punishment is sought for a work of cinematic art, strictly on legalistic grounds, by a person with no knowledge of the work's specific contents or artistic merit.

But the English widow knew her rights. And the copyright in *Dracula* was very nearly her only means of support. She had just granted a stage license to a man who toured the provinces, an actor-manager named Hamilton Deane. It wasn't really a first-rate company and it wasn't really much money and she didn't really like the adaptation. You couldn't really do a whole novel on stage, Deane had told her; practical stage conventions had to be observed. There would have to be cuts. Reading a book was different from watching a play. She remembered, of course, the tedious staged reading at the Lyceum that had been so important to Bram and had turned out so badly. And so she had given Hamilton Deane permission to do his surgery and make his play. She needed the money.

But at least she had given Deane her permission. This German thing was another matter. They had no rights—none!—and she would take her legal remedy.

In May 1925 there were more delays, and she was advised of the possibility of yet additional maneuvering and appeals. "I am quite prepared to carry on," she wrote to Thring.[29]

Finally, on July 20, word came from Berlin that Prana's liquidator had withdrawn its appeal. The prints and negatives of *Nosferatu* were ordered destroyed. The German lawyer's fees had been collected from the receiver, and Florence Stoker was in no further financial obligation. "The judgement now becomes a final one," the Berlin solicitor wrote, to which Thring added a fervent postscript: "I am glad this matter is now at an end." He had every reason to be: three years had now elapsed since the widow had first approached him.

But the widow's waking nightmare over *Nosferatu* had barely begun.

The German court had provided no tangible proof of the film's destruction, although the original negative never resurfaced. But as any reader of *Dracula* knows, a vampire has numerous hiding places, and unless the sanctifying rites are performed, he can live on indefinitely, watching and waiting, attacking at will.

In October, Florence Stoker received by mail the prospectus of a new organization that carried the name of her old acquaintance Ellen Terry—now Dame Ellen Terry—as one of the founding members. The Film Society, as it was called, also boasted the sponsorship of Bernard Shaw, H. G. Wells, and Julian Huxley. The Film Society was dedicated to preserving the art of the cinema, and would arrange screenings in a manner patterned after private theatre clubs that had long been in vogue. It sounded like a worthy cause indeed. Then she looked at the list of films that were to be shown.

Prominent among them was "*Dracula* by F. W. Murnau."

Not only had they stolen it—now they were claiming authorship as well!

She called Thring. He advised her to send a registered letter forbidding any performance of the film. The Society's organizer, a certain Ivor Montagu, whom she did not know, rang her up. The voice on the phone was unrepentant. As Stoker wrote Thring, "Montagu on the telephone contends as the performance will be private, they have a right to give it. He admits the film was purchased in Germany, but would not say from whom, or whether it was already in this country."[30] Thring advised Montagu that the proposed screening was not quite "private" from the standpoint of copyright law, and that

Mrs. Stoker was prepared to take full legal remedies.[31]

Vampires, according to literary and film tradition, are wise to secure an agent, slave, or protector in foreign lands they visit. In *Dracula* the point of contact is Renfield, who devours the flesh of small living things. However, in its travel to England and America as a film *Nosferatu* showed a distinct preference for vegetarians. The first was Ivor Montagu, the son of a wealthy, distinguished family who had turned communist as well as herbivorous. (In a bizarre misunderstanding, Montagu once let Shaw, another vegetarian, serve him a veal cutlet for luncheon. The young man was too intimidated by Shaw at the time to put up a fuss.) Montagu would later be an associate of both Hitchcock and Eisenstein, as well as an influential film historian. He was one of the earliest proponents of film preservation.

Florence Stoker as a young girl.

The last thing on Florence Stoker's mind was the preservation of *Nosferatu*. She wrote the American Society of Dramatists and Composers on the letterhead of her son's accounting firm, Williams, Stoker, Worssam and Holland, alerting them to the spreading pestilence of *Nosferatu*. "I have for a considerable time past been in negotiation for a film to be made from this novel . . . the fact that a pirated version thereof was in circulation would prove to be extremely prejudicial to me."[32] In actuality, there is no evidence (at least not in the Society of Authors' archives) of her having discussed film rights with anyone other than C. A. Bang, who was now handling her dramatic interests.

On October 10, Montagu wrote to Bang. "I must apologize for my shortness on the telephone yesterday . . . your call should not have been put through for I was in the middle of a meeting. But still, that is no excuse for me being rude." Montagu explained that since "we do not admit the public, but only show pictures to our members (exclusively) without charge, copyright does not affect us at all. Of course, it has never been settled with the films, because there has never been any private society showing them before, but on the precedent of the rights and powers of similar societies for the stage, I do not think there is any question of our losing a test case if one were brought." However, Montagu assured him "that if you could convince us that the showing of the film to our members would damage Mrs. Stoker in any way, we would not dream of sticking to our legal rights, and would probably abandon the film altogether rather than hurt somebody."[33]

A few days later, Montagu visited Bang, who was surprised at how young he was. Bang impressed upon him his view that the film he intended to show his members was "stolen goods." Bang also did some detective work of his own and learned that an importer—he couldn't learn the name—had tried to place the film at several London theatres, but ran into problems with the censor, "who has condemned it as too horrible. The film therefore has no

market value in this country and they have offered it to the Film Society free of charge."[34]

Montagu stonewalled on the matter of the agent. "No doubt he knows all about where the offer came from," Bang wrote Stoker, "but he is evidently shielding them."[35]

Like Seward, Van Helsing, and Harker scouring London for Dracula's safehouses, Bang, Thring, and company tracked the German vampire through commercial London, narrowing the search to an importer, Sargent's Trust Ltd., in Chancery Lane. But the film cannisters that contained *Nosferatu* were not to be found. By January, Thring informed Stoker, "I beg to inform you with great regret we must drop the case of the film *Dracula*. . . . The Sargent's Trust have already done everything to help us trace the man who actually held the film, but we find this person has disappeared entirely."[36]

For the moment, there was nothing that could be done. The creature had succeeded in crossing the channel, and had penetrated London. It could reappear at any time, to taunt and to torment. Whatever her legal rights, there were certain irrational aspects of *Dracula* that were beyond Florence Stoker's control. Uninvited, animated by the obsessions of others, the thing had achieved a life of its own and could move through her world as it pleased.

Chapter Three

"A NURSE WILL BE IN ATTENDANCE AT ALL PERFORMANCES..."

*In which the widow approves a proper vampire
in a proper venue, but yet has her doubts, and
still another foreigner scratches at her window,
this time with money and with an offer
to improve the product.*

WHEN HORACE LIVERIGHT, AMERICAN PUBLISHER AND THEATRICAL entrepreneur, took his seat at the Little Theatre in John Street, Adelphi, on a cold London night in early 1927, he would have been, in all probability, both uncomfortable and skeptical. Uncomfortable, because the clammy London winter and underheated buildings here would have made him yearn for his New York town house where he characteristically worked with his feet propped on a radiator, and where he wore woolen socks year-round in any case. Skeptical, because the reviews of this evening's offering were not very good, despite *Dracula*'s having barnstormed the provinces for two previous seasons to good business. The theatre itself was a former banking hall, converted for theatrical use with a small balcony and boxes added, but still clung to some of its former cramped and stuffy aspect. The stiff-backed stalls were a bit like those in a classroom or temperance lecture hall. Both associations would have irked Liveright; he was impatient with classrooms, and was himself completely self-educated—the cofounder of the Modern Library and publisher of five Nobel Prize winners had never graduated high school. As for

Dorothy Peterson's prominent necklace of garlic seems to pose no deterrent to Bela Lugosi's thirst in a dramatic but not altogether logical publicity photo. (Courtesy Ronald V. Borst/Hollywood Movie Posters)

*Horace Liveright, the legendary
publisher and Broadway producer of*
Dracula, *in a suitably atmospheric
portrait. (The Billy Rose Theatre
Collection, New York Public
Library at Lincoln Center, Astor,
Lenox and Tilden Foundations)*

temperance lectures, Horace Brisbin Liveright was one of the most celebrated party-givers of his age, Prohibition or not.

Though he was not the kind of notorious celebrity in London he was in New York, Liveright would have had little difficulty attracting the glances of his fellow theatregoers that winter evening—he was a tall man with a striking leonine profile and a backswept mane of hair. His wardrobe tended to vivid rainbow hues that he mixed as he pleased—a far cry from the sea of English tweeds that surrounded him. A magnetic, charismatic figure who inspired loyalty or enmity and rarely anything between, Horace Liveright was to many the flamboyant embodiment of the Gatsby-like excesses of his age. He was usually at the center of some controversy or another, the target of attacks by the guardians of public morality, and even his own authors. His wife would soon quite literally take a shot at him.

The houselights flashed and the audience quieted. A uniformed English nurse—could they really be *serious?*—stood reassuringly . . . no, *menacingly* in view of the house. (The gimmick was not original—Sybil Thorndike had introduced guardian nurses in this very theatre for her 1920 season of Grand Guignol.) The audience was impressed—it *wanted* to be impressed. This Hamilton Deane person, who had written, produced, and was even acting in the damned thing—he was said to be a cartoon of the English actor/manager—was simply operating without regard to the theatrical mainstream . . . and had found a whole new audience the mainstream had ignored—and the critics be damned. The gimmickry smacked more of a circus or sideshow than the legitimate theatre. It was the sort of show they called a "boob catcher" in the American trade. Of course, Liveright himself knew how to hawk his wares like a carnival barker—and frequently did.

The lights dimmed. Backstage, an actor imitated the low howling of a wolf by projecting his voice through a lamp chimney. The audience shuddered deliciously. Whatever this was, it was a far cry from Liveright's previous theatrical ventures, which had included an ambitious modern-dress *Hamlet* (his favorite play; he collected memorabilia of every actor who played the part) and a stage version of Theodore Dreiser's *An American Tragedy*. *Hamlet* in particular had not made money. Perhaps his approach had been too highbrow. Even Shakespeare, after all, knew how to play to the rabble when he had to.

Hamilton Deane had no reservations about pleasing audiences, and his barnstorming melodramas had gained him a loyal following in the provinces. As a former actor with the Henry Irving Vacation Company (he had made his debut with the touring ensemble in 1899), he was doubly acquainted with Bram Stoker, since his family owned an estate adjacent to that of Stoker's father, in Dublin. Deane did not, however, entertain the notion of a stage

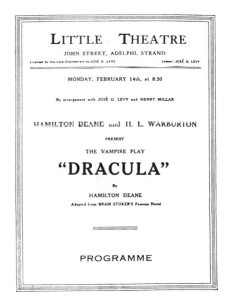

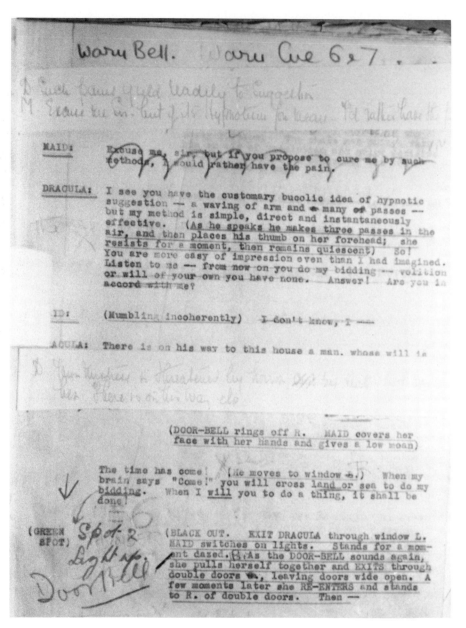

Edmund Blake, the first actor to portray Dracula in Hamilton Deane's adaptation, visible from the neck up in the trick coffin with an impalable dummy body that the Lord Chamberlain initially banned as too grisly an effect. (Courtesy of the Dracula Society)

A page from Hamilton Deane's original promptbook. (Courtesy of the Dracula Society)

version of *Dracula* until after his own troupe, the Hamilton Deane Company, was established in the early 1920s. Frustrated in his attempts to find a dramatist willing to tackle the project—the novel's large scope and complicated epistolary structure presented major technical problems—Deane, bedridden at the time and eager to get on with the project, decided to take on the job himself: "Fortunately," said Deane, "I then developed a severe cold, for it put me to bed and, idly at first, I began to write a draft of the play."[1]

At the time Deane was developing his proposal, Florence Stoker was still embroiled in her suit against Prana-Film over *Nosferatu*. She welcomed Deane's overture as a chance to reassert control over an authorized dramatization. (While the details of their contract are not available, their subsequent arrangement for the American production suggests that the license was far more lucrative to Stoker than Deane—though billed as co-dramatist, his financial participation would be limited to an almost unbelievably paltry 10 percent of Florence Stoker's royalties.[2])

Whatever reservations Deane may have had about his contract with Florence Stoker, he was enthusiastic about the play itself, and finished writing his script in a whirlwind four weeks. In order to make the play workable in a shoestring physical production, Deane reconceived the story as a conventional drawing-room melodrama, lopping off the opening and closing chapters of the book—ironically the best parts of the novel, involving Jonathan Harker's captivity at Castle Dracula, and the suspenseful climactic chase back to Transylvania. The novel's American character, the Texan Quincey Morris, one of Lucy's suitors, was recast as a woman, presumably to offer a third female part for a company member (the character was dropped in the American adaptation, but contemporary productions occasionally cast Dr. Seward as a woman for the same practical reason). Deane had initially intended a brief prologue showing Dracula emerging from the window of his castle like a huge, crawling bat, going so far as to include specific stage instructions for the proper execution of the effect. ("Trousers must be strapped under feet—one foot to be secured inside window to solid rostrum. The Inverness Cape which he wears must be heavily wired, so that when face downward it assumes the shape of a Bat's Wings."[3]) According to film historian Ivan Butler, who as a young man acted in one of Deane's many touring companies of *Dracula*, the prologue was never actually staged, owing to the cost it would incur.[4] It did not stop Deane, however, from using an artist's conception of the scene prominently on his posters.

Leslie Drayton, member of the Hamilton Deane Company who devised Dracula's trick stage coffin. Visible behind him is Deane's original poster, depicting the Count's descent from the castle, an effect cut from the play because of its expense. (Courtesy of Ivan Butler)

Deane's dramaturgical surgery served the purposes of the production he could afford to produce, but would wreak havoc with future stage and film adaptations. Like a macabre Halloween Humpty Dumpty, the scattered pieces of *Dracula* would not fit back easily—it would not be until the 1970s that a truly straightforward adaptation of the novel would even be attempted. Florence Stoker approved Deane's adaptation—one can assume she was comfortable with, or had even had a hand in creating, the "new" image of the master vampire in evening dress and opera cloak, one polite enough to be invited into a proper Knightsbridge living room. (That ghastly German thing ... it was better not to think about it.) Dracula might be a vampire, but if he was going to work in the English theatre, there were going to be some *limits*. Dracula's good manners are in rather short supply in the novel, and his hygiene and grooming are certainly problematic—Stoker gives him both bad breath and hair on the palms. Gentility and breeding added a new dimension to the character, and served a theatrical function—he was now able to interact with the characters, rather than merely hang outside their bedroom windows. But to what extent was the soup-and-fish characterization a reaction to the obscene, pestilential images of *Nosferatu,* over which the lawsuit was still raging at the time Deane made his play? Unlike the heroine of her husband's novel, Florence Stoker did not set down her thoughts on the matter in journals or letters. But it is clear that the characterization of Dracula that met with her approval was a remarkably domesticated one, an image almost perversely sanitized. Yet it is this particular interpretation that has had the greatest staying power.

Dracula was given a license by the Lord Chamberlain on August 5, 1924, for the Grand Theatre, Derby, where it had its preview-premiere. The censor insisted on one cut: the death of Dracula was not to be explicitly shown ("The five men close round the box, completely covering 'Dracula' from the audience, there is a movement of Harker's arm—but the audience sees nothing of the killing"[5]). However, Deane's trick coffin (devised by company member and magician Leslie Drayton), with its dummy body that seemed to disintegrate in a puff of Fuller's earth, eventually found its way around the censors and became one of the play's most memorable effects.

Deane had originally planned to play the vampire himself, but in his completed script the title part emerged as relatively small, and so he took on the meatier role of Abraham Van Helsing. Edmund Blake became the first actor to wear the now-familiar flowing cape of Dracula (Blake's performance was no doubt enhanced by a prominent gold front tooth) and Deane's future wife Dora Mary Patrick was cast as Mina. While financial advisors tried to discourage him, the initial audience response spurred Deane on until a properly mounted production could be staged in Wimbledon the following spring. The play was an immediate hit in its small venue, and while Deane received offers for a London production, he chose instead to keep to the road. He was justifiably concerned about the merciless London critics, who, he anticipated, would savage the show. (In time, they would do exactly that . . . with no impact whatsoever on attendance.)

In order to smooth his dealings with the notoriously difficult Florence Stoker, Deane approached her through her agent, C. A. Bang, who had been a manager at Heinemann when the firm had published several of Stoker's books, including the *Reminiscences.* Bang, a Dane by birth who was himself an author and translator, had been named to the Order of the British Empire and would soon be honored with the Crown of Italy for his contributions to science

Portrait study of Raymond Huntley as Dracula. (Courtesy of the Dracula Society)

and literature. He happened to be married at the time to a young woman whose brother was an aspiring actor. His name was Raymond Huntley.

"At the time I was playing in *The Farmer's Wife* at the Royal Court," recalled Huntley in a 1989 interview.[6] Still active on the London stage at the age of eighty-five, his memories were vivid. "I stayed with my sister and Bang at St. John's Wood, and Deane came up to discuss business. He subsequently offered me a job with his traveling repertory. I don't know whether he was currying favor with my brother-in-law by offering me this job, but I think he got a magnificent bargain. I was very enthusiastic and very naive—my salary was eight pounds a week, which was less than I had been getting previously. The parts I was to play are what are known in the trade as 'seconds,' that is, second leads, and this included Dracula."

Huntley admitted with a chuckle that "I have always considered the role of Count Dracula to have been an indiscretion of my youth." Indeed, he was very

Actor Raymond Huntley, the original Count Dracula of London's West End. The cape was a company prop, but Huntley had to provide his own evening clothes. (Courtesy of the Dracula Society)

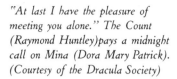

*"At last I have the pleasure of
meeting you alone." The Count
(Raymond Huntley)pays a midnight
call on Mina (Dora Mary Patrick).
(Courtesy of the Dracula Society)*

young—at twenty-two probably one of the youngest performers to ever tackle
the role outside of a college production. Tall, sharp-featured, and gifted with a
resonant voice, Huntley easily assumed older character parts. He remembered Deane as "a sort of minor god in the provinces [who] toured a fairly
large repertory in what were known as the number two and number three
dates—not your Manchesters and Liverpools and Birminghams, but less
important cities. I know I joined him at a horrible place called Morecambe on
a bank holiday."

The actor was required to provide his own costumes—though not the
flowing vampire cloak, which was considered a prop. "I had about four lounge
suits, full evening tails, full morning kit, short morning jacket, dinner jacket,
and silk hat. God knows how much it cost. I couldn't really tell you how I
managed it, but somehow I did." The standard makeup for Dracula in

Deane's productions included an effect that would be dropped in America—a wig with upward-sweeping gray streaks that suggested, perhaps too obviously, Mephistophelian horns. But it was this production that also introduced one of the most perennial features of the theatrical vampire—the big stand-up collar on the cape, a wardrobe idiosyncracy that has become almost synonymous with the character. Originally, the collar had a distinct theatrical function: to hide the actor's head when he stood with his back to the house, thus allowing him to slip out of the cape and down a trapdoor, effectively "disappearing" before the audience's eyes. Though the trick collar had no subsequent purpose in film adaptations, it has become a signature feature of vampire costuming for all time.

Soon *Dracula* began to take over Deane's repertory, pushing out the other productions as a matter of sheer economics. As an audience lure, *Dracula* overshadowed nearly anything else Deane served up. And, gradually, his resistance to a London production began to break down. As Huntley remembered, "I suppose José Levy, who owned and ran the Little Theatre in those days, saw the thing in the provinces, and thought it had curiosity or press value. I don't know how else it could have happened. It wasn't exactly a first class production."

The London engagement of *Dracula* opened at the Little Theatre on February 14, 1927, to generally hostile reviews. The important *Times* notice was particularly dismissive, judging the play's only strength to be in its

Rats, bats, and hypnotic hijinks: cartoonist Tom Titt's impression of an evening at the Little Theatre. (Courtesy of the Theatre Museum)

production of loud, startling noises. "In that respect, at least, this piece displays a sure sense of the theatre. There is very little of Bram Stoker in it. But most of us jumped in our seats at least once in every act." The review went on to criticize the play's "dreadfully stilted style of speech. This was so obtrusive that it almost seemed to be an intentional device to assist in making the flesh creep. The most extraordinary phrases came from the Professor's ready tongue. If they were part of a foreigner's English equipment, it is a pity that Mr. Hamilton Deane forgot all about his foreign accent during the interval."[7]

Another review went even further in its acid ridicule: the dialogue was "appallingly pompous" and singled out actors Stuart Lomath (as Seward) and Dora Mary Patrick as "life-long victims of elocutionists. They articulated each syllable in a clear, toneless manner, giving to each one precisely the same value. Mr. Lomath pronounced the word 'personally' as if it were spelt 'Pahrs O Nally' and said 'Sahr Vis' when he meant 'service.' Miss Patrick talked about a dreadful 'Leth Are Gee' which afflicted her 'Leems' . . ."[8]

Mina (Dora Mary Patrick) places her faith in Dr. Abraham Van Helsing (Hamilton Deane). (Courtesy of Jeanne Youngson)

But perhaps the most memorable brickbat of all was the one reserved for Raymond Huntley by the critic who complained of the actor's makeup. Huntley replied to the paper by letter, which was published:

"Sir—One of your dramatic critics was good enough to refer to the ill-fitting mask I am supposed to wear as Count Dracula in the play of that name at the Little Theatre.

"Although I shall not dispute with him that the face he saw may be both ill-fitting and mask-like, I should be glad of the hospitality of your column to assure him that at least it is my own."[9]

In his 1962 book *A Biography of Dracula: The Life Story of Bram Stoker* author Harry Ludlam, one of the few writers to have extensively interviewed Deane before his death in 1958, wrote that the uniformed nurse was a stunt inadvertently suggested to Deane by a newspaperman. Deane took the joke seriously, and rang up the Queen Alexandra Hospital, making it clear that he didn't want a glamour girl, "but a good, plain, upright woman, brisk and efficient. And I want one with medals, plenty of medals, please, if possible."[10] She arrived the same night, replete with medals and smelling salts.

Not all the press that *Dracula* generated was humorous. On April 25, 1927, *The Star* reported the suicide of a sixteen-year-old Russian boy who jumped into the path of a train at Victoria Station after attending a performance of the play. According to his guardian the disturbed boy's mother, a patient in a mental institution, had tried to take her life four times the year previously. The boy, the article stated, "was fond of morbid Russian books" and took his own life after witnessing the play (whose story concerned a madman and took place in an asylum). Hamilton Deane kept the clipping in his scrapbook, but made no attempt to exploit the macabre tragedy for publicity.

Florence Stoker was undoubtedly stung by the criticism and the generally tawdry level of public attention. *Dracula* was a far cry indeed from the glittering Lyceum openings around which her life and marriage once revolved. One indication that the production was an embarrassment to her was the fact that she never introduced herself to the actor in the title role. "It's absolute news to me that Bram Stoker ever married," said Raymond Huntley in 1989. "I'd never heard of her."

The show met with such faint praise that Deane assumed it would close immediately, until he looked at the box office receipts. *Dracula* was soon doing capacity business in the 300-seat playhouse and would need to be moved to the larger Duke of York's Theatre before the end of summer. The London *Evening News* noted that ". . . while glittering productions costing thousands of pounds have wilted and died after a week or so in the West End, *Dracula* has gone on drinking blood nightly. . . ."[11]

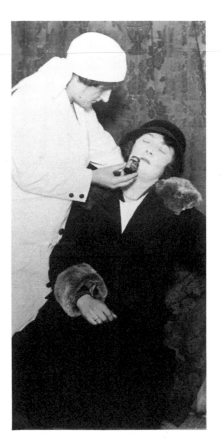

A uniformed nurse was ready to administer smelling salts to fainthearted patrons at all London performances of Dracula. *At one performance, thirty-nine audience members took advantage of the offer. (Courtesy of the Dracula Society)*

"We ran for some little time, for five months or so," recalled Huntley, "and then Deane got fed up with being a small frog in a big puddle and wanted to go back to his touring repertory, where he was happier. But his backer, a man named Harry Warburton, didn't like that idea at all—he thought he was being robbed of a London success." Unbeknownst to Deane, Warburton struck a deal with Mrs. Stoker to simply continue running the play without regard to Deane. *Dracula* was Mrs. Stoker's property, after all, wasn't it?

The following article appeared in the *Westminister Gazette:*

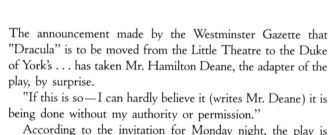

SURPRISE MOVE OF "DRACULA"

No Consultation of the Adapter

The announcement made by the Westminster Gazette that "Dracula" is to be moved from the Little Theatre to the Duke of York's . . . has taken Mr. Hamilton Deane, the adapter of the play, by surprise.

"If this is so—I can hardly believe it (writes Mr. Deane) it is being done without my authority or permission."

According to the invitation for Monday night, the play is being presented by Miss Violet Melnotte, the licensee of the Duke of York's, in association with Mr. Harry L. Warburton.

Mr. Warburton's manager told me yesterday (writes our theatrical correspondent) that the agreement between Mr. Deane and Mrs. Bram Stoker, the widow of the author of the novel, provided for an adaptation of the book and a run at the Little Theatre. As Mr. Deane had announced that the end of the run at the Little would be tomorrow that meant the agreement would then terminate. Mr. Warburton thereupon entered into an agreement with Mrs. Bram Stoker to present the play at the Duke of York's on Monday.

Mr. Hamilton Deane's name as adapter is given on the invitation issued for Monday next.[12]

A stylish caricature by E. S. Hynes, capturing the delicious spirit of fun and frenzy that Dracula *elicited in London's West End in 1927. (The Raymond Mander and Joe Mitchenson Theatre Collection)*

Now it was Hamilton Deane's turn to approach G. Herbert Thring and the Society of Authors with a complaint over the infringement of his own rights in *Dracula*. Thring, by this time an old hand in matters pertaining to *Dracula*, a veritable Van Helsing of literary contracts, urged mediation and told Mrs. Stoker he considered her position "rather hard."[13] Over the course of the ensuing year, a compromise was reached, extending Deane's touring

rights, but not before driving a permanent wedge between Deane and Huntley. The actor had accepted Warburton's offer to continue in the transferred
production, "which incurred Deane's lasting enmity. He hated me. Dora Mary
Patrick fairly spat her anger."

And Florence Stoker, no doubt, resented Deane. She resolved to end the
whole matter of licenses and split royalties—it was *her* husband, *her* book, *her*
money—and with Bang's help, quietly commissioned a playwright, Charles
Morrell, to make a new stage adapation, one that she would own outright.

The result was a peculiar vanity production, presented briefly by Harry
Warburton at the Royal Court Theatre, Warrington, in September 1927.
Morrell's manuscript[14] is clearly the work of an author working under the
widow's mandate, not of a professional dramatist following his own instincts.
Like the Deane piece, Morrell presented a drawing-room mystery, but unlike
Deane, lifted huge chunks of dialogue verbatim from the novel, creating a
static mise-en-scène that must have been excruciating to sit through (or to
perform). Numerous Shakespearean references were made, notably to *The
Tempest* and *A Midsummer Night's Dream*. A shipwreck occurs offstage. Like
Lady Macbeth, Mina sleepwalks. She also craves raw meat. Morrell includes
the obligatory laugh lines, though with less of a bludgeon than Deane. His line
for Dracula, "I have lived too long in Italy to care for the smell of Garlic" is
considerably more palatable than what Deane puts into the mouth of his
transsexualized American, Quincy Morris: "Well—sometimes—way back
home—I've caught a whiff of Garlic, from some 'Dago' or 'Mex' in the Subway—but I never 'saw red' like the Count, just now—that's got me beat!"

The Lord Chamberlain's office had many more objections to the Morrell
play, and demanded the striking of a scene in which the Host burns Mina's
forehead, as well as the famous set piece from the book, with Dracula feeding
Mina blood from his breast, while speaking Christ-like lines ("Come, drink of
my blood, that you may become even as I"). The blasphemous undertones of
the story were getting uncomfortably close to the surface.

The Morrell play was never produced again, and Florence Stoker grudg-
ingly accepted that if *Dracula* was to survive in the theatre, it could not do so
without the participation of Hamilton Deane.

Dracula continued its run in London, changing theatres several times, and
was revived under Bang's management the following year. On the occasion of
its 250th performance, at the Prince of Wales Theatre, audience members
each received a closed packet, with instructions not to break the seal before
the end of the third act. Contained therein was a surprise souvenir: a special
edition of Stoker's story collection *Dracula's Guest*, which in turn contained a
second surprise: a hidden cardboard bat that flew out of the book as it was
opened, propelled by an elastic band.[15]

*Actor Bernard Jukes, the theatre's original
Renfield, in and out of character.
(Courtesy of Jeanne Youngson)*

Hamilton Deane took the play to the provinces once more, where it was so successful that he at one point had three companies playing it in separate engagements. A few years later, the Lord Chamberlain would license a burlesque version, in verse:

> Here ye see a mighty drama
> Full of action and emotion,
> As can stir the public's feeling;
> Melodrama turned to marvel,
> Wonder of the Supernatural,
> Though the Critics snorted at it
> Jeered at it as blood and thunder
> And derided it as nonsense,
> Cried: "and is this Entertainment
> For the adult population?"
> Punch, The Times and the Observer
> All combined to prove it worthless.
> Yet *we feel they were mistaken.*
>
> And the play is one, soul stirring.
> True, unfit for babes and sucklings,
> Likewise, for all youth, improper;
> But to all matured persons
> Who can stand a meaty drama
> Very strong and very noble.
> Let's leave Irving his opinion.
> Can the Public err in Judgement?
> Shall not instinct safely guide us?
> Can there be a nobler subject
> For a play than here is handled?
> Innocence withstanding malice,
> Evil overcome by virtue?
> What is more sublime than this is
> As a subject for the writer?
>
> If this thrills our human marrow
> Must it not be mighty drama?
> Spake the mighty British Public.
> It knew better what it wanted.[16]

Actor-manager and playwright Hamilton Deane. (Courtesy of Jeanne Youngson)

Whatever it was, *Dracula* was certainly a phenomenon of the English theatre. Horace Liveright was immediately fascinated by the production's crude energy and unstoppable audience appeal. He saw it four times during his late winter business trip to London. "Although it was badly produced, I got a kick out of it each time," Liveright later recalled.[17] He was also impressed that the novel's sales had grown steadily in the thirty years it had been in print, and now averaged over 20,000 copies per year.[18]

There were problems, however. Much of the negative criticism had been earned. Whatever his talents as an actor or director, Deane as a writer did not have a gift for dialogue, and much of his script was thunderingly, amateurishly bad. Liveright knew it would be suicide to try to stage it in New York in its original form. But he knew that Deane's essential theatricality was a potential gold mine.

Liveright was no fool. As the publisher who had popularized Freud in America, it is inconceivable that he was unaware of *Dracula*'s psychosexual subtext and perverse manipulation of Christian iconography. Even if Hamilton Deane was an inept dramatist, the raw material was so highly charged that the "kick" Liveright described could well have been his realization that he had stumbled across a censor-proof way to present outrageous themes of oral sexuality, insanity, and borderline necrophilia (what, after all was the kiss of Dracula if not sex with a walking corpse?). The naive, supernatural trappings hid the real themes in plain sight. (At the same time he was negotiating for *Dracula*, Liveright gained considerable publicity by buying the rights to Edward Bourdet's play *The Captive*, a fairly tame drama about lesbianism that had nonetheless been closed by the local district attorney.[19] Although he was never able to produce the play, he reveled in any opportunity to clash with or outwit the censors of the time.)

Liveright visited Florence Stoker to make a proposition. He was willing to produce *Dracula* on Broadway, provided another dramatist could revise and improve the script.

Florence Stoker disliked him immediately.[20] Horace Liveright must have seemed to her as much like a reputable English publisher or producer as Hamilton Deane resembled Henry Irving. He was a flashy American with a vague air of scandal and disrepute. He didn't just want *Dracula*, he seemed to *be* Dracula in some undefined and unsavory way. Liveright was forced to employ his proposed adaptor, the London-based American John L. Balderston, as a go-between. Balderston, the London correspondent for the *New York World* and a playwright as well—his romantic ghost story *Berkeley Square* was already a success in London and New York—did his best to charm the widow through the course of Liveright's negotiations with the hard-nosed Stoker agent, C. A. Bang. Liveright, Stoker, and Bang finally agreed to terms: a $1,000 advance against a sliding percentage of the box office (5 percent on the first weekly $8,000, 7.5 percent on the next $2,000, and 10 percent on receipts over $10,000).[21]

Balderston, for his part, hesitated. The London production *was* fairly tacky, even if the crowds couldn't stay away. Finally, Balderston agreed to the assignment. On May 10, he wrote his New York agent, Harold Freedman, head of the Brandt and Brandt Dramatic Department: "The situation is that

John L. Balderston. (Billy Rose Theatre Collection, New York Public Library at Lincoln Center, Astor, Lenox and Tilden Foundations)

this play has been dramatized, very badly. . . . I have agreed to take the script and turn out another version by July 1 . . ." He added a postscript: ". . . at my suggestion, my name is not to go on *Dracula* as it is an extreme 'shocker,' and I do not think it would do *Berkeley Square* any good, though it ought to be a good shocker, and great fun."

Balderston agreed to a $300 advance to adapt the play, against 2.5 percent of gross receipts for all productions under Liveright's direction. He wrote his wife Marion on June 3, 1927, that he had finished the play, a month ahead of schedule. "*Dracula* leaves by the Olympic next Wednesday. I think it is a *damned* good shocker. It is finished but not copied. I will write by that boat my suggestions for preventing any Horace monkey business . . ." Balderston had already had difficulty collecting his advance from Liveright, whose cash flow could be wildly unpredictable. He wrote the producer on June 7: "I'm having a row with Bang—you'll not be surprised to hear that—he refuses to give up the original version of *Dracula* until I submit my version for him and Mrs. Stoker to pass before it goes to you. I have refused to do this, which is not according to the agreement, and I shan't send him my text, and I hope you won't, unless and until any contingent rights for England and the Continent, in

A cartoon from a 1927 issue of The Tatler, *depicting replacement cast members Frederick Keen and Dora Jay. (The Theatre Museum)*

case this version makes a hit and they want it, are safeguarded. Otherwise, I'd have no rights whatsoever, and neither would you, in a MSS signed simply Hamilton Deane. . . . If Bang won't give up the Deane version, all I can say is that I've used only twenty lines of it and don't think you lose much."

Balderston's script indeed amounted to a near-total rewrite. In the Deane version, for instance, the following line is given to Dracula, who has just frightened the maid with his entrance: "I have sorrow if I have given to you the alarm—perhaps my footfall sounds not so heavy as that of your English ploughman."[22] Balderston translated Deane's diction into standard English: "Forgive me. My footfall is not heavy, and your rugs are soft."[23] He also tightened the overall structure, eliminating extraneous characters and settings, and generally worked as an all-around play doctor.

Liveright was pleased with the results, but Stoker and Bang decided it was not in their interest to use the American version in London—whatever its flaws, the Deane original was a more lucrative proposition for them, at least in the short run. Unfortunately, the London production ran out of steam and was withdrawn from the West End only three months after the Broadway version opened. Using the American version could conceivably have extended the play's life and earnings in London—but Florence Stoker was not the kind to let foreigners whittle away at any of her share of the London proceeds. What the Germans had done to her was bad enough. (Though records are fragmentary, she did eventually permit Liveright some limited touring in England.)

The expatriate Hungarian actor Bela Lugosi cultivated a romantic stage persona in the 1920s. Dracula would change his image radically. (Courtesy of Richard Bojarski)

Balderston decided that a byline would no longer be a bad idea, and accepted co-billing with Deane, and Liveright announced a Broadway opening for October 1927. He offered Raymond Huntley and Bernard Jukes—the Dracula and Renfield of the London company—the chance to reprise their roles in New York, but only Jukes accepted (he would become the all-time marathon Renfield, playing the role in England and America more than 4,000 times). Huntley held out for more money than Liveright was willing to offer—$125 a week, to be precise—thus setting in motion what would become one of the most indelible acts of casting in theatrical history, the selection of the Hungarian character actor Bela Lugosi to portray Bram Stoker's bloodthirsty count.

Lugosi had arrived in New York as a political expatriate in 1920, a seasoned performer who had worked steadily in the Hungarian State Theatre as well as in Hungarian and German silent films. At the age of forty-six, he possessed a smoldering combination of dark good looks and piercing blue eyes. A strong, stubborn personality with inflexible work habits, Lugosi was fiercely proud of his national heritage. Rather than spend time to perfect his English, he instead learned English roles phonetically, and wondered why other European actors didn't do the same. Balderston later recalled that the actor had to be directed in French. (During *Dracula*'s run he took English lessons at Columbia University from director Arthur Lubin.) The result was the oddly inflected and deliberate style of speech now forever associated with the role of Dracula—and a professional albatross that would forever limit the roles that were offered him afterward. On stage, Lugosi was accustomed to playing romantic parts with an occasional turn as a villain. He worked steadily, but was in no sense a star or even well-known. An especially inattentive Alexander Woollcott, after seeming to praise the Lugosi performance in the 1926 production of *The Devil in the Cheese* as "excellent," went on to comment that "Miss Lugosi suggests a miniature Phyllis Povah, and that means to you whatever it means to you."[24]

Bela Lugosi first donned the cape of Dracula in 1927, not knowing he would eventually wear it to his grave. (Courtesy of Ronald V. Borst/Hollywood Movie Posters)

In his biography, *Lugosi: The Man Behind the Cape,* Robert Cremer offers an interesting, if not entirely verifiable, account of how Lugosi came to Liveright's attention, taken from an interview the actor gave to a Hungarian theatre magazine in 1928. Lugosi claimed that he was approached by Jean D. Williams, the well-known director of *Rain,* who was preparing a stage adaptation of *Dracula* "not like the one currently being shown in New York" and felt that Lugosi was "the only actor in America who was suitable for the part." However, "there were copyright difficulties . . . Replies from England concerning the sale of the copyright dragged on and the project was finally dropped."[25]

Had Florence Stoker attempted to sell the privately commissioned version of the play (which she owned outright) for production in America, thus cutting out Hamilton Deane (or any other writer) from any financial participation? The Society of Authors correspondence is sketchy, but there are definite indications that the sale fell through over Stoker's refusal to relinquish film rights along with stage rights.[26]

Whatever the reason, the Jean Williams production of *Dracula* was never realized. Lugosi told his magazine interviewer that Liveright had accidentally encountered Williams at the Harvard Club in the summer of 1927, discovered their overlapping interest, and that the director had given Lugosi such a glowing recommendation that Liveright auditioned him immediately.[27] Other accounts have Lugosi at first turning down the role because of its relatively limited dialogue (he later did turn down the part of the monster in the film version of *Frankenstein* because it was a nonspeaking part in which his features would be hidden by heavy makeup).

To Liveright's horror, Lugosi in rehearsal displayed none of the requisite power or magnetism the part required, and as time before an important backer's audition ran short, both Liveright and director Ira Hards were rapidly approaching panic. According to biographer Cremer, the cast grew increasingly nervous at the inscrutable actor's obvious lack of fire. "His only displays

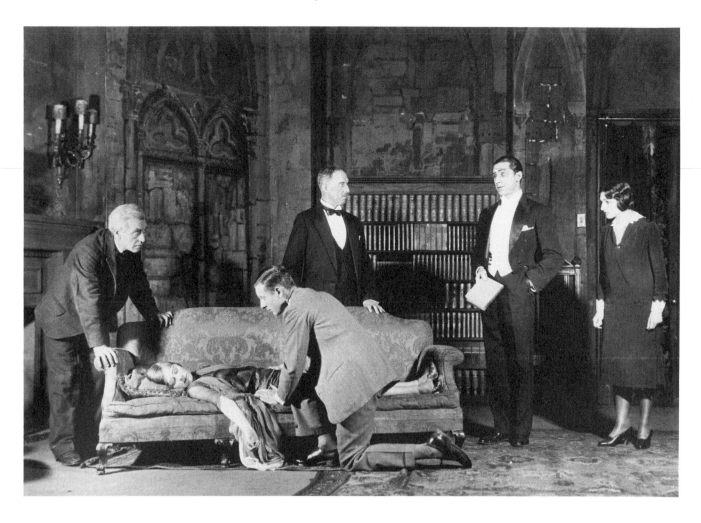

of emotion," wrote Cremer, "came when he reprimanded another actor for not pronouncing his cues carefully or for missing an entrance."

Finally, Liveright called Lugosi in for an uncomfortable talk, and tried to make his concern known in the most diplomatic fashion possible. Lugosi just stared at him. " 'Mr. Liveright,' Bela began in a tone verging on condescension, 'I understand your concern, but the performance is not until a week from tomorrow ev-e-nink.' The last words were delivered in deliberate, almost sinister tone that would have easily sent shudders through the cast, had they been present. Bela leaned forward, unintentionally menacing, towering over Liveright to emphasize his point. 'Now we work for position. Our lines must be perfect. Yes, we save the atmosphere for a week from tomorrow ev-e-nink.' "[28]

As usual, Bela did things his own way. The backer's preview was a resounding, riveting success. The show had a brief tryout at the Shubert Theatre in New Haven before opening at New York's Fulton Theatre (later

"The patient is feeling better, I hope?" Left to right: Edward Van Sloan, Dorothy Peterson, Terence Neill, Herbert Bunston, Bela Lugosi, and Nedda Harrigan. (Courtesy of Ronald V. Borst/ Hollywood Movie Posters)

Dorothy Peterson. (Billy Rose Theatre Collection, New York Public Library at Lincoln Center, Astor, Lenox and Tilden Foundations)

Artist Vernon Short's startling poster graphic for the Horace Liveright production. (Free Library of Philadelphia Theatre Collection)

the original Helen Hayes) on the night of October 5, 1927.

The New York critics were a bit more cordial in their reception, no doubt because they were viewing an essentially different play from the one that had been seen in London. Not all the changes were improvements, though, necessitating additional doctoring even after the opening. One effect in particular, that of Dracula in exotic werewolf form, looming over Lucy's bed, elicited only wolf-howls of laughter. Gilbert Gabriel wrote in the October 6 *New York Sun*: "It was jolly to see the Count . . . in a sort of dinner clothes cut from what looked to be the polar bear rug in the Boni and Liveright anteroom." The fanged fur was summarily banished, never to return. "If this whole production had not been staged with expert care, it is the kind of thing that would be laughed out of court at the first hearing," wrote Richard Dana Skinner in *The Commonweal*. "Instead, it manages to hold its audience almost petrified from first to last. . . . *Dracula* can hardly be recommended as a health diet for jaded nerves, but as a theatrical tour de force it is an outstanding achievement." Even Alexander Woollcott, who now had no difficulty recognizing Lugosi, was impressed. "Ye who have fits," he wrote, "prepare to throw them now."[29]

Dorothy Peterson and Terence Neill. (Free Library of Philadelphia Theatre Collection)

The New York cast, in addition to Lugosi, included Horace Liveright's longtime friend and companion Dorothy Peterson as Lucy (Balderston had dropped "Mina" in favor of a name that had twin connotations of light: the redeeming and the luciferic). Peterson would go on to a long career in films, specializing not in ingenues but rather in mothers and nurses. Terence Neill assumed the role of Jonathan Harker, Edward Van Sloan was Van Helsing, Herbert Bunston essayed the role of the ineffectual Seward, and Bernard Jukes as Renfield reprised the maniacal cackling that had won him plaudits in London. Albert Frith as Butterworth, the attendant, and Nedda Harrigan as Wells, the maid, supplied comic relief. She would later become Nedda Harrigan Logan as wife of Broadway's legendary director Joshua Logan, and president of the Actors' Fund until her death in 1989.

In addition to the rewritten script, the play had a much more substantial physical production, with sets by veteran designer Joseph Physioc, and elaborate effects. Hamilton Deane's need to keep down properties costs resulted in his vampire *almost* smashing a mirror, then thinking better of it; Liveright was able to spring for a new piece of glass for every performance (with the press agent quick to point out Lugosi's great good luck with the part, despite his breaking mirrors night after night). The London Dracula was middle-aged and malignant; Lugosi presented quite a different picture: sexy, continental, with slicked-back patent-leather hair and a weird green cast to his makeup — a Latin lover from beyond the grave, Valentino gone slightly rancid. It was a combination that worked, and audiences — especially female audiences —

Liveright's Dracula *was a constant presence in the theatre pages in 1927 and 1928.*

relished, even wallowed in, the romantic paradoxes.

With a hit on his hands, Liveright set his general manager Louis Cline into high gear, plastering the city with heralds and fliers, complete with a pronunciation guide to the title ("DRAK-u-la" the fliers advised, apparently for fear that the public might rhyme the name with "hula"). Artist Vernon Short painted a demon face with bat-wing ears that became one of the earliest Broadway show logos; it appeared on posters, fliers, the show's business letterhead, and was even manufactured as a souvenir mask. The prowling English nurse had been replaced with an American counterpart, and while the New York production never matched Hamilton Deane's record of thirty-nine "faints" at a single performance, eight patrons had to be treated for purported nervous shock. As *The New York Times* reported, "Cynical hints that the overcome spectators were in commercial collusion with the management were received in quiet dignity, or more likely by some further enterprise: a series of traffic tickets, perhaps, which, having been tied to an automobile, turned out to be not a summons to court but an order to appear at the Fulton at once. A baseball schedule, properly decorated with advertising. And stickers and hats and limerick contests. . . ."[30]

Despite the good press and good box office, Liveright was not convinced of the viability of a touring production. He was being overly cautious, or perhaps reacting to the volatile fortunes of his other business interests. His profit margin for *Dracula* began at $7,000 a week, an extremely low "nut" for a Broadway show of the time. "The play is doing extremely well," noted Harold Freedman to his partner Carl Brandt, "over $13,000 last week, and Horace is making a very large profit on it because of the cheapness of the company."[31] Nonetheless, Liveright hesitated on taking a chance with a tour.

Hamilton Deane, who had touring in his blood, and who was earning very little from the American production owing to the harsh terms of his contract with Florence Stoker, was frustrated by Horace's reluctance to take *Dracula* on the road. He let Balderston know that his patience was nearing its end, and he was prepared to take the same steps Mrs. Stoker had taken with the Morrell adaptation. He announced that he was preparing a new vampire play, one that had nothing to do with *Dracula* and which he would own outright. And he would tour it in America to capitalize on the publicity of the Liveright production if Liveright continued to sit on *Dracula*.

Balderston wrote Freedman that Deane's unfinished vampire play "will probably be snapped up and put on the road by somebody in New York, for, as I wrote Horace, you can't copyright the vampire idea, it is a new and effective one in the theatre, and there are probably a million people in the backwoods who will go to a theatre if they hear there's a vampire walking about in it, whether it is Dracula or some other . . ." It would be in Deane's

Horace Liveright *presents* The **Sensational Vampire Mystery Play**

Advertising art for the touring production. (Free Library of Philadelphia Theatre Collection)

The Count is effectively repelled by Van Helsing and the power of the Host. Bela Lugosi and Edward Van Sloan both would repeat their stage roles on film. (Courtesy of Ronald V. Borst/Hollywood Movie Posters)

interest, Balderston concluded, to "skim off the vampire cream ahead of Horace if he can, because he has been badly done by the Stoker executor and gets only 10% of their royalties from the American production."[32]

As the box office receipts began to wane in the spring of 1928, Liveright decided to gamble on the money-making potential of a tour, and sub-contracted the west coast rights to producer O. D. Woodward. The play closed at the Fulton after thirty-three weeks and 241 performances, earning a total of $350,857.50,[33] including its New Haven tryout. Lugosi and Jukes joined the west coast company, which played ten weeks in Los Angeles and San Francisco and grossed $108,080.[34] *Dracula* fever was a national epidemic no one wanted to resist. A Santa Barbara critic summed it up, calling the play "awesome, exciting, revolting and quite unhealthy, but so are many of the things that give us a kick these days."[35]

It was just the beginning. Encouraged by the California success, Liveright and Cline mounted their own tour of the eastern seaboard and the midwest. This time, Liveright was able to obtain Raymond Huntley, his first choice for New York, "very likely because Bela Lugosi wanted too much money," Huntley recalled. He accepted $250 a week for the tour—twice Liveright's original offer.

Huntley remembered Liveright as "slightly distant and austere," but had a vivid recollection of their one major clash. "I had a great disagreement with him because he wanted me to wear *green makeup* and I didn't take him seriously at all; I thought it was just bloody nonsense. We opened in Atlantic City and I put my usual makeup on and got a reminder that I was supposed to wear green, and a week or two later, on the 'subway circuit,' in the Bronx, I think, I got an extremely abrasive telephone call from Liveright that either I did as I was asked to do, in green makeup, or he would report me to Equity. Of course I was in no position to incur that kind of trouble so I went out and bought some green greasepaint."

Huntley would also be surprised by the lengths to which Louis Cline would go in fabricating press releases. For the Philadelphia engagement, the papers reported that Huntley was a master of theatrical makeup, inspired by Lon Chaney, who was even consulted by the police in their investigations. "I once converted the head of a famous detective into a fleshless skull," Huntley was quoted as having said. "He was then seated in a chair and a man charged with a murder was brought into the room. The criminal was so frightened that he made a complete confession." So advanced was Huntley's cosmetological magic, the story held, that he could "make a negro out of a white man, or vice versa, so convincingly that not even his best friend could tell the difference." Perhaps best of all was the claim that Huntley could "make a devil, a skeleton, or a woman out of any man in one hour," as if the first two forms led somehow

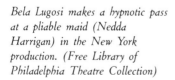

Bela Lugosi makes a hypnotic pass at a pliable maid (Nedda Harrigan) in the New York production. (Free Library of Philadelphia Theatre Collection)

naturally to the third.[36] Needless to say, Huntley knew nothing of his uncanny powers. It was just the great American hoopla machine doing its work.

Compared to his experiences in London, Huntley recalled the American production was "a complete change, a physically more expensive and I suppose you could say *managed* production." He never saw the Lugosi performance onstage, only on film. His reaction? "I thought it was way over the top, but I think Horace Liveright would have insisted on that." Did he have any regrets over turning down the Broadway role that had made Lugosi a star? "No, to tell you the truth, I was young and naive and *Dracula* was for many years after rather a sore spot with me because I really should have stayed here, you know, and worked with well-known directors and made authentic progress in my profession." (Huntley, of course, went on to a far happier career in the theatre than Lugosi would ever know, his hundreds of memorable characterizations including work in such films as *Rembrandt, Room at the Top,* and *Young Winston,* and innumerable West End appearances. As the 1990s opened, he had no plans for retirement.)

Touring, Horace Liveright knew, was expensive. *Dracula's* profit margin was offset to some extent by the increased advertising required by a "novelty" attraction. But the investment paid: manager Cline found that, consistently, the outlay of an extra $50 in promotion would translate into an additional $300 to $500 a week at the box office. And the number of publicity stunts that could be conjured up for *Dracula* appeared to be endless. At the Ohio Theatre in Cleveland, the uniformed nurse routine was augmented with "faint checks" refunding admission prices pro rata for performance time missed by patrons indisposed by shock for any portion of the evening.[37]

By May 1929, Liveright's total earnings on *Dracula* exceeded a million dollars. Less than a year later, the figure was reported to be approaching two million.

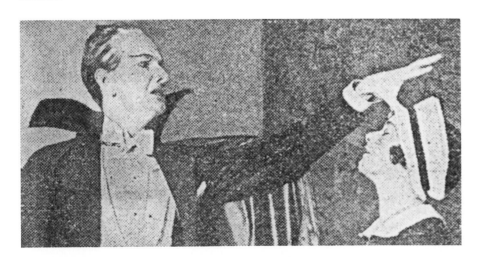

Raymond Huntley, meanwhile, interpreted the same moment for audiences in London. (Courtesy of the Dracula Society)

In spite of the income, Liveright's cash flow problems persisted. Both Stoker and Balderston were not receiving their royalties in a timely fashion from the mercurial showman. As Balderston complained to his agent, "He should realize, too, that he is dealing with some very temperamental people over here, the Stoker group . . . there is nothing to stop them from denouncing their contract in the middle of the run and compelling him to put up a big premium to renew it, for he is violating that contract right and left."[38]

Florence Stoker, of course, would have to be extremely hard-pressed to cancel the agreement—there would be no guarantee that Liveright *would* renew. He was as strapped financially in his way as Stoker was in hers. As it stood, however, there *was* income, however unpredictable.

Whatever fragile sense of control or predictability the widow possessed over *Dracula* in the autumn of 1928 was to be abruptly shattered. On December 16, without prior announcement, the Film Society entertained its

Left to right: Bernard Jukes, Edward Van Sloan, Herbert Bunston, Terence Neill and Dorothy Peterson. The American production dispensed with the trick dummy, Dracula instead providing a bloodcurdling offstage groan. (Free Library of Philadelphia Theatre Collection)

members with a private showing of *Nosferatu,* accompanied by an astounding statement: that they had obtained permission for the showing, not from Stoker, but from an American motion picture company, who now claimed to own the rights to *Dracula.*

What was happening? No one owned the rights but her! It was the nightmare, the whole German nightmare, it was happening again—

She made angry inquiries. She wrote to Thring. And finally she held close to her cataract-clouded eyes a press cutting that was like something out of a crazy dream. The article[39] had been published two months before—*two months,* and no one had told her! She read it over again and again, trying to make sense of the words it contained. Was she going mad? Was any of it possible?

"DRACULA" TO BE FILMED.

Universal Buy Screen Rights.

A PICTURE FOR VEIDT?

" Dracula," the famous thriller by the late Bram Stoker, which had such extraordinary success on the London stage and in the provinces recently, has been bought by Universal for the screen, and, it is understood, to be made into a full Unitone talking and sound picture.

The purchase of " Dracula " is in accordance with Carl Laemmle's policy of obtaining for the screen those famous novels which have proved themselves amazing magnets as stage productions as well. Prominent among the Universal plums for the coming year are " Show Boat," and " Broadway," the latter of which cost Laemmle £45,000.

No cast has been suggested yet, but the part of Count Dracula, the vampire, is stated to be admirable for Conrad Veidt.

Lies. All of it lies! But above all it was Germans again—new Germans, yes, but Germans all the same. And this time they were in Hollywood.

Chapter Four

A DEAL FOR THE DEVIL

or, Hollywood Bites

◆

*In which the picture people smell the blood, but
hesitate still, and say yes and no, and yes again, and in which
the German Count appears in New York, and Detroit, and
must be stopped, lest he spoil the occasion.*

"I CONSIDER NO TIME MUST BE LOST OVER ENCLOSED," WROTE FLO-
rence Stoker to G. Herbert Thring. She scribbled with feverish speed,
dropping prepositions and articles in her haste to reach the matter's meat. Her
handwriting was huge, fitting only a few sentences on each page; the widow's
eyesight was failing badly. "I have only just this minute learned that someone
has sold the pirated film of the German *Dracula* to an American
company . . ."[1]

This time, Thring was instantly supportive of the widow. "Whether the
performance was private or public does not matter. No person has a right to
retain a film which is an infringement of copyright," he assured her. He
examined the acknowledgment in the Film Society's program which Stoker
had sent him. "Can you tell me from whom the Universal Film Company of
America purchased the film rights? Whether *Dracula* is copyrighted in America, and who is Mr. J.V. Bryson who has so courteously given consent to an
infringing performance?"[2]

James Bryson, head of the European Film Company, was in fact Universal's point man in England, a flamboyant promoter and showman who had
already been embroiled in a bizarre scheme to smuggle into England a print of
Universal's *Phantom of the Opera* as a publicity stunt. He had misrepresented
the film as sensitive military material in order to obtain a British military
escort—a photo opportunity, in short. The scheme backfired, a scandal

*Actor Conrad Veidt, groomed by
Universal as the new Lon Chaney,
was the studio's first choice for
Dracula. His appearance in* The
Last Performance *(1929) was
virtually a screen test for the role.
(Photofest)*

ensued, and the Lon Chaney classic was actually banned from the British Empire for five years as a consequence.

After receiving an interrogating letter from the Society of Authors' solicitors, Messrs. Field Roscoe and Company, the Film Society retained lawyers of its own, Gilbert Samuel and Company, who made a formal reply. The Film Society had seen the front-page announcement in *To-Day's Cinema* (the lawyers explained) indicating that Mrs. Stoker had sold her rights to Universal.* They then approached Bryson, who confirmed the story and referred to a cable he had received from Carl Laemmle, head of Universal in America, stating that the rights had indeed been purchased, and that he, as Universal's British distributor, had no objections to *Nosferatu*'s being shown to members of the Film Society.

Florence Stoker was adamant. She had never heard of these people. She had never sold the rights to anyone.

C. D. Medley, of Field Roscoe and Company, told Thring he was skeptical of Bryson's story, "particularly as I find it was he, or his company, who forwarded the announcement to the cinema weekly."[3] Bryson now disclaimed that he had explicitly given permission for the performance.

Stoker did not have a face-to-face showdown with *Nosferatu*'s aiders and abettors until February 7, 1929, when the Bride of Dracula met Nosferatu's herbivorous henchman, their solicitors in tow. A tense meeting ensued, in which Montagu restated the history of the affair, and denied that he had been harboring the film since the previous controversy. (The program notes for the performance stated that the print of the film had been discovered, by chance, as stock footage being readied for export to Australia in a safe located in the same room the Society's technical staff happened to use.) He produced the original statement from Bryson's office concerning the alleged Universal purchase, which only compounded the insult to Stoker: the draft notice contained a paragraph, struck before publication, to the effect that Stoker had been asking £50,000, but Universal had been able to have its way with her for a considerably lesser sum.

Fifty thousand pounds! Stoker could not believe what she was hearing . . . the lies were bad enough, but . . . was it possible that she might be able to ask that much? The draft did not, however, reveal the final terms of the fictitious sale. But . . . £50,000!

Montagu, round-faced, round-spectacled, an enfant terrible with artistic pretensions and communist leanings, must have been an almost incomprehensible figure to Stoker, and she to him. Stoker was born poor and had spent her

Ivor Montagu, pioneer film preservationist and Florence Stoker's nemesis. (The Library of Congress)

---

*According to film historian Richard Koszarski, a noted expert on Universal, the studio had flirted with the idea of filming *Dracula* as early as 1915.

life maintaining a precarious foothold on the middle class; Montagu had been born rich and now dabbled fashionably in socialist circles! He didn't seem to understand the difference between art and thievery. He insisted that what he had done was completely innocent. He had probably been plotting this for years!

Stoker demanded that the film be turned over. Montagu replied that it would be distinctly hard for him to give up the film without being compensated for it—the Film Society had, after all, paid £40 for the print. The insolence of this creature! Was she now to pay for the privilege of being robbed? (Subsidizing thieves—it was socialism at its essence!) Stoker's lawyer pointed out that the film was quite useless to him since he couldn't exhibit it again, but Montagu explained that one of the objects of the Film Society was to collect and preserve films of artistic or scientific interest. *Nosferatu* in his opinion fit these criteria. He would, however, be prepared to give them a warrant that no future use of the film would be made of the film during the period of *Dracula's* copyright without Stoker's express permission.

Stoker was outraged. She told Montagu precisely her opinion of the character of his infringement. The rights in the matter were hers, and not his to bargain. The film was not something to be preserved, but to be destroyed.

Medley pressed Montagu for information about additional prints of the film that might exist. Montagu alluded to one copy in use in France—he had no direct knowledge of it, but had seen the advertisements in the Parisian newspapers. As for America, yes, he believed it had traveled there as well, by way of an organization called the International Film Arts Guild. At least one copy, and very likely more.

So it had already happened, exactly as she feared: *Nosferatu* had reached America with its relentless, infringing pestilence.

Medley advised Mrs. Stoker to ignore Montagu's suggestion that they be permitted to hold the film "as a sort of curiosity upon an understanding not to exhibit." He further advised her that, while the Film Society had made no profit worth mentioning in the affair, formal legal action might well be taken against Bryson and Universal, as a warning to the cinema trade that Stoker alone held the film rights and that "any person who attempts to interfere with her will be dealt with."[4]

The widow, however, backed off. "I am not anxious to go to law," she wrote Medley, concerned that the Film Society might not be financially strong enough to pay the costs on both sides in the event of their losing an action brought against them.[5] If they would pay the costs already incurred, the matter might be dropped. Bryson and Universal were unresponsive to requests for an explanation of their behavior. Stoker made no move to challenge them further. She couldn't afford to alienate them. However outrageous their

TO-DAY'S CINEMA

Tuesday, December 18, 1928.

"DRACULA."

Six-Year-Old Revival Fails to Make Flesh Creep.

FILM SOCIETY'S SHOW PIRATED VERSION.

Our flesh might have crept six years ago when Murnau put "Nosferatu" before a thrill-thirsty world. On Sunday, when it was revived by the Film Society, it proved interesting, but not altogether impressive. Bram Stoker's "Dracula," of which the film is a pirated version, more or less, contains ample material for the shivering of spines. In the kindergarten days of 1922 the producer of "Sunrise" had not quite caught the technique. This was evident less in the crude use of irises and alternate cuts that in its utter absence of flow, a sign that the essential quality of the cinema film is less in its pictures as in their relation to one another. There is a succession of pictures of the most beautiful composition and brilliant photography in the picture. But they are nearer to a photo album than a film. It will be doubly interesting in this respect to see that up-to-the-minute version of "Dracula" which is scheduled for production by Universal. The sanguine exploits of the blood-sucking Count should make an eerie but an entertaining feature.

Of the shorts shown the most fascinating was "A Glass of Water," one of British Instructional's best efforts, in which the horrors that lie in our drinking water before it is filtered by the M.W.B. proved both dreadful and decorative.

Other items included a bright little silhouette film of a Grimm fairly tale, an excellent subject for Yuletide amusement, and a "nearly abstract" in which bowler hats defied gravity and men walked into lamp-posts and disappeared.

behavior, they were interested in *Dracula,* and they had more money to spend than she had ever seen at one time in her life.

By late March, the Film Society had agreed to turn over the positive print of *Nosferatu* in its possession. Stoker expressed some ambivalence or confusion over the means by which she might destroy the film. The matter was handed over to the lawyers. Field Roscoe and Company were similarly unversed in the requisite rituals. "I do not myself know how these films are destroyed or whether I have any means of doing it," Medley wrote Thring, "but will consider the matter when I get it."[6] The record is silent on the exact fate of the film, but presumably the English print of *Nosferatu* was consigned to the flames around the first of April, 1929.

Did Florence Stoker ever actually see *Nosferatu*? After seven long years of doing battle, and finally capturing the enemy, it would seem strange indeed if she didn't insist on looking the thing in the face. But her letters leave the distinct impression that she considered the film beneath contempt. To look at it might dignify it. Silent movie vampires could not be heard, and they were better not seen. If she had once been Oscar Wilde's Cecily Cardew, she was now his Lady Bracknell, on this point, as indeed on all points, firm.

Nosferatu, of course, would go on to be recognized as a landmark of world cinema, elevating the estimation of *Dracula* in a way no other dramatic adaptation ever would, or ever could. With Hamilton Deane's constricted adaptation, the piece had begun its descent into kitsch; *Nosferatu,* however, had mined *Dracula*'s metaphors and focused its meanings into visual poetry. It had achieved for the material what Florence Stoker herself would never

A vampire is destroyed by sunlight for the first time in Nosferatu. *Unfortunately for Florence Stoker, the film itself was not so easily dealt with. (Photofest)*

achieve: artistic legitimacy. For all its popular fascination, *Dracula* would forever be an object of critical condescension.

Nosferatu was not Stoker's only contretemps over the film rights. She had turned against C. A. Bang, who had been advising her on motion picture matters, when it was brought to her attention that his commission of 25 percent of her earnings might be vampirically high. A lawsuit and countersuit ensued.[7] Stoker engaged the representation of the well-known play broker Dorothea Fassett, a principal of the London Play Company. "The Stokers were suspicious of all agents after the Bang business," she later wrote. Fassett acknowledged that she had been instrumental in their getting rid of Bang, and had employed her own solicitors, at some expense, to lobby the Stokers' lawyers and vouch for her good intentions.[8]

The cynical, chain-smoking, business-savvy Fassett was in many ways a caricature of the hard-nosed theatrical agent, and a sharp contrast to the Victorian Knightsbridge widow. But they had something in common: both women liked a fight. "Dorothea wasn't truly happy unless she was in the middle of a row, and she always seemed to have five or six of them going," remembered Laurence Fitch, a veteran British agent who worked for Fassett as an office assistant at the time of the Hollywood interest in *Dracula*. He remembered the regal F. A. L. Bram Stoker (as she often signed papers) "sweeping in and out" of Fassett's Picadilly office. "To a seventeen-year-old boy, one old lady tends to look like any other. But Florence Stoker certainly had *presence*," Fitch recalled.[9]

The alignment with Fassett was fortuitous for Stoker, and it is unlikely that a film sale for *Dracula* could have been made without Fassett as a mediating presence. But more important still was Harold Freedman, head of the Brandt and Brandt Dramatic Department in New York. Freedman, who came into the *Dracula* film deal as John Balderston's agent, displayed in many ways the antithesis of the aggressive, abrasive style that marked the wheeler-dealers of the period. Freedman was famous in literary circles for the under-stated, almost conspiratorial whisper in which he held client discussions. Discretion, tact, and quiet persistence were the Freedman hallmarks, and would eventually earn him a legendary status among agents. (Among his biggest coups would be the film sale of *My Fair Lady* for $5.5 million plus a percentage, a staggering figure for the time.)

Fassett in London and Freedman in New York would be the two individuals most responsible for *Dracula*'s film sale to Universal. While most accounts credit the interest of Carl Laemmle, Jr., or the director Tod Browning's supposed dedication to the project, it was Fassett's hand-holding in London and Freedman's quiet behind-the-scenes efforts in New York and Hollywood that would actually close the deal. The story, told here for the first time,

Harold Freedman, the literary agent who stage-managed Dracula's *difficult sale to Hollywood. (Courtesy of Robert A. Freedman)*

provides a fascinating look at the reality of Hollywood deal-making in the days of the early talkies.

Even before her falling-out with Bang, Stoker had received some inquiries about film rights to *Dracula*. The vexing thing was, it was the success of the play in London and New York that was spurring the interest, not a renewed appreciation of the novel. The play was the thing, and the play and the book were very different animals indeed.

John Balderston was among the first to realize that Stoker was going to try to sell the film rights to the novel alone, and rid herself of any claims by himself and Hamilton Deane. Ironically, he had been aware of the Universal story for over a month before Stoker—and had in fact had his agent Harold Freedman contact Universal directly to confirm that they had not purchased the rights. Balderston was nonetheless sure that Stoker *had* been negotiating, with the desire to cut him out. He feared that "these people are so pig-headed and so stupid that they might let the film go smash rather than give us a percentage," he wrote Freedman. "There remains the point, whether the film people wouldn't pay us something on the side when they understood the position?" He suggested that there was a fine chance for Freedman's "Machiavellian diplomacy."[10]

Examples of the many transatlantic cables that fueled the film deal.

It was the beginning of a long string of mutual misunderstandings and mistrusts between Stoker, Deane, Balderston, and Liveright that would haunt the negotiations for a screen version of *Dracula*. Balderston was particularly stung by the seeming discounting of his own contributions. "Owing to the peculiarities of the people concerned, this play would not have got on in New York at all if I had not exercised my well-known powers of diplomacy," Balderston wrote to Louis Cline. "Horace would be the first to admit that he was several times on the verge of chucking the thing. I did get around the old lady then, and I think I can do it again, but I doubt very much whether anybody else can."[11]

Deane and Balderston had had a previous, informal agreement to split equally any proceeds from a film sale. But now, Balderston learned, Stoker and her son had proposed to Deane that they sell the Deane version of the play, not the Balderston. Balderston tried to disabuse Deane of this notion, pointing out that the Dramatists' Guild would undoubtedly back Balderston's own claim. Hollywood would buy one thing and one thing only—equity in a success. "The Deane version not only would not have been a success [in New York] but was actually turned down by Liveright and everybody else before I came along."[12]

Liveright had by this point realized his terrible oversight in not negotiating any film rights in his theatrical contract. He, too, had presumed that a film version would go back to the book. Now he was faced with the necessity of having to purchase the film rights from Stoker in order to have any interest in them at all.

Balderston wrote Freedman: "Mrs. Stoker and I have become very friendly over the inequities of Bang, her confidential agent who has been robbing her for years . . . and she realizes that I have not been trying to rob her, as of course Bang told her I was, over the film. Her son also seems a decent chap and I am having lunch with him on Friday. He has the film thing in hand, and is dealing with Horace . . .

"Mrs. Stoker, after some hesitation and consultation with her son, told me on Sunday that she has decided to sell all the rights to Horace. The price is, I believe, £4200 . . . this includes all the rights, talkies and everything. As she seemed friendly, although entirely ignorant on the whole subject, I explained to her that Deane and myself have a distinct interest in the matter, if the play is to be turned into a talkie. This seemed a new idea to her. She had been previously led to believe that we were a pair of robbers trying to get the film rights away from her. I think I made her see that it is a matter of joint equity."

Stoker asked Balderston if she should sell Horace the rights. "I didn't give a definite answer, but I told her he undoubtably wanted to resell, which seemed a novel idea to her. She thought he wanted to produce the film himself." Balderston pointed out the need to delay the release of any film for a few years, "as otherwise Horace might sacrifice all our royalties for a large price for the film people."[13] Liveright had, in fact, begun quietly negotiating with at least one studio. Stoker and her son took the matter under advisement, and delayed signing.

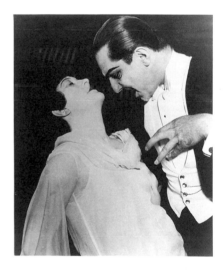

Lugosi with actress Hazel Whitmore during the west coast tour.

They decided instead to increase their asking price of Liveright to £6,000.

Liveright didn't have the money, and the first, lower offer was probably bluster. His finances, as usual, were in chaos. Instead, he appealed to Harold Freedman to offer Stoker an advance of $1,000 if she would permit him to continue his studio negotiations. He proposed a three-way split, a third to Stoker, a third to the playwrights, and a third to himself. It was a ludicrous, desperate offer and went nowhere. In addition, Liveright's second road company of *Dracula* had gone bust due to bad planning and he was badly in arrears in royalties owed. He simply had no credibility. No doubt, he felt that *Dracula*'s stage success and subsequent attractiveness to Hollywood were largely his doing. But there was no denying that he had simply waived the film rights in what would become one of the great money-spinning literary properties of the twentieth century. Liveright's fortunes in publishing were also at a low ebb, and his days with Boni and Liveright were numbered. One of the advertising illustrations that was traveling on the road with *Dracula* showed the vampire attacking a girl in flapper-style attire. Now, on the brink of the stock market crash, the picture had another, more resonant portent for Liveright, himself one of the leading symbols of the jazz age and its excesses.

Meanwhile, Dorothea Fassett had received a firm offer of £6,000 from an agent named Wilkes. The Stokers hesitated. Universal hadn't been heard from, after all. They bided their time through the spring of 1929, convinced that the value of *Dracula* could only increase. Their agents thought otherwise, and urged them to take the tide at the flood.

The negotiations, however, were about to be interrupted by the Banquo-like appearance of an unwelcome shadow.

Nosferatu had surfaced in America.

First in New York with its teeming millions, then, emboldened, in Detroit, the German Count was seeking audiences with impunity. During the first week in June an advertisement ran in *The New York Times*: the "First Showing in America," the ad proclaimed. "Inspired by *Dracula*," the film was said to be "A thrilling mystery masterpiece—a chilling psychodrama of bloodlust." Max Schreck's face adorned the ad like the image on a postal stamp from hell.

Horace Liveright was among the first to take notice, and sent Louis Cline to see the film. It was showing at the Film Guild Cinema, on Eighth Street in Greenwich Village (decades later, as the Eighth Street Playhouse, the same site would be haunted by the long-running *Rocky Horror Picture Show*). The little-cinema movement had been gaining American momentum as reaction against the commercial giantism of picture palaces like the Roxy, and the Film Guild was one of New York's jewels. Architect Frederick Kiesler (1890–1965) had created a Bauhaus-deco extravangaza of a theatre, despite its small size. The screen was completely encircled by an iris-like proscenium Kiesler called a "screenoscope" with curtains that seemed to dilate rather than raise. The severe black and white color scheme was intended as a metaphor of the cinema's essence of light and shadow. Constructivist-looking placards advertised "100% CINEMA—UNIQUE IN DESIGN—RADICAL IN FORM—THE HOUSE OF SHADOW SILENCE—REST FOR WEARY EARDRUMS." All in all, it must have been one of the most delirious places imaginable to watch an expressionist film like *Nosferatu*.[14]

Louis Cline had no impressions of the decor, at least not that he reported. He wrote a memo to Liveright on June 4: "There is no question . . . that Murnau made this film from the book by Stoker and he has put most of the book into the film except the three women in white [who] are conspicuous by their absence." However, he concluded, "there is nothing as far as I can see that infringes on our version of the story. Of course the use of the word Dracula evidently enticed people into the small house. I had to stand almost through the first show [but] . . . when people saw what a boring picture *Nosferatu* turned out to be, there were plenty of seats in the theatre during the second showing last night."[15] Cline was not alone in his opinion of the film—a

Nosferatu's sudden appearance in a Greenwich Village theatre threatened to derail the film deal.

critical fashion for *Nosferatu* would not develop until after World War II. *The New York Times* called it "more of a soporific than a thriller" and commented on two audibly dozing audience members. The overall effect of the film, in the *Times'* opinion, was "like cardboard puppets doing all they can to be horrible on papier-mâché settings."[16] The *Herald Tribune* called it "jumbled and confused," and, while praising its visual compositions, complained that the story "flopped woefully due to inexpert cutting or bad continuity."[17] Only the *New York Post* anticipated the film's eventual classic status: "Not since *Caligari* has this reviewer been so taken with a foreign horror film as with F. W. Murnau's *Nosferatu the Vampire* . . . taken from *Dracula*, recently seen on the stage . . . and infinitely more subtly horrible than the stage edition. Mr. Murnau's is no momentary horror, bringing shrieks from suburban ladies in the balcony, but a pestilential horror coming from a fear of things only rarely seen."[18]

Despite the predominantly bad reviews (or perhaps a partial cause of them) the 1929 American print, re-titled *Nosferatu the Vampire*, may have been

A rare glimpse inside New York's Film Guild Cinema, "the house of shadow silence" where Nosferatu *made its American debut. Architect Frederick Kiesler's symbolist designs included an iris-shaped proscenium. (Courtesy of Mrs. Frederick Kiesler)*

a substantially variant cut of the film. In Europe, a completely reedited version of *Nosferatu* was released the same year under the title *The Twelfth Hour*. The work of a former student of Murnau's, *The Twelfth Hour* incorporated new footage as well as Murnau outtakes. On the basis of the published credits, the American print, too, varied substantially from the original—at least in terms of its titles and character names. For one thing, most of the character names were changed again. Count Orlok became "Count Nosferatu," while the Renfield character, Knock, was called "Vorlock." Other character names underwent changes as well, and the doomed ship, formerly the *Emprusa*, became the none-too-subtle *Vamprusa*. New York State Archives records show that the film was otherwise of virtually identical length to the original, and there is no record of whether the film was color-tinted, whether any specific music accompanied it, etc. One indication that some reediting may have occurred is the appearance in a French account[19] of the name "Symon Gould" as being responsible for the *montage*, or editing, of the American version. The American intertitles—and perhaps the character names—were provided by Benjamin De Casseres (who had done the dialogue cards for such silent classics as *The Phantom of the Opera*), with Conrad West listed as "scenarist."

Symon Gould was the founder and director of the International Film Arts Guild, and proprietor of the Eighth Street theatre. A pioneer exhibitor of the art film movement in the United States, Gould had founded the Guild in New York at almost the same time as Ivor Montagu's Film Society in London was formed. He was also the second vegetarian who would intercede on behalf of the German vampire. Far more ardent a herbivore than Montagu, Gould would eventually mount a quixotic presidential campaign against John Ken-

Symon Gould, founder of the Film Guild Cinema, provided Nosferatu *with a safe haven in America. (The Billy Rose Theatre Collection, New York Public Library at Lincoln Center, Astor, Lenox and Tilden Foundations)*

nedy and Richard Nixon, running on the ticket of the American Vegetarian Party in 1960. Gould's interest in blood themes led him eventually to take over the American distribution of Franju's gruesome slaughterhouse documentary *Blood of the Beasts*.

Florence Stoker proposed to write once more to the newspapers of America, alerting them to the menace of *Nosferatu*, but G. Herbert Thring stilled her hand: ". . . you might not only prejudice your position but might lay yourself open to an action for libel if it is subsequently proved that the film was not an infringement of your copyright. We have at present no real evidence upon which to base a claim."[20] Thring's opinion would prove prescient a few years later, when the American copyright status of *Dracula* would indeed come under serious question.

Harold Freedman drafted a letter to the Dramatists' Guild on behalf of Balderston and Deane over the *Nosferatu* piracy, but it was never sent. The film was no longer being exhibited, and in any event was not taken seriously by most of the main players in the *Dracula* negotiations. As usual, however, the matter was far from at an end.

Florence Stoker's worsening eyesight had progressed to the point that required surgery, and October 1929 found her recovering in a nursing home. She thereafter moved to what would be her final residence, a small mews house off Wilton Place in Knightsbridge, a few blocks from Hyde Park Corner. Carriage houses in 1929 had less of today's aura of urban chic and more the feeling of a back entrance. The address, in short, was distinctly in the shadow of the elegant homes surrounding it. But at least it was still Knightsbridge, and if she didn't have money or a fashionable front door, she still had her paintings and treasured souvenirs from the days of the Lyceum and Cheyne Walk. Unable to read or write—she dictated a few letters to her son and a companion—Stoker's anxiety over *Nosferatu* may have been assuaged by her not being able to readily communicate about it.

By December, Balderston updated her on the affair. Gould had scheduled *Nosferatu* for a return engagement on Eighth Street. "I am sorry to worry you again about this thing, but we have all tried our best to scotch this snake without complete success . . . if it ever came to a fight I should, of course, be willing to associate myself with you to the extent of my interest in the rights."[21] He assured her the following day that Gould and company were "small people who are quite irresponsible and they only show the thing on the sly in small houses and run away when you chase them. This is annoying and damaging no doubt, but it ought not to kill the market for the film when done properly and in a big way."[22]

Freedman worried, however, that *Nosferatu* had the potential to cloud negotiations for *Dracula*. The value of the sale was the offering of a clear title to the property. But when *Nosferatu* had surfaced in Detroit, Louis Cline wrote Balderston that it had been "advertised frankly as *Dracula*." Cline, who hadn't been following the *Nosferatu* affair very closely, asked Balderston "if there is any dope you can get from Mrs. Stoker about who made the film she rejected. I intend booking *Dracula* . . . on a swing out through Detroit, Milwaukee, Kansas City and Denver, but if this film is going to beat us into these places, it is going to hurt us."[23]

Freedman contacted Gould. Unlike Ivor Montagu, Gould did not seem interested in retaining the film as a curiosity, or for any other reason, if cash could change hands. Furthermore, Gould contended that accepting anything less than $500 was not worth his while—he could easily get that much by sending the film back to Germany. Freedman wrote Balderston, "I am trying to get him down to about $300—if not, I'll pay him $400 on the following basis: that, if during the next six months no positive print appears in this country, I will turn the money over to him."[24] Meanwhile, Gould was to relinquish his positive print and all information as to the location of the negative and the prevention of any further piracy that might interfere with the film negotiations.

Gould made no immediate response. The German Count could repose in his film cannisters until the most advantageous moment.

Dorothea Fassett was getting very nervous. "I am strongly of the opinion that the value of this property is going down every minute . . . if any of us are to make anything out of the film rights, we ought to do it now." She reported that an offer was being tendered to Stoker through the International Copyright Bureau—but only if they would bring the price below £9,000 (a pound sterling was worth about $4.75 at the time). The offer was refused.[25] Raymond Huntley's name appeared in cables as a suspected party to negotiations with Columbia Pictures.[26] The offering price quoted was $25,000. (Huntley remembers nothing of the affair.) Stoker insisted on $35,000, with three-fifths guaranteed to her, and two-fifths to Balderston and Deane.[27] The deal fell through. In the matter of actors, Universal had lost Conrad Veidt, who returned to Europe rather than risk the talkies with his heavy accent, and their next choice, Lon Chaney, was under contract to Metro. And above all, Freedman's direct contacts with various picture executives produced a consensus: the price of *Dracula* was simply too high.

Stoker, however, trusted her Bracknellian instincts on *Dracula*: the floor for the property was now $35,000. Stock market crash or no.

In January, Freedman apprised Balderston of the situation. The film rights, he wrote, "still seems to narrow itself down to the Universal proposition. The Laemmles are coming here next week and I am going into it with them then. Lon Chaney has finally decided to do a talkie with Metro.

Universal were unable to wean him away at the time this thing was hot here . . . If he doesn't get along with Metro on his first picture, then I suppose there will be some chance of Universal's getting him."[28]

By mid-February the situation hadn't changed. "Universal are still very interested in it," Freedman wrote, "but won't do anything unless they can get Chaney."[29]

In March, Dorothea Fassett wrote Freedman that Stoker's sleep was once more being disturbed by thoughts of *Nosferatu*. "She would like to have details as to the film's career," wrote Fassett dryly, "and know whether it just died or whether some arrangement was made to kill it."[30]

Neither had occurred. And Gould was nowhere closer to revealing the film cannisters' whereabouts.

By early spring, possibly because of the growing awareness of the enor-

Lon Chaney, the Man of a Thousand Faces, seen here with his own. Chaney was Universal's second choice for Dracula following Conrad Veidt's departure. Unfortunately, Chaney was under contract to Metro. (Courtesy of Scott MacQueen)

Chaney's Dracula would likely have been a very different creature than the one with which we are now familiar. Here, for example, is Chaney's pop-eyed conception of a vampire in London After Midnight.

Actor Bernard Jukes campaigned unsuccessfully for a studio sale. This maniacal publicity portrait was his calling card.

mous potential in talking pictures, and despite the international financial mess, the nibbling started again. On March 13, Freedman cabled Balderston: INFORMED HORACE DRACULA CAN BE BOUGHT REASONABLY I HAVE MATTER UP WITH METRO UNIVERSAL PATHE COLUMBIA. On April 8, both Bela Lugosi—who had earlier been denied an option—and his manager Harry Weber wired Freedman that they had lined up a deal for $40,000, cryptically promising the biggest studio, an excellent, reputable director, and most importantly, a willingness to buy and produce *Dracula* with Lugosi as the star. The name of the studio was revealed two days later when a west coast play broker named William Dolloff wired Freedman with a counteroffer: BELA LUGOSI SPOKE TO ME IN REFERENCE PICTURE RIGHTS DRACULA

STOP CAN OBTAIN HIGHER FIGURE FOR RIGHTS THAN METROS OFFER STOP PLEASE HOLD OFF NEGOTIATIONS. Dolloff's deal—allegedly for $50,000—fell through when his purchaser grew skittish over Horace Liveright's lingering involvement in the project and confusion over who indeed was representing the rights. Liveright had sold his publishing interests and was now on the west coast working for Paramount Publix Corporation on salary as a "production associate," and still vainly trying to raise the purchase price for *Dracula.* Although Paramount boss Ben Schulberg had some interest in a film version—possibly as a result of Liveright's prodding—almost no one else on the lot was enthusiastic. In April Paramount story editor E. J. Montagne gave Schulberg his opinion that the theme was "strictly morbid" and might run into problems with the recently inaugurated Production Code. Montagne felt that "the very things which made people gasp and talk about it [on stage], such as the blood-sucking scenes, would be prohibited by the code and also by censors because of the effect of these scenes on children."[31]

The fact that Metro considered *Dracula* with Lugosi and not Lon Chaney, whom they had under contract, is interesting and suggests that his director, Tod Browning, was fully aware of his star's failing health—Chaney had throat cancer—so much so that he, and the studio, were willing to do *Dracula* without their most bankable asset, the Man of a Thousand Faces.

Bernard Jukes, the actor who was making a career out of playing Renfield on the stage, also became party to the negotiations in the spring of 1930, and apparently came close to securing a studio offer. The actor seems to have promoted the property, and himself, fairly aggressively; a series of startling publicity portraits of Jukes as the fly-eating maniac made the rounds of the studios, but finally were of no avail.

Discouraged with the sluggish, approach-avoidance stance of the studios, Harold Freedman decided to visit the coast in person to bring the matter to a head. Arriving in May, he found the Universal situation "fairly cold" with Metro and Paramount-Famous-Lasky as the more likely candidates. However, he "had to get several directors interested in the proposition and one or two individual producers" before Universal agreed, in late June, to take *Dracula* for $40,000 rather than see it go to a rival company.[32] It was not an easy sale. As Freedman later explained, "I finally put through the sale in face of Mr. Laemmle, Sr.'s definite written objection to the purchase of the picture."[33] So much for Laemmle, Sr.'s oft-cited fondness for the shadowy tradition of German expressionism. As the elder Laemmle later told an interviewer in a discussion of *Frankenstein,* which Universal produced the following year, "I don't believe in horror pictures. It's morbid. None of our officers are for it. People don't want that sort of thing," he said. "Only Junior wanted it."[34]

Junior hadn't always been a junior. Born Julius Laemmle, the son of the

Agent Harold Freedman rarely posed for photographs, but his wife May sketched this likeness around the time of the negotiations for Dracula. *(Courtesy of Robert A. Freedman)*

former Oshkosh, Wisconsin, haberdasher and self-made movie mogul had inherited the control of the studio on his twenty-first birthday. In a bizarre reciprocal gesture that suggests a plot from a morbid German doppelgänger film, the diminutive young man relinquished his own name and identity: Julius died and was resurrected as Carl Laemmle, Jr. His abilities and achievements are still a matter of debate,[35] but he made one indelible contribution to American culture: the Hollywood horror movie, an obsessive new genre revolving around threatening, controlling, supernaturally powerful male monstrosities.

It would be fascinating to know Freedman's precise tactic for mediating between father and son over *Dracula,* but even with Balderston he is tantalizingly reticent, stating only with implied exasperation that "there is no use going through the various things that had to be done to get the thing over."[36]

Universal had agreed to agree, but the contracts had yet to be signed. And it was at this juncture that two unwelcome guests decided to make their presences known, and perhaps to spoil the occasion. One was Nosferatu, the vampire. The other was Horace Liveright, the producer.

Symon Gould had decided to bypass Freedman and approach Universal's New York office directly, asking a flat payment of $1,000 to relinquish his print of *Nosferatu.* Universal balked. Associate producer E. M. Asher was under some pressure to obtain the film; on July 19, he wired Freedman asking for assistance in obtaining Symon Gould's print of the Murnau film on a rush basis at a reasonable fee. Asher seems to have been more interested in studying the film rather than destroying it; the Universal scenario department was already encountering major difficulties over its screenplay treatment. Why not see what had already been produced?

Gould wouldn't budge. Asher asked Freedman to employ some personal diplomacy. Universal was willing to pay $200 for a ninety-day "rental." Freedman warned Gould that the film had no future commercial use, and that he could be enjoined against exhibiting it. Gould responded by wiring Carl Laemmle, Jr., directly: PLEASE WIRE DECISION REGARDING DRACULA PRINT. Laemmle told Gould his terms were unreasonable. Asher authorized Freedman to pay up to $400—and to rush the print by airmail to Universal City.

Simultaneously, Horace Liveright, stung over being closed out of the *Dracula* negotiations, told Freedman that unless he received a financial consideration, he would file a lawsuit against Universal on the basis that its film adaptation constituted unfair competition to the stage version, in which he still held rights.[37] He knew that Universal would never sign if there was even the slightest possibility of litigation that might prevent the film from being released. He also insisted that his share be paid not by Universal but by the owners—Stoker, Balderston, and Deane, with whom he clearly felt the need to settle a score.

To Freedman's relief, he did not hold out for an exorbitant amount of money—Liveright wanted cash, needed it badly, and was not really looking for a protracted fight. The producer finally accepted $4,500 in exchange for a quit claim waiving all future film rights in *Dracula*. Freedman was not, however, able to persuade Stoker and the playwrights to pay any more than $1,000. Universal quietly made up the rest. Liveright was never told how little his partners had actually paid him. "It will be fatal if Liveright should know before the execution of this deal that the owners are only paying $1000," wrote Freedman to Fassett on August 13. Fifty percent of the $39,000 balance, minus agent commissions, went to Stoker, and 25 percent to each of the playwrights.

That left only the matter of Symon Gould and his vampire shadow in nitrate.

Freedman continued his dickering with the exhibitor. He wired E. M. Asher: BELIEVE CAN GET PRINT FOR FOUR HUNDRED DOLLARS DOUBT WHETHER ANOTHER IN EXISTENCE WIRE ME IF WILLING PAY THIS.[38] Universal was willing. On August 13, Universal forwarded a check for $400 to Brandt and Brandt, and, two days later, they took possession of the film. Harold Freedman's covering letter took no chances, legalistically: "This, I presume, is the print you intended when you wrote me about sending you a print of *Dracula*. We have no print of *Dracula*, as you know, as we have made a deal with you for the motion picture rights of this play.

"*Nosferatu, the Vampire* has been adjudged by the courts to be a violation of Mrs. Stoker's rights, and the courts have ordered the prints destroyed. I am turning it over to you for the purposes of destruction and in view of our contract with you for the delivering over to you of the rights to *Dracula* for motion picture purposes."[39]

No doubt, Harold Freedman didn't believe for a second that Universal was actually going to perform a sacrifical rite over the film—their interest in *Nosferatu* was a far more practical one. *Nosferatu* had infringed, and now might be infringed upon itself, cannibalized and reborn. In its marriage with the cinema, *Dracula* would become an unstoppable, unquenchable fixture of the public imagination.

The nuptials, however, would prove a bumpy nightmare indeed.

Florence Stoker, John L. Balderston, Hamilton Deane and Symon Gould signed a cinematic "death warrant" for Nosferatu *in the summer of 1930.*

Say "DRACULA" to them and their hair stands on end in delightful anticipation of the mystery and thrills to come. Say "DRACULA" and you're talking of a stage play that broke records for attendance in New York and every road-show city on the map. Louis Bromfield author of "The Green Bay Tree" and other best sellers is adapting it for the screen . . . The director is Tod Browning who gave you THE UNHOLY THREE and OUTSIDE THE LAW (now breaking records in first run houses everywhere).

DRACULA

UNIVERSAL PICTURES

Chapter Five

THE GHOST GOES WEST

———————— ◆ ————————

*In which the Laemmles build a castle, but have no tenant,
and in which the cinematic rites are finally administered,
but the director is odd, and requires armadillos,
and the thing costs too much, but needs to be finished.*

———————— ————————

IN ACCORDANCE WITH ITS INTENTIONS THAT *DRACULA* BE A "PRES-
tige" effort ("A Universal Super Production," as they put it in the trades), the
studio announced the signing of Pulitzer Prize–winning novelist Louis Bromfield to write the screenplay. Bromfield had been lured to Hollywood by
Samuel Goldwyn some months earlier, but after being given nothing to do for
nearly half a year, he paid Goldwyn $10,000 to be released from his contract.[1]
Junior Laemmle claimed to have hired him on the strength of his Pulitzer
novel, a New England family saga called *Early Autumn* (which Laemmle's
publicists purported the mogul had actually read), and his established reputation as a Broadway dramatist.

It is difficult to imagine a writer farther removed from the world of
Dracula—or Hollywood, for that matter—than Louis Bromfield, and it is
likely that Universal wanted to exploit the publicity value of Bromfield's name
and his serendipitous leave-taking of a rival studio. Although his novels are
largely forgotten today, Bromfield was a prolific and popular writer of a
versatile temperament, though his tendencies toward political reaction and the
championing of the "natural aristocracy" would begin to put him out of public
favor during the years of the New Deal.[2] Genuinely curious and enthusiastic
about the creative potential of talking pictures, Bromfield recorded his impressions of the film colony in a Sunday feature in the March 30, 1930, issue of
The New York Times. "There is an intelligence and talent gathering in
Hollywood as it never gathered before. It is most hopeful, most promising.
The talkies offer a new style, much more interesting to work in . . . I believe
that some day they will assume proportions as an art form as great as Anglo-
Saxon literature. I really do."

Bromfield, who had never been west of the Mississippi, was entranced by

*The preproduction trade
advertisement for* Dracula
*promised a film both literary and
erotic. Little of either quality
survived the filming. (Courtesy of
Ronald V. Borst/Hollywood Movie
Posters)*

the benevolent climate, the clean air and sunlight, the endless groves and flowering plants. Later in life he would devote much of his energy and writing to farming, agrarian reform, and conservation; it is easy to understand the seductive spell California cast over him. Friends, he said, had tried to warn him. "I was told that I was about to lose myself in a world that consisted physically of a valley between some mountains owned entirely by picture actors, directors, oil speculators and realtors and built over with dwellings that vaguely resembled yurts, pagodas, tepees, pueblos, igloos and medieval castles. Spiritually, the place was simply desert. All art, all spirituality withered when brought within ten miles of Hollywood."

Like Harker on his way to Transylvania, Bromfield jotted down his impressions of the local landowners and peasants. He saw his newly adopted milieu as stratified into three separate castes—the native Californians, whom he idealized; the glamorous picture people; and desolate emigrés from the American elsewhere. The castes never mixed. And, as if in anticipation of Nathanael West, over them all hovered "a swarm of locusts composed of realtors, cult-leaders, religious prophets and radio announcers, who talk far too much."

Elsewhere in the article—which vacillates weirdly between wide-eyed optimism and revealing cynicism—Bromfield notes with evident distaste the "religious cranks, the dog poisoners, and in general the collection of freaks who have descended on Southern California . . . It is cheap and easy to accuse the picture industry of fantastic houses and fantastic decoration, but it's a false accusation . . . The responsibility lies with fat, middle-aged and elderly women from the Middle West, who after years of prairie life have released their sublimated libidos in a perfect orgy of overstuffed sofas, Grand Rapids Louis Seize and boudoirs that would have put Anna Held to shame."

Bromfield, at this point, had no conception of the degree to which *Dracula*—and horror movies in general—would eclipse Grand Rapids Louis Seize as an outlet for sublimated libidos. Horror movies—of the genuinely fantastic, supernatural variety—had not been invented yet, at least not in America, where conventions dictated that supernatural occurrences always be "explained away," usually as the disguise or machinations of a criminal. In a sense, Bromfield was being asked to create a genre, and his first, intuitive effort has a certain significance.

In late July, before the rights to the novel and the play had been formally acquired, Bromfield was set to work under Erwin Gelsey, head of Universal's scenario department. Glowing press releases were submitted to the trades heralding the arrival of Junior Laemmle's literary pet, and the formidable battle he faced. According to the July 26 *Hollywood Filmograph,* "*Dracula,* one of the most unique stories brought to the stage in years, requires not only the

Novelist Louis Bromfield, engaged by Universal to produce a "prestige" treatment of Dracula, *had a vision too ambitious for the studio's budget. (Billy Rose Theatre Collection, New York Public Library at Lincoln Center, Astor, Lenox and Tilden Foundations)*

sympathetic understanding of its screen adaptor but the technical skill of a writer experienced in the development of extraordinary dramatic plots." The assignment was regarded, ominously, as "particularly difficult."

Bromfield soon found out why. Universal was in the process of buying the rights to both the novel and the stage play . . . the problem was, neither had very much to do with the other. The Deane dramatization had dispensed with most of the novel in order to make it producible on a shoestring, and its dialogue was almost literally unspeakable. The Balderston adaptation was a vast improvement, but the play doctoring required for Broadway had resulted in a piece that was even further removed from the book.

It would have been much better to throw out the play and start with the book. But Universal was spending $40,000 on three separate properties—no, not just three, there were four! A novel and *three* different stage adaptations, including that ghastly vanity production of Mrs. Stoker's, the Morrell thing— and the studio wanted its money's worth out of all of them.

In addition, two treatments had been already prepared, one by Frederick "Fritz" Stephani and another by Louis Stevens. Stephani had grappled somewhat listlessly with both the novel and the Broadway play, and added a few surreal touches of his own—Dracula, for instance, was to make the trip from Transylvania to England in an airplane outfitted with enormous bat-wings. Stephani's aerodynamic imagination would find its niche a few years later at Universal, when he worked on the first *Flash Gordon* serial.

Bromfield followed his instincts as a novelist, and turned directly to Stoker's book for inspiration. The material was certainly rich, though the epistolary style was a problem. Paying lip service to Stoker's conceit, Bromfield's treatment opens with an over-the-shoulder shot of Jonathan Harker writing a letter from his room in a Transylvanian inn at the height of a raging blizzard. Thereafter, the technique is dropped, and Bromfield continues with an enormously visual and evocative recreation of Harker's journey to Castle Dracula, with detailed descriptions of fantastic settings and winding, torch-lit staircases, all perched on a two-thousand-foot precipice.

Some early concept sketches by the artist John Ivan Hoffman—quite possibly inspired by the Bromfield treatment—have survived, showing a caped superman dashing down a gargoyle-decorated staircase. Bromfield's visions would prove ultimately too ambitious for the studio's budget, but they are certainly in keeping with the spirit of Stoker's original. The screenwriter obviously had in mind the kind of meticulous adaptation of an English novel in which MGM would later specialize. Unfortunately, Universal's financial health was becoming increasingly precarious. A year after the stock market crash, the studio had sharply curtailed its activities, producing fewer features on smaller budgets. *Dracula* would be a "Super Production" in relative terms

Carl Laemmle, Jr., the "baby mogul" who established Universal's horror tradition over his father's strenuous objections. (Courtesy of Scott MacQueen)

only; its $355,000 budget was above average for the new streamlined opera-
tion, but only a fraction of the $1.45 million Universal had spent on its last
"prestige" film, *All Quiet on the Western Front.*[3]

Bromfield began with Stoker's Dracula—a towering, cadaverous old man
with white hair and drooping mustache, a completely different figure from the
suave Mephisto in evening clothes that had been popularized on the stage.
How, then, was Bromfield to reconcile the book and the play? In a clever bit
of inspiration, Bromfield found the means—Dracula *would* be two people.
Traveling to London and drinking new blood, he would simply be rejuvenated
into "Count de Ville," the drawing-room Dracula of the theatre. Only in
moments of blood-lust would he revert to his former, novelistic aspect. Thus,
the studio could have things both ways, and get a free dollop of *Dr. Jekyll and
Mr. Hyde* to boot.

It was an uneasy dramatic device, but probably a good political move on
Bromfield's part, since it seemed to reconcile the unreconcilable. Other
Bromfield choices are less than inspired. He introduced dubious comic relief
in the guise of a new character in London, a neighbor of the Sewards known as
"Mrs. Triplett." The part was specifically intended—at least by Bromfield—
for the hefty comedienne Alison Skipworth, a performer who could easily
have been cast as one of Bromfield's overstuffed prairie emigrés. Mrs. Triplett
was to be the owner of Carfax Abbey, landlord and bridge partner to
Bromfield's supernatural aristocrat. Due to his extrasensory powers, Dracula
puts Charles Goren to shame. Yet the vampire is unmasked during a card
game, when Dracula fails to reflect in a compact mirror which Mrs. Triplett
uses to powder her nose.

It is not known whether Bromfield added this material due to studio
demand or as his own cynical sop to the compromising realities of the project.
For Samuel Goldwyn, he had been given nothing to do; for Universal, he was
being asked to do the impossible. And whatever their literary and cinematic
merit, his contributions, if filmed, would enhance the studio's prestige at the
expense of its budget—the construction of the oversized sets for Dracula's
London and Transylvanian lairs, as envisioned by Bromfield, would render the
film unproducible. Bromfield's honeymoon with the studio was short. Within a
few weeks of his arrival at Universal City, he was being shadowed by
screenwriter Dudley Murphy, who accompanied Bromfield and Universal
associate producer E. M. Asher to Oakland, where Bela Lugosi was appearing
in a stock production of *Dracula* at the Fulton Theatre. Lugosi was no longer
associated with the national road company, then playing the east, having held
out for more money than Liveright was willing to pay. Raymond Huntley,
despite his misgivings about the production, had accepted the role. The Fulton
venue was probably not the best showcase for Lugosi to be seen in by

*A bridge partner for the Count?
Comedienne Alison Skipworth would have
provided comic relief in Louis Bromfield's
conception of* Dracula. *(Photofest)*

Universal; aside from the second-string cast, there were half-empty houses during the Oakland engagement—weak evidence indeed of Lugosi's box office appeal to an increasingly cost-conscious studio. Despite some unofficial mumbling in the press that Lugosi had won the film role, the real point of the Bromfield/Asher/Murphy trip was most likely to study the cost-saving possibilities of the stage version over the book.

Bromfield was not the first literary author to be pulled into the crushing machinery of the Hollywood studio system, and he would not be the last. Several months later he told a fan magazine, "Work in Hollywood from the writer's point of view can be colossally unsatisfactory and there are plenty of discouraging moments when bit by bit you see your idea being transformed into something that seems new and unfamiliar."[4] With passing years, his view of Hollywood would become even more negative.

Shortly before Bromfield began work on *Dracula,* Universal formally announced Tod Browning as director. Browning had been Lon Chaney's director at Metro, and it is possible that Universal signed him for a three-picture deal in anticipation of also obtaining Chaney for *Dracula.* A Chaney picture—any Chaney picture—spelled box office, and a Browning/Chaney collaboration would be considered all the more bankable. Chaney's endless fascination with twisted, deformed, and grotesque characterizations was rivaled only by the public's bottomless appetite for more. Chaney's rise to fame in the 20s was the result of one of the oddest psychological bonds between a star and his public that Hollywood has ever seen (and a phenomenon of popular culture that has not yet been examined at sufficient depth). Chaney, of course, had turned down Universal's offer to buy him *Dracula* as his first talkie, and instead remained at Metro to make the carnival crime drama *The Unholy Three,* which Browning had already directed once as a silent.

To this day, Browning remains a maddeningly difficult director to assess. On one hand, his films possess a thematic consistency almost unparalleled in film history; an obsession with the bizarre and grotesque, with the plight and vengeance of the social outsider, and a fascination with the tawdrier aspects of show business—carnivals, sideshows, fake mediums, and confidence games—all of which become skewed metaphors for unhealthy human relationships. These obsessions reached a climax in 1932 with *Freaks,* one of the most notorious films ever made, featuring real circus freaks cast as the sideshow denizens who gruesomely avenge themselves on a beautiful, treacherous woman. To many cineastes, Browning is a major *auteur* in a minor key; others, however, point out that his technical execution rarely does justice to the brilliance of his concepts. His films *should* be good. But more often than not the Browning end product is an unholy mess. There is no denying, however, the enduring fascination of his work, even if the fascination is akin to watching an auto wreck.

Louis Bromfield's enthusiasm for Dracula *soured as his screenplay was revised beyond recognition. (Free Library of Philadelphia Theatre Collection)*

The reclusive, alcohol-tormented director Tod Browning produced one of the most obsessive bodies of work in film history. Dracula would be his most famous film, but hardly his best. (The British Film Institute)

Browning had a reputation as an alcoholic, which may account for the slipshod manner in which many of his films were executed; his drinking had caused him to be blacklisted for two years in the early 20s, and it was widely believed that Irving Thalberg had fired him from Metro in 1929 for the same reason. His drunken escapades also engendered a kind of perverse awe among his drinking pals, who told and retold (and undoubtedly embellished) tales of his inebriated exploits. In one of the most colorful, Browning confronted a stuffy assistant manager at the St. Francis Hotel in San Francisco during a New Year's Eve party, who was evidently displeased with the director's obstreperous demeanor. "As the evening waned, the animosity waxed. Tod yanked out his false teeth — uppers and lowers — and hurled them at the A.M. with the suggestion: 'Go bite yourself!'"[5]

Browning cultivated a flamboyant persona, favoring loud socks, louder shirts, and the loudest ties. Actress Carroll Borland, who worked for him in 1935's *Mark of the Vampire*, recalled that he usually "dressed like he was going to the racetrack." He was evidently skilled at deflecting attention from his self-sabotaging behavior — he was known to provide his own impromptu sawdust and tinsel on the set, often breaking into song (an a capella rendition of "When the Moon Comes Over the Mountain" was his specialty), sometimes a card trick or carny routine. Over the years he had developed a network of cronies who indulged his behavior and kept him in assignments.

There is evidence to suggest that Browning and Chaney had begun work on an unauthorized version of *Dracula* at Metro in 1927, or a project so similar that it created serious concern for Irving Thalberg, who was aware of the bitter legal battle Florence Stoker had waged over *Nosferatu*. According to film historian and archivist Philip J. Riley, "Browning's story called for the vampire to attack by drifting into the room as a mist as in *Dracula*. Both lead female characters were named Lucy and they had the vampire calling on them from the ruins of an old estate next door. In both stories they brought in an older expert who tried to save the heroine by placing garlic around the room while the maid and the groom stood watch over her. Also, the young male leads, Jonathan Harker and Arthur Hibbs, were very similar." Thalberg's reaction was quick and to the point: "Change it."[6]

The production that emerged was filmed as *The Hypnotist*, and finally released as *London After Midnight*. While it still featured Chaney as a "vampire," the character was really a double role for Chaney; he also played the detective intent on solving the mystery. Chaney's makeup was one of the most startling creations of his career, rivaling even his Opera phantom: a scuttling figure in a beaver hat and bat-winged coat, a shock of white hair, pointed dentures, and eyes kept bulging by painful wire-and-plastic appliances.

London After Midnight: *Metro was worried about another infringement debacle, à la* Nosferatu. *(Courtesy of Philip J. Riley)*

What, we must wonder, would have been Chaney's concept of *Dracula*?

Undoubtedly, the Man of a Thousand Faces would have balked at a role requiring nothing more than evening clothes and a menacing stare, and a Chaney *Dracula* would almost certainly have been significantly reshaped for its star, making full use of man-into-bat transformations and other spectacular makeup effects. Bromfield's treatment, with its double-faced vampire, hints at the sort of approach that would have maintained the Chaney mystique. Perhaps Chaney would have insisted on playing both Dracula *and* Van Helsing, aided by two voices, doubles, and split screens — the double-casting of Chaney in *London After Midnight* certainly suggests the possibility. Alternately, Chaney might have been quite effectively cast against another Metro contract

star (Lionel Barrymore immediately comes to mind—and Barrymore would in fact play a memorable variation on Van Helsing in Browning's 1935 remake of *London After Midnight,* called *Mark of the Vampire*).

Unfortunately, any possibility of Chaney's ever assuming the role for Universal or anyone else evaporated when his chronic throat ailment was diagnosed as terminal cancer. A few days later, *Variety* contained the following announcement:

Wray, the Neck-Biter
Hollywood, June 21.
John Wray will play the neck-biting monster in "Dracula" for Universal.
Tod Browning will direct.

Wray, who had played the vicious drill sergeant Himmelstosse in Junior Laemmle's triumph *All Quiet on the Western Front,* was an extremely unlikely choice for *Dracula,* and he was not mentioned again.

It was only the beginning, however, of silly season in the matter of *Dracula* casting.

Conrad Veidt, the performer originally mentioned by Universal in connection with *Dracula,* had decided to return to Europe rather than brave talkies in English, in which he was not completely fluent and which he regarded as a professional risk. Although his accent would not have hampered *Dracula* in the slightest, he was probably correct to believe his career would be distinctly limited by the coming of sound. Later, of course, his English perfected, he would return to Hollywood as a specialist in wartime villains. But it is clear that a brilliant opportunity was lost when Universal lost Conrad Veidt; judging from his many fine silent performances, ranging from the murderous somnambulist in *The Cabinet of Dr. Caligari* to the tragic Gwyneplaine in *The Man Who Laughs,* Veidt might well have elevated the role of Dracula to pantheon status.

While Bela Lugosi should have seemed the obvious choice for the part, it was as true in 1930 as it is today that a stage success did not guarantee an actor a chance to play the same role on film. Universal considered a number of actors for the part, foremost among them Ian Keith, a magnetic, classically trained actor with a troubled personal life, whose best-remembered film role would be the alcoholic carny in *Nightmare Alley,* a part that so eerily reflected the performer's own circumstances that it is uncomfortable to watch. Another front-runner was William Courtenay, a distinguished New York actor who had just enjoyed a successful New York run and national tour as a cloaked magician in *The Spider.* Perhaps the most unusual Dracula of all would have been Paul Muni, mentioned in several accounts as one of Universal's serious

The devil in black pajamas. A publicity shot used by Lugosi as he campaigned for the film role. (Free Library of Philadelphia Theatre Collection)

HOLLYWOOD FILMOGRAPH

Ian Keith To Play "Dracula"

Bela Lugosi and William Courtney Are Being Considered

There has been so much said and done about who will play Dracula for Universal, that everybody has sort of watched with interest who the powers that be will select.

Dame Rumor has it that Universal has selected Ian Keith, who just finished a picture on their lot. Prior to this he appeared in "The Big Trail" for Fox Films and is right now working at the RKO in "Sheeps Clothing," directed by Louis Wolheim.

For some time it has been rumored that Bela Lugosi was to have the leading role, since he played it so well on the stage, both here and abroad. Then William Courtney was mentioned as the man who was liable to gain the part on demand from the New York offices of the firm.

Maybe we are a bit premature with our announcement, but we have every reason to believe that Ian Keith has been selected and unless some unforeseen thing happens will play Dracula.

contenders. Muni, who was widely touted as "The New Lon Chaney" after his multifaceted appearance in *Seven Faces* for William Fox in 1929, insisted repeatedly in print that he had no interest in enacting grotesques, and it is difficult to imagine him actually accepting such a role. At the time of the film's casting, Muni was appearing on stage at the Pasadena Playhouse in the pre-Broadway run of a split-personality drama, *This One Man*, and was certainly within the range of Universal's viewfinder (in a related bit of inspired casting, Muni was followed at the Pasadena Playhouse by *Dracula* with saturnine Victor Jory as the Count and the then-juvenile Robert Young as Harker).

Harold Freedman attempted to exercise some leverage on behalf of yet another performer early in negotiations with Universal: "It appears to me that Joseph Schildkraut might be a brilliant piece of casting in the name part of *Dracula*," he wired the studio. ". . . Casting an attractive leading man in this part might be infinitely more effective than putting a character man into it."[7] Schildkraut was one of Universal's top leading men at the time, and coincidentally had married the former Mrs. Horace Liveright, Elise Bartlett.

Bela Lugosi continued to lobby energetically for the role, despite Universal's expressed lack of enthusiasm; Junior Laemmle had flatly told the agents he just wasn't interested in the actor. Lugosi went so far as to donate his services to Universal's foreign-language unit, dubbing Conrad Veidt's role in *The Last Performance* into Hungarian, and at some point during Universal's negotiations with Florence Stoker was asked—or took it upon himself—to intercede with Stoker on Universal's behalf. At the time the sale was closed, Lugosi wired Harold Freedman that he had spent months promoting Universal to Florence Stoker via cables to London, trying to bring down her asking price. Would Freedman please express an opinion to Universal for his being the logical choice for the part?

Lugosi apparently did not understand that donating services and acting as an unpaid intermediary in negotiations was putting him in a terrible bargaining position. He didn't comprehend that expressing enthusiasm for the film in press interviews, and even offering script suggestions (as he did to the *Oakland Tribune*, giving his own enthusiastic mini-treatment of how Dracula's sea voyage to England might be translated to the screen[8] might also be interpreted as a particularly nervy kind of butting-in. Lugosi seems to have assumed, with a certain touching naiveté, that magnanimous gestures would be repaid in kind, but the message Universal was receiving was not one he intended. Lugosi was simply proving that he was desperate for the part and might be had very, very cheaply.

Several years later, he related a somewhat distorted account of the affair to a *New York Post* reporter, who printed the entire interview in a bizarre phonetic interpretation of a "Hungarian" accent: "De Bram Stoker heirs

Thirsty frontrunner: Ian Keith. (Photofest)

Chester Morris: the studio was willing. (Courtesy of Scott MacQueen and the UCLA Film Archives)

Agent's choice: Joseph Schildkraut. (Photofest)

John Wray: the initial announcement. (Photofest)

Paul Muni: not very likely. (Photofest)

The distinguished stage actor William Courtenay was another leading contender for Dracula. (Free Library of Philadelphia Theatre Collection)

asked $200,000 for de film reidts, but Universal didn't like to pay dat much. Zo dey asked me would I correspond wid Mrs. Stoker, de widow, and get it maybe a liddle cheaper. I wreidt and wreidt until I get cramps, and after aboudt two months, Mrs. Stoker says O.K., we can haff it for $60,000. Zo what does Uniwersal do from graddidude? From graddidude dey start to test two dozens fellows for *Dragula*—but not me! And who was tested? De cousins and brodder-in-laws of de Laemmles—all deir pets and the pets of DEIR pets!"

Actually, the search extended considerably beyond Laemmle pets— indecision over *Dracula* persisted until just weeks before shooting began, leading E. M. ("Efe") Asher, Universal's associate producer now in charge of *Dracula,* to send the following letter to director Roland West, who had just directed *The Bat Whispers* (a creepy mystery released by United Artists, with a masked, cloaked title character who would be a direct inspiration for Batman):

"Dear Roland,

"We will start Dracula in about three weeks. Is there any possibility of getting Chester Morris to play Dracula?"

The tough-guy specialist's role in *The Bat Whispers* had been a caped villain, after all. And a bat was a bat, wasn't it?

The director responded:

"Dear Efe,

"Don't think I'd care for that part for Chester as we are looking for romance."[9]

Meanwhile, although Louis Bromfield remained the "official" scenarist for several more weeks, screenwriter Garrett Fort (who had just completed work with Browning on *Outside the Law,* another remake of a silent Lon Chaney gangster film, this time starring Edward G. Robinson) took out a prominent trade advertisement announcing his assignment to *Dracula* for "Adaptation and Dialogue." Bromfield's enforced collaboration with Dudley Murphy yielded a script that bore almost no connection to Bromfield's treatment. The means for melding the novel and stage play was now the substitution of Renfield as the real estate agent who travels to Transylvania. (This, of course, left the novel's leading man, Jonathan Harker, with precious little to do.) Browning took a hand in the script as well, and, under an apparent mandate to save as much money as possible, cut some of the most cinematic sequences, including the climactic chase back to Castle Dracula. As Universal's financial situation became even more fragile, and initial enthusiasm for the project waned, the de facto goal was apparently to find a way to film *Dracula* without having to spend money.

Bromfield, disillusioned and drained by his encounter with *Dracula,* soon left Hollywood, never to return. Though one of his books, *The Rains Came,*

Garrett Fort. (Billy Rose Theatre Collection, New York Public Library at Lincoln Center, Astor, Lenox and Tilden Foundations)

would enjoy a cinematic success as *The Rains of Ranchipur*, his attitude toward Hollywood remained sour. "Out of nothing into nothing" is how he summed it up for *Life* magazine in 1948.[10] Dudley Murphy developed a similarly jaundiced view. He criticized the "misdirected energy" of the Hollywood creative community, "full of people, often brilliant, making compromises. Money and the greed of the place cause them to lose their perspective and gradually lose their integrity. I want to pull out before it's too late."[11]

Dudley did pull out, and set himself up as an independent producer, never to return to Hollywood again. Murphy's most memorable effort would be his landmark production of Eugene O'Neill's *The Emperor Jones*, filmed in New York in 1933. (Murphy would later relocate his operations to Mexico, where he spent the rest of his life.)

The casting process for *Dracula* had reached a state of total paralysis. Former actress and Lugosi protégée Carroll Borland, is probably the last person living who knew the actor at the time *Dracula* was being filmed. She had first seen Lugosi in the original touring production at the age of fifteen. "I think all adolescent girls go through a period where they fall in love with horses or monsters or whatever," she recalled in a 1989 interview. "And I thought that Bela Lugosi was the most exciting person I had ever seen. He was certainly the most magnetic man I have ever known. We would just sit in a room and all the women would go . . . whoom! And he did the same thing on stage." The precocious Borland was inspired to compose a full-length novel, an unauthorized sequel to Stoker entitled *Countess Dracula*, which she sent to Lugosi at his Oakland hotel when he made a return stage engagement the following year.

"I wrote all the characters fifty years later, made it modern in the 1930s. I wrote him a letter and asked if he would be interested in seeing it. I don't know what his education was—I think it was the equivalent of a high school education—but he never read English well, and at that time he didn't speak it very well, but he understood. He was very impressed that I was going to the university—I went to Berkeley on a Shakespeare scholarship at sixteen—the European concept of the 'university' was a much more exclusive one than ours."

Borland was thrilled when she received an invitation to lunch at the Leamington Hotel, his residence during the stock production of *Dracula* that Asher, Bromfield, and Murphy had seen. "He invited me—*and* my mother. Remember, this man was always the European gentleman, observing all the forms and manners and codes and requirements. He decided he wanted to hear the novel, thinking it might have some possibilities as a new stage vehicle to follow up *Dracula*. So he came to the house in a taxi and stretched out on this very sofa and snapped his fingers for coffee. It took about three days to read it to him." Borland insists to this day that Lugosi's interest in her was strictly professional and "avuncular." She and her mother had no idea that the Hungarian gentleman stretched out on their sofa had been linked romantically in a scandal as a lover of the "Brooklyn Bonfire" Clara Bow—in company with such other notables as Gary Cooper, and the entire football team of the University of Southern California. Bow had fallen for Bela after seeing him onstage in *Dracula.*

Lugosi later told Borland that he had contacted the Stoker estate and that their demands were too high. His anxieties about *Dracula* were at their peak—the film was about to be made, and still, no answer! He kept his tensions to himself, however. "He was superstitious and didn't want to talk about it." she said. Giving up on any possibility of the film role coming to fruition (*Hollywood Filmograph,* which had editorialized repeatedly in support of Lugosi's casting, had gone so far as to print the news that Ian Keith had in all likelihood won the part) he told Borland he was preparing a stock tour of *Dracula.* Would she like to try out for the part of Lucy?

The star-smitten Borland was thrilled, but the touring production was called off* when Lugosi suddenly received word from Universal. He was to be offered the part.

Lugosi's elation was brief. The terms of the contract were grotesque. Universal was offering a flat $500 a week for a seven-week shooting schedule. $3,500, for the title role in a major studio film that had been the focus of nearly three years of cross-continental and transatlantic negotiations. It was a studio power play at its baldest and nastiest: in all his scraping and bowing and supplicating the actor had more than tipped his hand, and blown the poker game: Universal knew it could dictate terms; the Dracula they desired was far too hungry to put up a fuss.

And here, Bela Lugosi reached a Faustian crossroads. In accepting the contract he would almost certainly achieve worldwide fame for a role with which he had spent years in obsessive identification, the role itself a variation on Mephistopheles. But here the roles were reversed, and reversed again, as if in a crazy, cobwebby hall of mirrors—a Faustian bargain with the devil represented on both sides. He had already been stung, by Liveright, for holding out for too much money. That actor—almost a boy, that Huntley from England—had been all too eager to take his place. An actor's life had always been problematic, even in good times, but this year was one of the worst, economically, that anyone could remember.

And Universal wouldn't budge.

Carroll Borland, Bela Lugosi's avid protegée, seen here in a test makeup for MGM's Mark of the Vampire. *Borland's appearance would later inspire many media imitations, including the cartoons of Charles Addams. (Courtesy of Carroll Borland.)*

---

*Lugosi did, however, offer Borland the chance to play Lucy in a condensed version of *Dracula* he prepared for the vaudeville circuit in 1932.

ALL THE MOTION PICTURE NEWS—EVERY PAGE A FRONT PAGE

HOLLYWOOD filmograph 10¢

Copyright 1928—Hollywood Filmograph—Established 1922

VOL. 10, NO. 30   SATURDAY, AUGUST 9, 1930   PUBLISHED WEEKLY

BELA LUGOSI

Hollywood Filmograph *had high hopes for* Dracula *and lobbied energetically for Lugosi's casting. The paper, however, was less than enthusiastic about the finished film. (The Library of Congress)*

No doubt, Lugosi rationalized. A financial concession, yes, but what an investment! The exposure. The acclaim. The future! Well-meaning friends, no doubt, urged him to sign. How could anyone turn down work, these days? And a starring part in a movie by the Laemmles! There were actors on breadlines. He'd be crazy to turn it down.

A Universal Super Production!

Was there any choice?

Lugosi signed, in ink, not realizing he had made a pact in blood.

Filming began on *Dracula* on September 29, 1930. In addition to Lugosi's daredevil last-minute casting, there were still many unresolved problems, not the least of which were the lack of a hero and second female lead.

The lead actress had already been cast. At the age of twenty, Helen Chandler was an immensely popular New York actress, having spent most of her life on stage (she made her debut at the age of eight, her child roles including a stint as the boy prince opposite John Barrymore's Richard III, and, a few years later, as Ophelia in Horace Liveright's controversial, modern-dress *Hamlet*). Tod Browning had seen her opening night performance in the mysterious stage play *Silent House,* and was no doubt aware of her current appearance in Warner Bros.' screen adaptation of Sutton Vane's stage hit *Outward Bound,* in which Chandler played opposite Douglas Fairbanks, Jr., as a pair of suicides on their way to judgment on a mysterious ship. Viewed today, *Outward Bound* is an excruciating gabfest of middlebrow metaphysics, but was nonetheless immensely popular as a play and film, a weird prefiguration of *No Exit.* It certainly served to link Chandler in the public mind with themes of the supernatural. The actress had a fragile, wistful quality that perfectly suited the role of Mina as it was now written—gone completely was any hint of the "New Woman" of the novel; the character was now a complete milksop.

"In *Dracula,* I played one of those bewildered little girls who go around pale, hollow-eyed and anguished, wondering about things," she told an interviewer in 1932. What she really was wondering about was how to schedule surgery for chronic appendicitis without holding up the film. She managed to put off surgery until after the film's completion.[12]

Too hot for Harker: the forty-one-year-old "juvenile" Robert Ames was dropped by the studio in the midst of a messy and highly publicized divorce trial. (Free Library of Philadelphia Theatre Collection)

Lew Ayres, who had scored such a hit in Universal's last blockbuster, *All Quiet on the Western Front,* originally announced for the role of Jonathan Harker (or what remained of the role of Jonathan Harker), was dropped; in later years he said that the part that really interested him was "the guy who ate the flies and spiders."[13]

In desperation, Universal turned to RKO star Robert Ames, who at the age of forty-one was probably Hollywood's oldest employable "juvenile." (No one seemed to mind that Ames was old enough to be Helen Chandler's father.) His casting was announced in the October 18 issue of *Billboard,* but almost simultaneously was eclipsed by front-page news of his messy matrimonial travails and impending divorce—his fourth, and messiest. Ames' wife, Muriel Oakes, complained in public that Ames was "sulky, bad-tempered and wouldn't stop drinking."[14] Ames, she claimed, had been on a marathon drinking spree since they left the altar. Robert Ames suddenly disappeared from any of Universal's announcements on *Dracula.* (On November 27 of the following year, while engaged to actress Ina Claire, he would be found dead of a hemorrhaged bladder at the Hotel Delmonico in New York, his suite littered with whisky bottles and sedative powders.)

The third, and final, Jonathan Harker was to be David Manners, the former Rauf de Ryther Daun Acklom of Halifax, Nova Scotia, a rising young performer brought to Hollywood the year before by director James Whale for the film version of the West End stage success *Journey's End.* (Whale, a gifted, idiosyncratic, and finally tragic talent, would create two masterpieces for Universal: *Frankenstein* (1931) and its deliriously perverse sequel *Bride of Frankenstein* in 1935.) Manners was highly in demand as a specific type of romantic lead, aptly described by Gregory Mank in a 1977 profile: "Hollywood was in the era of the Leading Lady—lacquered goddesses who aimed their best profiles at the camera as their capped teeth gnashed at the scenery (and all too often) the leading man. The dream of these high-heeled deities was to have a romantic screen partner who was handsome without being distractingly sexy, and a polished actor who would not be a scene stealer. Manners was to serve their fantasy."[15] (The fantasy didn't come cheap; Universal had to pay a fee to Jack Warner for the loan of his contract star, as well as Manners' $2,000-a-week salary[16]—four times the earnings of the film's nominal star—for an anemic supporting part.)

Another latecomer to the cast was Frances Dade, who would play the doomed Lucy Weston (Westenra being too much of a mouthful for the scriptwriters, apparently). Dade, a twenty-one-year-old ingenue from a prominent Philadelphia family, had enjoyed a stage success in *Gentlemen Prefer Blondes* and made her film debut opposite Ronald Coleman in *Raffles.* The smoky-voiced, blue-eyed blonde could trace her looks to her grandmother, Mrs. Clifford Pemberton, who had been the model for the profile on the Liberty dollar.

As for Renfield, Lew Ayres was right in recognizing the film's plum role. The part went to New York stage actor Dwight Frye, who had recently moved west with his wife, the actress Laura Bullivant, following the failure of the theatrical tearoom they operated on West 69th Street and the general downturn of the theater economy. Frye's surviving scrapbooks reveal a performer of remarkable range and popularity; like Helen Chandler, he enjoyed excellent press and was in frequent demand, receiving kudos for his work in *Six Characters in Search of an Author* and comedies like *A Man's a Man.* The role of Renfield, with its shifting moods and explosive outbursts, would be an ideal showcase for Frye's versatility. He could not anticipate, however, the extent to which the part would limit his Hollywood options. On the strength of *Dracula* he would attract the attention of James Whale, who cast him as *Frankenstein's* demented hunchback . . . and thus sealed forever the actor's niche of wild-eyed lunatics and monsters' assistants.

Edward Van Sloan reprised his stage role as Dr. Van Helsing, along with

Ames' replacement was the aptly named David Manners, a popular leading man on loan from First National. (Free Library of Philadelphia Theatre Collection)

Herbert Bunston as Dr. Seward. Van Sloan's screen test consisted of his standing in front of a mantelpiece and mirror, speaking lines from the stage play and ducking when an offscreen "Dracula" smashed the mirror with a vase. The clip was later used as part of the film's preview trailer (trailers at that time were customarily made from outtakes or specially shot material, since duping original negatives was a cumbersome process). Other supporting players included Michael Visaroff as the innkeeper; Charles Gerrard and Moon Carroll as the comic attendant and maid; Joan Standing, who had withstood the rigors of filming Erich Von Stroheim's *Greed*, played the English nurse; and Carl Laemmle's teenaged niece, Rebecca Beth Laemmle, who worked under the professional name of Carla. Like her cousin Julius, she had also changed her name in tribute to the older Laemmle. A few years earlier Carla had appeared as a ballerina in the silent *The Phantom of the Opera*; in *Dracula* she would have the distinction of speaking the first words of dialogue ever uttered in a talking horror movie ("Among the rugged peaks that frown down upon the Borgo Pass are found crumbling castles of a bygone age").

Edna Tichenor, seen here in London After Midnight, *represented Tod Browning's ideal of feminine evil. He created the look meticulously for* Dracula. *(Photofest)*

As one of Dracula's undead brides, Browning cast none other than Greta Garbo's regular stand-in at Metro, Jeraldine Dvorak. The resulting cameo amounted to a perverse caricature of the glacial persona Garbo cultivated at Browning's former studio.

The supervising art director was Charles D. Hall, who had designed Chaplin's *The Gold Rush* and other classic films; in *Dracula* he also drew upon the talents of designers Hermann Rosse (who had won an Academy Award for *The King of Jazz*) and the aforementioned John Ivan Hoffman. Several of the sets pushed Universal's physical capacity to the limits. David Manners recalled that the massive setting for Dracula's castle, with its huge staircase and eighteen-foot-wide spiderweb "filled the sound stage up to the roof."[17] In the finished film the height of this set was extended to Westminster-like proportions through the use of a painting on glass mounted in front of the camera. (While not credited, the glass shots in *Dracula* closely resemble the rendering style of Conrad Tritschler, a former stage designer from Britain whom Hall would have known. Tritschler created similar glass effects for the marvelously atmospheric *White Zombie*, filmed the following year by the Halperin Brothers on the Universal lot and using Universal technicians and sets, including some interiors left over from *Dracula*. Tritschler died in 1939.)

Dracula's cinematographer, Karl Freund, was not announced to the trade press until filming had already commenced. Browning's assistant director was Scott Beal (the veteran assistant director, who would have had the most revealing insights of all into the making of *Dracula*, died in the early 1970s). Symon Gould's illicit print of *Nosferatu* had arrived in Los Angeles, and had almost certainly been studied by all the key creative personnel.

Although the name of the woman on the right remains a mystery, two of Dracula's vampire wives have finally been identified. Jeraldine Dvorak, former stand-in for Greta Garbo, found it difficult to escape the star's shadow and establish a screen persona of her own. Dismissed by Garbo, she found professional refuge in the vaults of Dracula. Dvorak also doubled for Marlene Dietrich and Madeline Carroll, and finally left Hollywood for a more rewarding career on stage.

A noted character actress of the 1930s and 40s, Dorothy Tree made her first unbilled film appearance as one of Dracula's corpselike consorts. A dark contralto who would later would corner the market on wartime villainesses, Tree had her career cut short in the early 1950s, a victim of the McCarthy era blacklists. She gave up acting for a successful career as a New York voice coach and speech therapist. (The Billy Rose Theatre Collection, New York Public Library at Lincoln Center, Astor, Lenox, and Tilden Foundations.)

Cinematographer Karl Freund, a Prussian taskmaster in the tradition of Von Stroheim, whose talents were largely wasted on Dracula. *(Photofest)*

The published shooting script for *Dracula*[18] reveals vividly the extent to which Browning circumvented and undermined the story's cinematic possibilities. The film was shot roughly in sequence—an odd and inefficient way to work, then as today—and Freund clearly was given some degree of creative latitude with the opening scenes at Castle Dracula, during the first days of shooting when schedules and budget considerations would not have been weighed so heavily. But even these scenes—and they are the core of whatever interest the film retains—are shot in a flat and highly restrictive manner. In scene after scene the script demonstrates just how much Browning cut, trimmed, ignored, and generally sabotaged the screenplay's visual potentials, insisting on static camera setups, eliminating reaction shots and special effects, and generally taking the lazy way out at every opportunity. In one story that circulated around Hollywood—possibly apocryphal, since it has no firm attribution—Freund became so fed up with Browning's static ways that he finally just turned on the camera and let it run unattended. Indeed, there is one endless take in the finished film featuring Manners, Chandler, and Van Sloan that runs 251 feet, nearly three minutes without a cut[19] that was clearly meant to be broken up with closeups and reaction shots. At one point Chandler tells Manners, "Oh, no—don't look at me like that," in an apparent reference to a dramatic change in his expression. The two-shot, however, shows Manners as motionless as a wax dummy—as if oblivious that the camera is even catching his face.

Freund's work on *Dracula* has been wildly overpraised, as if to enforce a preconceived notion that Freund provides a significant link between German expressionism and the American horror film. Freund was certainly talented, both as a photographer and a director—he had worked behind the camera on Fritz Lang's *Metropolis* and with F. W. Murnau himself on *The Last Laugh*, and Freund's directorial work on 1935's *Mad Love* remains a perfectly controlled and creepily evocative homage to expressionist horror. In *Dracula*, however, whatever inspiration Freund might have brought to bear appears to have been effectively hampered by Tod Browning.

Browning's treatment of the material is odd indeed for someone purported to have coveted the project for years. "To be quite honest," recalled Manners, "Tod Browning was always off to the side somewhere. I remember being directed by Karl Freund, the photographer who came from Germany and had a great sense for film. I believe that he is the one who is mainly responsible for *Dracula* being watchable today."[20] Carroll Borland, who worked with Browning and Lugosi in MGM's *Mark of the Vampire* in 1935, found the director equally enigmatic. "I don't remember him doing a thing. He was this little man who sat there. I was used to stage directors who would take you aside and talk about the character and whatnot, but it was Jimmy Howe [James Wong

Howe, the cinematographer] who had much more to do with creating the mood of my scenes. People are always asking me what it was like to work with Tod Browning—and I have to tell them I don't know!" Lugosi, who had worked with Browning once before, in *The Thirteenth Chair* for Metro, offered a more sympathetic appraisal of Browning's position vis-à-vis Universal on *Dracula:* "The studios were hell-bent on saving money—they even cut rubber-erasers in offices in half—everything that Tod Browning wanted to do was queried. Couldn't it be done cheaper? Wouldn't it be just as effective if . . . ? That sort of thing. It was most dispiriting."[21]

In *The Genius of the System: Hollywood Filmmaking in the Studio Era,* film historian Thomas Schatz relates that "Browning was devastated by Chaney's death, and he never really recovered his professional footing."[22] Less comfortable with actors who did not direct themselves, Browning seems to have indulged himself in peculiar, nonhuman details. For *London After Midnight,* he had, for some eccentric reason, been determined to include armadillos as animal bit players, and made special arrangements to have the creatures shipped from Texas. Unfortunately, they had been packed together with live rattlesnakes and arrived in no condition to act.[23] (Their naive handler had apparently wildly overestimated the toughness of their natural armor.) No matter that armadillos were equally out of place in Transylvania as they would have been in London, Browning nonetheless did things his own way, and Bela Lugosi's momentous first appearance on the huge Castle Dracula staircase would be heralded by a mini-stampede of *dasypi novemcincti.*

Dasypus novemcinctus, *the nine-banded armadillo, a memorable bit player in* Dracula. *(Courtesy of the Cowgirl Hall of Fame)*

Karl Freund seems to have shown some enthusiasm for *Dracula* before caving in to Browning's wet-towel approach. According to the veteran Hollywood model-maker William Davison, the cameraman delivered in person a sketch of a castle he wanted built for the film, which Davison's shop turned around in twenty-four hours at an approximate cost of $2,000.[24] The five-foot-tall model appears for a few seconds in the finished film—somewhat jarringly in that it bears no similarity whatsoever to the soaring gothic fantasias Charles Hall and company had created for the interiors. It looks, in fact, remarkably like the chateau glimpsed in *Nosferatu*.

Among the actors, Bela Lugosi remained characteristically aloof from the company. He had already clashed with Universal's makeup man, Jack Pierce, over the character's appearance (the script, for example, called for fangs), and insisted on doing his makeup himself.[25] He agreed to wear a hairpiece, however, that added a slight widow's peak to his somewhat thinning hairline. On the set, David Manners recalled the actor at work: "I mainly remember Lugosi standing in front of a full-length mirror between scenes, intoning 'I am Dracula.' He was mysterious and never really said anything to the other members of the cast except good morning when he arrived and good night when he left. He was polite, but always distant."[26] Lugosi struck Manners as a vain, eccentric performer. "I never thought he was acting, but being the odd man he was."[27]

Carroll Borland offered another explanation for Lugosi's reclusive professional behavior, which other actors commented on throughout his career. "He was simply afraid of his English," said Borland. The old crutch of learning parts phonetically was hampering his ability to interact professionally off-camera. He even dictated all of his correspondence to a secretary, who was responsible for correcting his usage and grammar.

Journalist Lillian Shirley, after visiting Lugosi on the set, reported in the March 1931 issue of *Modern Screen* that the actor had reached the point of actually hating the part. "I was with him when a telegram arrived. It was from Henry Duffy, the Pacific Coast theatre impresario, who wanted Mr. Lugosi to play *Dracula* for sixteen weeks," Shirley wrote. Lugosi threw down the message in disgust, his face visibly reddening, even beneath the gray-green makeup. " 'No! Not at any price. . . . When I am through with this picture I hope never to hear of Dracula again. I cannot stand it. . . . I do not intend that it shall possess me. No one knows what I suffer from this role.' " He was certainly suffering financially; a full realization of the inequity of his salary *vis-à-vis* the other performers' had no doubt set in.

For its part, *Hollywood Filmograph* continued to give increasingly overheated accounts of the filming, culminating in the nonsense of October 11: "So horrible is this grotesque monster that everyone on the Big U lot is

"Is this the coach from Count Dracula?"
A close encounter at the Borgo Pass.

terrified whenever Bela Lugosi emerges from his dressing room. . . . Child prodigies scamper into prop rooms . . . even hard-riding cowboys stand at the heads of their trembling steeds."

The story, as filmed, contained considerably less blood and thunder. The film opens with a familiar theme from *Swan Lake*, heard over the titles. The musical passage, which had been arranged and abridged by Universal's music director Heinz Roemheld, had been used in the silent era as a generic *misterioso* accompaniment.[28] Except for a brief passage in a concert hall, *Dracula*, like many early talkies, is often deathly quiet, and many of its pantomimic sequences could have been lifted directly out of a silent film. The

*Transylvanian peasants are less than
pleased at the prospect of nightfall.
The careful attention to costume
and production detail in the opening
sequences of Dracula deteriorated
badly as the film progressed.*

first shot is a carriage rumbling up a mountain pass. Inside, the real estate
agent Renfield is warned that the coach must reach the inn by sundown—it is
Walpurgis night, he is told, the evil time of *nosferatu*. At the inn, Renfield
shocks the local peasants with the news that he must continue traveling after
dark for a midnight rendevous with a carriage sent by a local nobleman, Count
Dracula.

At the mention of the name, the peasants cross themselves in shock and
beg Renfield to stay. When they realize that he cannot be dissuaded from his
journey, the innkeeper's wife gives him a rosary to wear around his neck, in the
hope that it will protect him against the vampires at Dracula's castle. Renfield's
carriage rumbles off toward the Borgo Pass, and the scene dissolves to the
castle and its vaults, where, just as promised, Dracula and his three corpselike

wives rise from their coffins to strike macabre poses. In partial disguise, Dracula is the coachman whom Renfield meets at the Borgo Pass and who drives him to the castle; when the ride proves a bit too bumpy and Renfield leans out the window to beg the driver to slow down, he sees that the horses are being led not by a man but by a huge, flapping bat. The coach pulls into the courtyard of an ancient castle, the driver vanished. Renfield enters the huge, partially ruined, and cobweb-festooned main hall of the castle, where he is greeted on a monumental staircase by a cloaked figure in black carrying a taper. "I am . . . Dracula," he announces, with an ambiguous smile. The Count motions Renfield to follow him to the chambers above, where food awaits him, along with a comfortable bed. The details of the lease on Carfax Abbey meet with the Count's satisfaction. A ship has been chartered to take them to England the following evening. Renfield accidentally cuts his finger on a paper clip, and doesn't notice the predatory change that comes over his host, or how he is repelled by the rosary he wears. Regaining his poise, Dracula pours only a single glass of wine. "I never drink—wine," he explains.

The wine, however, is drugged, and Renfield collapses in front of a window while a bat flaps mockingly in his face. The three weird women from the vaults approach him with a strange, gliding motion, only to be repelled by the returning Dracula, who claims the young man's blood as his own. The scene dissolves to a storm at sea, and the hold of a ship where Dracula's earth-box is being protected by Renfield, now a raving madman. Dracula rises, and Renfield begs him for "lives, small ones, with blood in them" when they arrive in England. Dracula magisterially ignores his slave, and focuses his attention instead on the stock footage of sailors battling the storm. The scene fades, and we next hear the voices of the men who have boarded the derelict vessel that has drifted into Whitby harbor, all its crewmen dead, the captain lashed to the wheel. The only survivor is a lunatic with a bizarre craving to devour flies and spiders. Renfield is committed to a local mental hospital, the Seward Sanitarium.

Meanwhile, Dracula moves freely about London, blending inconspicuously with his cloak and evening clothes among the elegant, theatregoing crowds. A flower girl on a side street offers him a buttonhole, but gives the vampire her life instead. Refreshed from his snack, Dracula moves on to a concert hall, where he contrives an introduction at the box of Dr. Seward, owner of the sanitarium which adjoins the grounds of Carfax Abbey. Seward presents his daughter, Mina, her fiancé, John Harker, and Mina's attractive friend, Lucy. Lucy is immediately fascinated by the Count, and he by her. Later that night, he enters her bedroom window in bat-form and bestows his fatal kiss.

From this point on, the film falls back on the style and conventions of the

"Wear this — for your mother's sake."
Renfield (Dwight Frye) receives a warning
and a blessing from the innkeeper's wife.
(Photofest)

(Overleaf) Upstairs/Downstairs: Dracula
invites his guest to partake of vampiric
knowledge in the chambers above.
(Photofest)

*Bela Lugosi stalks Florence
Stoker's London, as recreated on
the Universal backlot. (Photofest)*

stage play. Mina begins to have bad dreams, and believes that Lucy has returned from the dead. Dracula has insinuated himself into the Seward household as a frequent guest whom Mina welcomes but whom Harker resents. Dr. Van Helsing, a colleague of Dr. Seward's, suspects a vampire and quickly exposes the Count by confronting him with a mirrored cigarette box, in which he does not reflect. Dracula smashes the box. "For one who has lived not even a single lifetime, you are a wise man, Van Helsing," he sneers, recognizing his match. With Renfield's assistance, Dracula continues to drain Mina's blood, and finally abducts her to Carfax Abbey to complete her transformation into his vampire bride. The men follow, and Dracula, thinking that Renfield has betrayed him, strangles the lunatic and escapes with Mina into the Carfax vaults. The sun rises, Dracula's coffin is discovered, and he is perfunctorily staked, offscreen. Mina's trance lifts, the lovers are reunited, and the film ends—or seems to. Halfway through the end title of the film during its original release, Dr. Van Helsing appeared on screen, standing against the proscenium of a motion picture theatre, and delivered the verbatim epilogue from the stage play. "Just a moment, ladies and gentlemen! Just a word before you go. We hope the memories of Dracula and Renfield won't give you bad dreams, so just a word of reassurance. When you get home tonight and the lights have been turned out and you are afraid to look behind the curtains and you dread to see a face appear at the window—why, just pull yourself together and remember that after all *there are such things*."[29]

Dracula finished principal photography November 15, 1930, six days over schedule but almost $14,000 under budget.[30] Some additional scenes and retakes were shot in December and January. The editing process may have further truncated the story. One entire, expensive set—a secondary staircase and hall in Carfax Abbey—was simply not used in the film, though scene stills indicate that footage was shot. The whole subplot involving the discovery and destruction of Lucy as a vampire is simply dropped in mid-film and never resolved. A costly glass shot of Carfax Abbey overlooking the crashing sea was similarly not used. Renfield is shown attacking the maid, yet she turns up hale and unharmed a few minutes later. For some reason—revenge by Freund on an inattentive director?—a large, ragged piece of cardboard apparently used to reduce the glare of a practical lamp in Mina's bedroom is fully visible to the camera in two shots—in one, it occupies almost a quarter of the screen, in the foreground, as Dracula makes his approach. Dracula's demise was reduced to a series of offscreen groans. And there would be problems to come. The finished titles, as transcribed in continuity dated at the beginning of February, made no mention of Hamilton Deane or John L. Balderston. They did, however, give Lugosi a solo billing under the title. Balderston's correspondence file on this matter has not survived, but it seems obvious that an

Trance macabre: Helen Chandler succumbs to a dream of ecstacy and horror. (Photofest)

objection was raised citing the terms of the contract. Universal would have
been forced to remake the main titles at the last moment, reinstating the
playwrights and relegating Lugosi to the third-title cast list. There is some
tangible indication of the credits being assembled hurriedly—Carl Laemmle's
title is actually misspelled as PRESIENT.

According to one published account, Laemmle, Sr., had "violent heebie-
jeebies" over the finished picture when it was screened for him.[31] In *The
Genius of the System,* film historian Thomas Schatz reports that a November
1930 preview took place,[32] and this may account for the two running times
that have been persistently cited for the film—eighty-four minutes versus the
actual running time of seventy-five minutes. Laemmle may well have demanded cuts in order to increase the film's funereal pace, which would explain
the missing scenes, continuity problems, and discrepancies of running time.
The final negative cost of *Dracula,* not including exploitation, was
$441,984.90.

The world premiere of *Dracula* was set for Friday, February 13, at the
country's unofficial cathedral of the motion picture, the Roxy Theatre in New
York. The ball was now squarely in the court of Paul Gulick, Universal's head
of promotion in New York. He had already placed a number of lurid trade ads
in *Variety, Motion Picture Herald,* and elsewhere featuring an artist's conception
of Bela Lugosi, eyes glowing and hairpiece blowing as he leaned over a
sleeping woman with prominent nipples. The same breasts would also be given
play on the cover of a tie-in edition of the novel, to be published by Grosset
and Dunlap . . . no matter that the actual women in the film were corseted to
the throat. Ballyhoo was ballyhoo. Anyway, no one knew *what* kind of picture
this was . . . a horror story? A love story? Was it going to be bats or beds . . .
or a little of both?

Joe Weil, head of Universal's exploitation department, arranged to have
the island of Manhattan "sniped" with teaser advertisements printed in drip-
ping red letters: GOOD TO THE LAST GASP—DRACULA—ROXY THEATRE
and I'LL BE ON YOUR NECK FRIDAY THE 13TH—DRACULA. Department
stores sported lavish window displays of the photoplay edition of the novel
surrounded by photos and window card posters (these advertising graphics, so
liberally distributed—and discarded—at the time of the film's release, can
today fetch as much as $10,000 apiece from die-hard collectors). Contrary to
many previous accounts of the film's release, Universal planned *Dracula* as a
Friday the 13th tie-in, and completely ignored the possibilities of Friday the
13th, 1931, falling next to Valentine's Day. On February 11, an ad was taken
out in *The New York Times* featuring the leering face of Bela Lugosi behind a
fake telegram to S. L. "Roxy" Rothaphel: DEAR ROXY DON'T BLAME ME
BUT I WAS BORN SUPERSTITIOUS STOP JUST HEARD YOU ARE OPENING

*Making midnight whoopee: Bela
Lugosi carries Helen Chandler up
the elaborate Carfax Abbey
staircase which was never seen in
the finished film. (Collection of the
Cinémathèque Française)*

DRACULA FRIDAY STOP THAT BAD ENOUGH BUT FRIDAY THE THIR-
TEENTH IS TERRIBLE STOP I HAVE PUT EVERYTHING I HAVE INTO THIS
PICTURE AND AS A FAVOR TO ME CANT YOU OPEN YOUR PRESENTATION
THURSDAY STOP BEST REGARDS TOD BROWNING.

And Universal's *Dracula* was released to a trembling world on February
12, 1931. It was a world that trembled for a number of other reasons than for
fear of the un-dead. Throughout most of 1930, the country had been in a
trancelike state of denial about the economy—a general awareness of the
Depression's reality dawned only gradually. The public's entertainment tastes
were becoming increasingly stylized and escapist; Radio City Music Hall, then
under construction, reflected this impulse vividly, as did the nationwide mania
for miniature golf, which even film exhibitors viewed as a threat.

*A Depression-age Dracula eclipses jazz
baby Frances Dade in a pantomimic
exorcism of the roaring twenties. (Courtesy
of Ronald V. Borst/Hollywood Movie
Posters)*

Dracula's trajectory as a film encompassed and reflected both the pre-crash
days of dizzying optimism and the bottomless pit of economic stagnation. The
film can be read as an unconscious allegory of encroaching, paralyzing force,
not unlike the Depression itself. The film becomes paralyzed, numb, and
static, enervating both to the viewer and the performers. When Bela Lugosi
draws his black cape over sleeping jazz baby Frances Dade—the image of the
Liberty dollar, according to her publicity—he is performing a rite of economic extreme unction. (Soon after *Dracula*, Lugosi appeared in a humorous
short subject that made the same point even more sharply: approaching the
quintessential flapper icon Mae "Betty Boop" Questal, he informs her that
"you have booped your last boop" and summarily sinks in his fangs.)

Dracula has always been a lightning rod for prevailing social anxieties. In
the absence of a strong director, the film would become even more susceptible
to the half-conscious projections of its creators, its public, and its critics.
Dracula would provide a particular social catharsis for the moviegoing public
of 1931. But that would be far from the limit of its appeal.

The film's first two reels are without question its strongest, and provide the
main reason for the film's enduring fascination. The Transylvania sequences
have, however, been routinely overpraised in terms of their direction and
cinematography. Browning's direction is heavy-handed as usual and Freund's
camerawork shines only in relation to the mediocrity of the balance of the film.
What, then, brings commentators back again and again to these scenes, trying
to capture validity or meaning?

Part of the explanation must lie in the rather extraordinary number and
layers of visual symbols. Renfield's visit to Castle Dracula is densely packed
with evocative visual cues: the high gothic architecture is unmistakably
ecclesiastical—Castle Dracula is religion in ruins. Dracula meets the traveler
on a huge staircase, a figure of illumination with a tapering candle, and guides
him to a higher level. A huge spiraling spiderweb—an ancient symbol for the

"My blood now flows through her veins . . ." Edward Van Sloan and Bela Lugosi reprise the classic dramatic standoff they perfected on stage. (Photofest)

fabric of reality—is a barrier that must be crossed. An unholy trinity of bats is observed. The castle's vaults, the audience already knows, are places of death and resurrection. Above, the young man is conducted to an altarlike table and offered a chalice. There is talk of wine and blood, and secret understandings. The power of the crucifix is demonstrated. Three silent women who approach are banished, and a male-to-male blood ritual is performed.

The religio-mythic trappings, the initiation/corruption of an innocent, the evocation of a Grail quest that culminates in a blood sacrifice and homoerotic rite of passage are all motifs powerful enough in and of themselves, but brought together within a space of ten minutes they achieve a kind of psychological critical mass unprecedented in the cinema. Exactly why Tod Browning decided to have Dracula attack Renfield is unclear—the script called for the vampire women to do the deed—but consciously or unconsciously he tapped directly into Stoker's subtext, and the film takes on a decidedly homoerotic tone. Renfield is the only character in the film who actually undergoes any change or development; the real "story" is Renfield's tragic, unrequited love for the Count.

The press reaction to *Dracula* was mixed at best. The trade papers, especially those based on the west coast, were much more candid in their appraisals than the general readership dailies, many of which seemed to be acting as pipelines for Universal's publicity office. Norbert Lusk, reviewing the New York premiere for the *Los Angeles Times* on February 22, commented that "in spite of pronounced merit the story of human vampires who feast on the blood of living victims is too extreme to provide entertainment that causes word-of-mouth advertising. Plainly a freak picture, it must be accepted as a curiosity devoid of the important element of sympathy that causes the widest appeal." *Hollywood Filmograph,* which had lobbied so energetically for Lugosi's casting, did not preview the film and made no appraisal at all until after *Dracula's* west coast release at the end of March. Universal in the interim took out trade ads with puff quotes from the New York dailies. The *Filmograph's* reviewer, Harold Weight, pulled few punches. "Tod Browning directed—although we cannot believe that the same man was responsible for both the first and latter parts of the picture," he wrote. "Had the rest of the picture lived up to the first sequence in the ruined castle in Transylvania, *Dracula* . . . would have been a horror and thrill classic long remembered."[34] Predictably, at least one reviewer took the totally perverse stance that it was the opening sequences that lagged, but that Browning had redeemed himself with the *second* part of the film.

Variety[35] reported that *Dracula* grossed $112,000 in its inaugural engagement at the Roxy (though Universal claimed a higher figure in its trade ads). The earnings were, in any case, quite respectable but not a sellout, and the Roxy dropped *Dracula* after eight days. At this point no one at Universal dreamed the film would be its top money-maker of the year. The picture went into national distribution during March. At the New Haven opening, Yale students let loose a flock of bats they had smuggled into the theatre. The audience thought the stunt was a publicity gag, and complimented the management.[36] In San Francisco, "Midnight Whoopee Shows" were scheduled. And so on.

To cover all possible venues, Universal had prepared a silent version of the film with dialogue titles for theatres, especially those in small towns, not yet

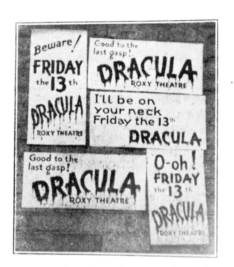

Universal's publicity department plastered Times Square with blood-red advertising snipes intended to draw audiences to the Roxy Theatre. (Free Library of Philadelphia Theatre Collection)

Dwight Frye's performance as the fly-eating Renfield was so definitive and convincing that it hindered the versatile actor's future opportunities in Hollywood.

Pencil self-portrait by Dwight Frye, from the actor's personal scrapbook. (Courtesy of Dwight D. Frye)

wired for sound. The version was nearly identical to the talkie, save for the condensed dialogue and the inclusion of a brief shot, from a distance, of Van Helsing pounding the stake into Dracula's heart—an offscreen groan being a clear impossibility in a silent picture. In keeping with the practice of the time, this version would have been accompanied by a continuous recorded musical score, in all likelihood drawn from classical scores in the public domain.[37]

By the time *Dracula* reached Los Angeles, Universal was in the middle of a work shutdown, yet another austerity measure. None of the usual display advertising was taken out in the *Los Angeles Times* when the film opened at the Orpheum. "It was a theatre in downtown Los Angeles—God knows what it is today," recalled the late Lillian Lugosi, Bela's fourth wife. "It really wasn't a big deal. No ballyhoo, no nothing!"[38] In the *Times* local review, Philip K. Scheuer was hardly sanguine: "Bram Stoker's classic of a generation, *Dracula*, is now an audible movie, and you may hear and see it at the Orpheum if you are so minded." Scheuer politely praised several elements, but called the film "a somewhat less than grisly affair."[39] Coincidentally, the same page of the paper contained a brief notice that Tod Browning was leaving Universal, having completed his contract and would shortly return to Metro.

Dracula outperformed almost everyone's expectations, and certainly vindicated Carl Laemmle, Jr., in the eyes of his many critics. Morbid or not, talking horror films were a new and evidently profitable genre. Next on Laemmle's list would be *Frankenstein,* based on a John Balderston adaptation of a play by Peggy Webling that Hamilton Deane had produced in England. Horace Liveright had announced it for Broadway, but had been unable to raise the capital. His efforts in Hollywood had produced very little, he was drinking heavily and was about to embark on his final, downhill slide into oblivion and death. Liveright's efforts as a producer had been directly responsible for bringing both *Dracula* and *Frankenstein* to Hollywood's attention. The two properties would spin more money for others than Liveright had ever dreamed of at the height of his own career. But Liveright, like his discovery Bela Lugosi, would never share in the windfall. And in October 1931, Liveright lost even his stage interests. Florence Stoker and the playwrights finally moved against the producer for nonpayment of royalties, and the stage rights were recontracted to Alfred Wallerstein, who assumed Liveright's debt. Liveright had grossed over two million dollars on *Dracula,* and lost the property over a delinquent sum of $678.01.[40]

By the end of fiscal 1931, on the strength of *Dracula,* it was clear that Universal would make a profit for the first time in two years. In its first domestic release the film would gross almost $700,000, nearly double its investment.[41] World receipts by 1936 were $1,012,189.[42] Although financial

The best scenes were saved for staircases: here Renfield realizes, too late, that Dracula's designs no longer require the services of an insect-eating slave. (Photofest)

Broken down by Broadway, Hollywood, and the stock market crash, the near-destitute producer Horace Liveright visited the set of Dracula and posed for publicity pictures, despite his having lost all rights in the property. Left to right: Tod Browning, Bela Lugosi, Liveright, and screenwriter Dudley Murphy.

The world premiere of Dracula in New York was heralded with a hammy—and effective—advertising campaign.

The Feminine Love *of* Horror

Have You Ever Watched A Woman
Talk About Death? "Don't!" Warns Bela Lugosi

By GLADYS HALL

"BUT it is *women* who love horror. Gloat over it. Feed on it. Are nourished by it. Shudder and cling and cry out—*and come back for more*.

"*Women have a predestination to suffering.*

"It is women who bear the race in bloody agony. Suffering is a kind of horror. Blood is a kind of horror. Therefore women are born with a predestination to horror in their very blood stream. It is a biological thing."

Thus Bela Lugosi. Thus **Dracula**. Thus the Horror Man, the Mystery Man of Hollywood.

The tall, too-pallid man with the enormous predatory hands, the narrow, red-lit pale blue eyes, the soft, caressing voice, the atmosphere of charnel house and carnival surrounding him, a rank miasma.

Bela Lugosi from Hungary—the saga of the vampire, the lore of demonology, the dark secrets of the state of trance a part of his daily life.

The man who never sleeps at night. The man who lies alone in his darkened house. *The man to whom no woman can stay married—why not?*

No answer. No answer. No answer. There are questions better not put to Bela Lugosi. There are answers far better not heard. There are secrets better—much better—left interred.

Does he eat food, make love, work, play, hope, struggle as other men? No answer. No answer. *No answer.*

Why the Women Came Back

LUGOSI sat in a deep chair in my library. (One does not go to his house!) A single light burned above him, making his pallid face more pallid, obliterating all but the red lights burning ceaselessly in his too-pale blue eyes. The windows were opened and there came the mournful sound of the wind in the tall boughs of the eucalyptus. . .Was it only the wind playing in the boughs of the trees . . . or was it . . . ? No answer. No answer. Better not ask.

His voice came, remote and far away, dying down, rising to a penetrating cry.

He said, "When I was playing **Dracula** on the stage, my audiences were women. *Women.* There were men, too. Escorts the women *had brought with them*. For reasons only their dark subconscious knew. In order to establish a subtle sex intimacy. Contact. In order to cling and to feel the sensuous thrill of protection. Men did not come of their own volition. *Women did.* Came—and knew an ecstasy dragged from the depths of unspeakable things. Came—*and then came back again. And again.*" (Was there gloating in his voice? Or was it my chilled imagination playing me tricks, feverish and fantastical?)

"Women wrote me letters. Ah, what letters women wrote me! Young girls. Women from seventeen to thirty. Letters of a horrible hun-

ger. *Asking me if I cared only for maidens' blood.* Asking me if I had done the play because I was in reality that sort of Thing. And through these letters, couched in terms of shuddering, transparent fear, there ran the hideous note of—*hope.*

"They hoped that I was **Dracula**. They hoped that my love was the love of **Dracula**. They gloated over the Thing

(Continued on page 86)

Freulich

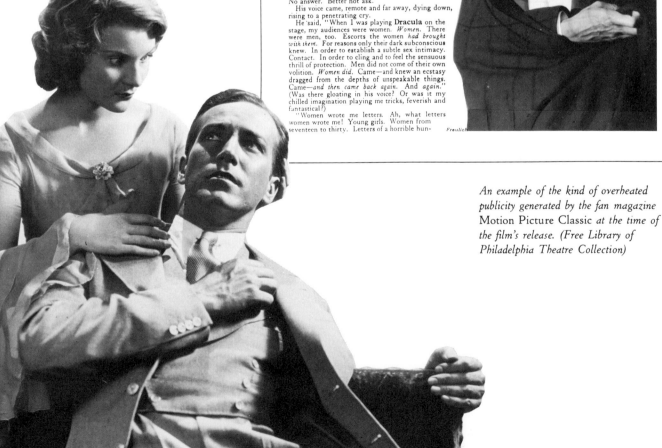

Helen Chandler and David Manners managed to generate more passion for the publicity photographer than they did for director Tod Browning. (Photofest)

An example of the kind of overheated publicity generated by the fan magazine Motion Picture Classic at the time of the film's release. (Free Library of Philadelphia Theatre Collection)

February 12, 1931: Dracula *enjoys its long-awaited premiere at New York's Roxy Theatre. (Free Library of Philadelphia Theatre Collection)*

problems would continue to dog Universal throughout the 1930s, it is generally acknowledged that the bright year of 1931 prevented the studio from folding, and that *Dracula* had much to do with stabilizing Universal's fortunes.

As should be abundantly clear, *Dracula* was a far from satisfactory film from an artistic standpoint. Almost everything about its production and direction had been seriously compromised or undermined. And no doubt, there were those who wished it could have all been done over again in a way that did justice to the possibilities of the material.

It was, therefore, in the best tradition of Hollywood wish fulfillment that that is exactly what happened.

Chapter Six

THE SPANISH DRACULA

*In which we discover Hollywood, in transtition and translation, where
a bright young man sleeps by day and works by night,
uses cobwebs to catch a wife, and does better by the Count than
the others, in a tongue he does not naturally speak.*

LUPITA TOVAR WAS VERY FRIGHTENED.

It would prove to be good practice.

The seventeen-year-old aspiring actress from Mexico clutched a letter in English, which she could not read, a letter of introduction to Universal Pictures from Fox Films, where she had done some bit parts in silent pictures. Tovar had won a talent competition as a schoolgirl in Mexico and had come to Hollywood with her grandmother the previous year, but now the spectre of talking pictures was threatening to dash her hopes. In the silent days, film had been a truly international medium. Now, Fox was bringing English-speaking actors from New York, and her contract was not to be renewed.

The ingenue waited nervously. The producer Tovar was scheduled to see had not arrived—she was told he was in a meeting. But as she sat in the bungalow-style office on the Universal lot, a tall man with a penetrating gaze passed through the room again and again. Watching. Looking.

Unnerved by the silent, menacing attention, Tovar left her letter of introduction and went home.

A message was waiting for her when she arrived. It was the producer. He was sorry his meeting had gone on so long, but would she mind coming back? The letter from Fox had been extremely complimentary, it seemed.

Tovar hesitated. She didn't want to subject herself to any more ocular advances from that strange man. "I went to my dancing teacher, Eduardo Cansino, the father of Rita Hayworth. Rita was a little girl then, and Cansino and his wife were terribly nice to me. I told them what had happened at Universal and that I was afraid to go back alone. All right, they said, we'll take

Lupita Tovar resists the un-dead advances of Carlos Villarias in the Spanish-language version of Dracula. Offscreen, the film's producer would pursue her with a similar, hot-blooded zeal. (The Paul Kohner collection, courtesy of Lupita Tovar)

you. But when we finally got to meet the producer, Paul Kohner — it was the man who had been staring at me!"[1]

At the age of twenty-seven, Paul Kohner was an ambitious young presence at Universal. Born in Czechoslovakia and educated in Vienna, Kohner had risen through the Universal ranks as office boy, publicist, and personal assistant to Carl Laemmle, Sr. As a production supervisor, he had been responsible for Paul Leni's lush costume spectacle *The Man Who Laughs*, with Conrad Veidt. In many ways, Laemmle treated Kohner like a son . . . with all the complexities and ambivalences built into a family relationship. In reality, Kohner felt himself to be the low man on the Universal totem pole. Though he had worked for Laemmle for years, he had no formal contract — and had never asked for one. "My salary is puny compared to those in other studios. But I cannot demand more money, nor do I dare to quit," he confided to his brother and biographer, Frederick Kohner. "I probably couldn't get a job anywhere else because everyone around Hollywood believes that I'm a nephew of the Old Man."[2] Kohner wasn't, but nepotism at Universal was a standing joke in the industry and beyond (Ogden Nash was inspired, memorably, to comment on the situation in verse, rhyming "Laemmle" with "faemmle"). Not only did the payroll swell with Laemmles, but the studio went so far as to house selected relatives in bungalows on the lot.

Kohner had achieved his position through hard work. However, with the rise of Junior Laemmle to head of production in 1928, Kohner's niche became less secure. Junior was distinctly less interested in European properties, talent, and directors, which were Kohner's strong suit, if not his passion. "Junior's running this joint now," said one director, "and if there's one thing the kid can't stand, it's 'great' European producers and directors."[3]

One German director Universal had imported was Paul Leni, whose work in Europe had included the expressionist classic *Waxworks*. For Universal he directed the highly stylized and atmospheric old-house chiller *The Cat and the Canary*, adapted from the long-running mystery play about an eccentric who makes his heirs wait twenty years for the reading of his will, with tensions escalating commensurately. *Cat* was followed by *The Man Who Laughs* starring Conrad Veidt as Victor Hugo's tragic grotesque Gwyneplaine, whose face was carved into a permanent grin in childhood. The film had probably been planned for Lon Chaney before his decision to return to Metro after *The Phantom of the Opera*. Kohner had been the production supervisor for *The Man Who Laughs* and was responsible in no small part for the film's sumptuous look and meticulous execution. Leni was single-handedly creating a new style, moody and macabre, and was Universal's resident horror specialist at the time the studio leaked its bogus story about acquiring the rights to *Dracula*, with Veidt as the film's probable star. If Veidt and Leni were involved in *Dracula*, it

Paul Kohner as a confident mogul-apparent. (The Paul Kohner collection, courtesy of Lupita Tovar)

Lupita Tovar in the Spanish version of The Cat Creeps. Kohner's foreign-language adaptation was so atmospherically lit that Carl Laemmle, Sr., ordered the American film to be reshot in the same manner. (The Paul Kohner collection, courtesy of Lupita Tovar)

Actor Conrad Veidt, left, and director Paul Leni would likely have made Dracula on a grand scale under Paul Kohner's supervision had Leni not unexpectedly died. (Photofest)

is inconceivable that Paul Kohner was not also involved, perhaps leaking the trade paper story himself in an attempt to get *Dracula* on the Big U's front burner.

The project came to nothing, however, with the untimely death of Paul Leni by blood poisoning in 1929.

Following Leni's death, Kohner's recommendations to Junior for projects went unanswered.[4] Finally, in frustration, Kohner went directly to his "Uncle Carl" with a proposition.

During the silent era, Universal had made half its revenues from foreign countries. Talking pictures posed a severe threat to this market. Dubbing was not yet practical—ordinary sound recording and synchronization presented problems enough. Moreover, much of the attraction and novelty of talking pictures derived from hearing actors speak in their natural voices. The international film markets were in chaos over talkies. Some countries were

The Spanish Dracula's *supervising producer Paul Kohner with his mentor, Carl Laemmle, Sr. (The Paul Kohner collection, courtesy of Lupita Tovar)*

"Yo no bebo . . . vino." El Conde Dracula (Carlos Villarias) serves Renfield (Pablo Alvarez Rubio) some Spanish wine of unexpected potency.

proposing embargos and punitive tariffs if quotas of films in their own languages were not met. Some commentators even lobbied in print for Esperanto as "the new universal language of film."

Kohner suggested, more realistically, that Universal follow the lead of other studios, and begin producing simultaneous foreign-language versions of its domestic talkies. These versions could be produced at a small fraction of the original costs—from $40,000 to $70,000[5]—owing largely to the costs saved on new sets and cheaper foreign talent.

Uncle Carl was impressed, and immediately named Kohner head of foreign production, at a salary raise of $25 a week. Laemmle was puzzled, though, at how Kohner planned to handle his daytime duties and supervise the foreign-language films, which he intended to shoot at night, after the American units had left for the day. "You have to sleep, Kohner—how can you do it?" asked Uncle Carl. "Oh, I know how to do it," the ambitious young man replied. "I can sleep between shifts on a couch in my office."[6]

The first project was to be a Spanish-language adaptation of Rupert Julian's *The Cat Creeps,* a sound remake of Leni's mystery melodrama *The Cat and the Canary,* made by Universal in 1927. Kohner was confident of his logistics. What he needed now was a Spanish-speaking star.

Lupita Tovar struck him immediately as a personality of extraordinary possibilities. She was astonishingly photogenic, and totally unaffected—a truly ingenuous ingenue. But even with Eduardo and Volga Cansino standing by as bodyguards, Tovar mistrusted the producer. She held tight to her resumé photos. Kohner asked if he might keep one. "They're for business!" Tovar snapped. "I mean for business," replied Kohner. "And I'd like your telephone number, too." He offered to take them to dinner, but to Tovar's relief, the Cansinos demurred.

The next day they returned to view some of her work from Fox. "You could tell he was looking at me and not the screen," Tovar recalled. "Well," said Kohner. "You photograph well. Now how about dinner?" They refused again, invoking Tovar's grandmother. They would need permission. Kohner called the grandmother. "Hello, Mrs. Sullivan? This is Paul Kohner at Universal Pictures. With your permission, I'd like to take your granddaughter to dinner." Mrs. Sullivan's only objection was that Tovar had not taken a coat. Kohner promised she would not get cold.

Tovar was terrified. She took the phone and talked to her grandmother in Spanish. "Grandma! What have you done?"

"Oh, he sounds like a very nice person. It's all right."

Kohner took her to dinner at the Universal commissary.

"There was a whole bunch grouped there, these young directors— William Wyler, Ernst Laemmle, Kurt Neumann—and I was the only girl.

Advertisement for the Spanish Dracula *during its Mexico City engagement.*

And they were all talking in German among themselves—about me! Apparently they hadn't approved of his previous girlfriend, but they did approve of me." Kohner had earlier broken an engagement to Mary Philbin, the ingenue who tore the mask from Lon Chaney's face in *The Phantom of the Opera*.

Kohner paid Tovar $25 a night to film Spanish introductory sequences for Universal's musical variety extravaganza *The King of Jazz*. Tovar decided there was no money in films and prepared to return to Mexico. Kohner convinced Laemmle to give her a contract. On the basis of Kohner's enthusiasm, she was cast as the female lead in *The Cat Creeps* without a screen test.

The Cat Creeps—to be known as *La Voluntad del Muerto* in Spanish—gave Paul Kohner the heady opportunity to second-guess artistic decisions of the English-language unit, which he did with great gusto. Finding Rupert Julian's daily rushes to be lacking in atmosphere, he completely re-dressed and relit the sets *à la* Leni, making extensive use of candles, cobwebs, and shadows. "The result was very eerie," recalled Tovar. Laemmle was so impressed with the foreign version that he ordered the English material to be reshot, with Kohner acting as artistic advisor. Unfortunately, neither version of the film has survived, though scene stills give some indication of the drama and chiaroscuro of Kohner's mise-en-scène.

Tovar, whose English was nearly nonexistent at the time, was fairly well-shielded from the obvious political nuances of the situation. "All I knew in English was how to say 'No,'" Tovar recalled. "The first night on the set, everyone went to dinner, but I didn't know that, and just sat waiting for them to come back. Paul came over to me. 'Aren't you hungry?' he asked. 'No—thank you.' 'Well, come on anyway,' he said. He tried to get me to order something but I was embarrassed. I just had coffee. I didn't know the tickets we had been given were for free meals, and I didn't have the money to pay."

Tovar soon got used to the regular free meals, but the public attention that came with the job remained unsettling. She still thought of herself as a schoolgirl, not a movie star. *The Cat Creeps* was a sensation in Mexico, and one of Tovar's public appearances there nearly created a riot. She had to be lifted out of the mob atop a police car.

Throughout the film's production and promotion, Kohner had bombarded her almost daily with flowers and candies. At the Mexico City premiere, telephonic speakers were set up in the theatre, to convey live congratulations from Carl Laemmle, Sr., and stars like Ramon Novarro. Kohner couldn't help but dominate much of the long-distance chatter himself. Laemmle kidded him about it "on air." What *was* his interest in this starlet, anyway? "I just want to encourage her," Kohner replied.

Following *The Cat Creeps,* Tovar's family gave her an ultimatum. "My father said, All right, you have proven you can do something—now come

back to the family and back to school." Kohner was not about to lose her so easily. Universal's legal department informed Tovar's father that they were invoking their contract option on his daughter. Her next picture would be a Spanish-language version of *Dracula*.

Kohner's treatment of *Dracula* was nothing if not ambitious, and today can be read as an almost shot-by-shot scathing critique of the Browning version. And whatever else it is, the Spanish *Dracula* remains one of the few examples in world cinema of a simultaneous, alternate rendition of a familiar classic, richly illustrating the interpretive possibilities of a single script.

Kohner's director for *Dracula* was George Melford, well-known for his work on Westerns and perhaps best remembered as the director of Rudolph Valentino in *The Sheik*. Melford did not speak Spanish, but gave instructions through an on-set interpreter, or "dialogue director" named E. Tovar Avalos. Cinematographer George Robinson brought a highly developed visual sensibility to the assignment, employing a highly mobile camera, complex compositions, and deep shadows. He would later shoot many of Universal's most memorable horror classics, including all the Dracula follow-ups, from *Dracula's Daughter* through *Abbott and Costello Meet Frankenstein*.

Kohner, Melford, and Robinson worked as a closely knit team, Tovar recalled, each taking turns peering through the viewfinder. She remembered Kohner as a meticulous perfectionist during *Dracula*, "determined to improve everything." Indeed, the degree to which the team felt it necessary to rework the American film bordered on the obsessive. If Browning and Freund composed a shot from right to left, the Spanish film would reverse it, as if by reflex. The American compositions are remarkably flat, like a play performed on a narrow stage apron. Robinson's camera work is distinguished by its use of multiple planes of focus and action. Foreground objects create tension and depth, while middle-ground devices (cobwebs, windows, branches, bars, etc.) further split and define the visual field. His work is especially flattering to Charles D. Hall's sets; the angles use the decor for inspiration rather than cropping it arbitrarily. Much of the traditional criticism of *Dracula* has blamed the American film's deficiencies on the presumed technical limitations imposed by the early talkies. But even a cursory viewing of the Spanish film (a stunning, though incomplete archival print at the Library of Congress was struck from the original nitrate negative in 1977) demonstrates without question that there was no dearth of capabilities on the Universal lot, only a misuse of them.

For the title role, Kohner and Melford selected a thirty-eight-year-old stage actor from Cordoba, Carlos Villarias Llano, who worked under the name Carlos Villarias (for some inexplicable reason, probably a mistake, his name on the opening credits of the film itself would be further shortened, to "Carlos Villar"). Villarias would later be seen occasionally in English-

The opening credits of the Spanish film were superimposed over the live image of a guttering candle. (Courtesy the Cinemateca de Cuba)

Carlos Villarías recreates Bela Lugosi's classic pose on the castle staircase.

language roles during the thirties and early forties, including the part of the headwaiter in *Bordertown* with Paul Muni and Bette Davis in 1935.

For "Juan Harker" the choice was Barry Norton, a multilingual juvenile whose publicity painted him as the truant son of a wealthy Argentine family. Norton, the former Alfredo Biraben, had been directed by F. W. Murnau in the circus drama *Four Devils* for Fox and was also seen in *What Price Glory*. Dr. Van Helsing was played by Eduardo Arozamena, a popular Mexican character actor whose career would last until the early 1950s. The role of Renfield went to Pablo Alvarez Rubio, a prizewinning actor, journalist, and orator from Spain who began his work in films in 1927. As the raven-haired Lucia, Carmen Guerrero was beginning a film career that would bring her a popularity among Spanish-speaking audiences rivaling Lupita Tovar's.

The Spanish version of *Dracula* follows the original shooting script far more carefully than the American film, enhancing its visual suggestions rather than undermining them. The independent mood of the two films is established with the main titles. Instead of the static art deco bat of the Browning version, the Spanish film superimposes its credits over a guttering candle that is quickly extinguished, transporting us from the illuminated world into a realm of darkness.

The film opens with outtake footage of the same glass shot that opens the American film, with a coach rumbling up a desolate mountain pass. (Contrary to some accounts, the two versions of the film actually have no footage in common, though the Spanish film does employ unused negative from the Browning film.) The scenes with the Transylvanian peasants are rather flatly played, but by the time Renfield (for some reason the name is spelled in publicity materials and pronounced in the film as "Rendfield") is on his way to Castle Dracula, the film comes into its own. We are shown the King Vampire rising from his earth-box in a glowing cloud of mist — a flawlessly executed double exposure, and a grand effect. (Instead of dealing with such technical

Having risen from his earth-box in a cloud of mist, Carlos Villarias prepares to terrorize the Transylvanian countryside.

challenges, Browning and Freund simply averted their camera's gaze at the first hint of a trembling coffin lid.)

The mysterious driver who meets the traveler at the Borgo Pass is muffled with a black scarf (unlike the American film, in which Lugosi's face is inexplicably uncovered and completely recognizable as Dracula). The ride to the castle is longer and bumpier than in the American film, and Pablo Alvarez Rubio as Renfield is considerably more frightened than his American counterpart, Dwight Frye. All doors, even coach doors, creak as though they weigh a ton. Renfield finds the great hall of the castle empty—and devoid of armadillos. As he approaches the base of the huge staircase, a bat swoops down at him again and again. He waves it off with his cane, turns—and then, in one of the film's supreme visual moments, the camera pulls back to reveal Dracula, who has appeared out of nowhere, holding a candle at the top of the stairs and framed by the giant, backlit spiderweb. Without a cut (the camera was mounted on a moving crane*) our field of vision rushes forward up the steps, until the full-length figure of the vampire fills the screen. A familiar exchange of dialogue ensues (adapted in Spanish by B. Fernandez Cue), including the reminder that "*sangre es la vida*" and praise for the night-music of "*los hijos de la noche.*" The scene in Dracula's chambers is marked by more fluid camera work and enhanced lighting. Robinson's camera pulls back into an arched alcove for a *Nosferatu*-like composition. A tall, ornate chair that was featured in both *The Cat and the Canary* and *The Cat Creeps* is placed centrally in the room, and the dead branches outside the looming windows are lit in ghostly relief. Robinson also makes dramatic use of firelight and candles as Dracula and Renfield discuss the terms of the Carfax Abbey lease. Instead of a paper clip, Renfield cuts his hand on a knife he is using to demolish a roast chicken. As he does so, Dracula's eyes fill the screen in an intense, quivering closeup.

The third reel of the Spanish *Dracula* has been a matter of some speculation in American film circles for a number of years. The negative had fallen prey to nitrate decomposition by the time the American Film Institute made an archival print for the Universal retrospective at the Museum of Modern Art in 1977. Sadly, this reel contained some of the most interesting material, including Dracula's vampire wives, the scene aboard the doomed ship, and the scene at the London concert hall where Dracula first encounters the main characters.

A complete print, however, had been long rumored to be in the possession of the Cuban Film Archives in Havana. With the generous cooperation of the

The mysterious coach driver, as seen in the Spanish film as well as in Nosferatu.

*This remarkable piece of equipment was specially built for *Broadway* in 1929 by its director Paul Fejos and cameraman Hal Mohr. It became a venerated fixture on the Universal backlot and was often put to effective use, notably for the opening shot of Orson Welles' *A Touch of Evil.*

Frame enlargements from the Spanish film demonstrate the degree to which Kohner, Melford, and Robinson reworked the compositions of the American film, employing a highly mobile camera, extreme closeups, and deep chiaroscuro. (Courtesy of the Cinemateca de Cuba)

Charles D. Hall's impressive Castle Dracula set was re-dressed and relit for the Spanish production. The towering chair upstage center appeared in Paul Leni's silent classic The Cat and the Canary *as well as in its talking remake,* The Cat Creeps. *(Courtesy of Ronald V. Borst/Hollywood Movie Posters)*

Cinemateca de Cuba and the permission of the U.S. Treasury Department (whose regulations restrict the travel of United States citizens to Cuba) this author was able to visit Havana in June 1989 to study in detail the only complete print of the Spanish *Dracula* in existence. It had, coincidentally, just enjoyed a brief public revival at the Cinemateca's theatre, the Rampas, in downtown Havana. And it was no disappointment.

Following Dracula's exit (dramatically framed in an arched door—a distinct homage to *Nosferatu*), Renfield begins to feel the effects of the drugged wine. He pulls at his collar, and the crucifix falls away from his neck (Browning never explained how Dracula was able to attack Renfield when the cross that had just repelled him was still so snugly in place). Renfield staggers toward the window. Robinson then sets his camera outside the window, shooting in as Renfield struggles with the latch. He doesn't see the three vampire women who have suddenly materialized, approaching him from be-

Seen here for the first time in almost sixty years, the three vampire sisters from the "lost" reel of the Spanish Dracula. (Courtesy of the Cinemateca de Cuba)

hind. He opens the window, only to encounter a flapping bat in the foreground. (This shot is one of the best, and most nightmarish, uses of Robinson's three-field technique, involving the viewer in a complicated, participatory conspiracy. The audience can see what the focal character cannot, its attention being pulled in three directions simultaneously.)

Unlike the actresses in the American film (zombie schoolmarms with tight braids and robotic demeanor) the Spanish *vampiras* are wild, exotic creatures with flowing hair and low-cut gowns. As they slither forth, there is one dramatic closeup of their faces—one with teeth bared, and another—the center of the image—backlit in such a way that her nimbus of blonde hair frames not a face but a shadow. It is, without question, one of the great, if hitherto unheralded, images from the horror films of the 1930s, and a marvelous evocation of Stoker's original vision: "Two were dark, and had high aquiline noses, like the Count's, and great dark, piercing eyes. . . . The other was fair, as fair as can be, with great wavy masses of hair and eyes like pale sapphires. I seemed to know her face, and to know it in connection with some dreamy fear, but I could not recollect at the moment how or where. All three had brilliant white teeth, that shone like pearls against the ruby of their voluptuous lips."[7]

Renfield looks into the courtyard and sees the Count watching an earth-box as it is lowered onto a wagon. The scene is shot from a low angle, through a stylized clutch of dead branches echoing the art direction of *The Cabinet of Dr. Caligari*. Renfield falls in a faint and the vampire women swirl around him, swooping for his throat as the scene fades out.

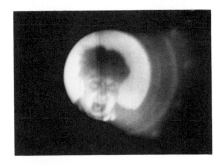

In contrast to the American film, the Spanish *Dracula* establishes the ship scene en route to England without the formality of a title card, and without dialogue. Both films intercut separate storm-at-sea clips from the same silent maritime drama. Although this sequence is composed of almost the identical number of shots in both versions, the Spanish is by far the more chilling and evocative, and is quite obviously influenced by the analogous scene in *Nosferatu*. Neither version achieves quite the effect of the screenplay's am-

bitious concept (sailors being stalked, one by one, and leaping into the sea; a triumphant Dracula on the bow of the ship, his cape open to the storm like a billowing black sail) but the Spanish film provides the superior treatment. While we don't see the sailors' watery death-leaps, we do see their terrified faces in closeup. A snarling Dracula emerges from the ship's hold in another *Nosferatu*-inspired image, while Renfield's face is glimpsed in a porthole, laughing maniacally. Real rats add to the occasion, crawling on Dracula's coffin lid and swarming around Renfield when he is discovered in the ship's hold.

The sequence aboard the doomed ship was greatly influenced by the analagous scene in Nosferatu. (Courtesy of the Cinemateca de Cuba)

Left to right: director George Melford and cinematographer George Robinson prepare to shoot a scene with performers Barry Norton and Lupita Tovar. (The Paul Kohner collection, courtesy of Lupita Tovar)

Carlos Villarias

When the hatch is opened, he screams as if scalded by the sunlight.

Ensconced at Carfax Abbey, Dracula once more emerges from his earth-box in a halo of glowing mist. A brief outtake of Bela Lugosi in the American film is intercut, showing Dracula's arrival at the London concert hall. Robinson makes a striking triangular composition of actors, curtains, and an overhead light fixture as the vampire peers into the box where the principal characters are seated. His fateful lines to Lucy (Lucia here)—"There are far . . . worse things . . . awaiting man . . . than . . . death"—are delivered as the houselights dim, leaving Dracula almost completely in shadow and Lucia's face isolated in darkness by a tight oval spot. The third reel ends with an outtake from the 1925 *The Phantom of the Opera,* showing the curtain rising on a corps de ballet.

The film does suffer from the same stage-bound sluggishness as the American film, but Melford, Robinson, and Kohner are consistently resourceful in enhancing the mood and action. The women's costumes are startlingly sheer and revealing for a film of the period (Tovar recalled, "My negligee was very low-cut. When my grandson saw the film, he said, '*Now* I know why Grandpapa married you!'"). The sexual aspects of the story are accentuated rather than minimized: when Dracula attacks Lucy in her bedroom, he covers her with his cape like a huge crawling bat, an image both ugly and erotic. The American film settles for a discreet fadeout. Tovar's Eva—once more, the heroine has undergone a change of name—becomes sexually animated as the vampire's spell overtakes her. Helen Chandler, by contrast, seems merely dazed. There is a rather more generous use of fog and mist, and shots are framed to take full advantage of the high, detailed interiors. Issues left dangling in the American film are resolved: Renfield's attack on the fainting maid is merely a bit of comic relief (he's only after a fly that has alighted on her), and the vampire Lucy is tracked to her crypt and properly dispatched (Browning leaves her wandering in the night, as if looking for a sequel). A glass shot of Carfax by the rolling sea is seen twice in the film; the huge upstairs staircase that Browning wasted is used, though briefly.

The death of Renfield is handled particularly well. Browning stages a rather inept stunt with Renfield's body flopping down a flight of stone steps, the "stone" thumping hollowly as he does; in the Spanish film, Dracula hurls his unfortunate slave over the side of the steps in a completely unexpected and violent *coup de théâtre.*

The Spanish *Dracula* began shooting the night of October 10, 1930. "The American crew left at six and we were ready," Tovar recollected. "We started shooting at eight. At midnight, they would call for dinner." Kohner had wisely seen that he could save a great deal of time by shooting out of sequence, and scheduled scenes and sets accordingly. Tovar recalled that a moviola was kept on the set, on which footage shot for the American film could be viewed by the

"There are . . . far . . . worse things . . . awaiting man . . . than . . . death." Carmen Guerrero and Carlos Villarias take a slow dive into darkness. (Courtesy of the Cinemateca de Cuba)

Unaware that Dracula stands below her bedroom window, Lucia (Carmen Guerrero) prepares for her final sleep. The composition of the shot is typical of cameraman George Robinson's use of foreground elements to convey depth and visual tension. The lamp, incidentally, appears next to the heroine's bed in Karl Freund's The Mummy—*one of several set pieces borrowed from* Dracula *(along with the title music and most of the plot).*

Unlike the same scene in the American version, which ends in a discreet fadeout, the Spanish vampire spreads his cape across the bed of his prey like a huge crawling bat—an image both ugly and erotic. (Courtesy of the Cinemateca de Cuba)

The drawing room sets were re-dressed and more flatteringly photographed in the Spanish film. Left to right: Jose Soriano Viosca as Dr. Seward, Carlos Villarias, Lupita Tovar, Barry Norton and Eduardo Arozamena. (Photofest)

A still from the Spanish film and a frame enlargement from Nosferatu, *showing a striking similarity of set designs.* Nosferatu *was studied carefully by Universal's artistic and technical crew.*

Publicity portrait of Carlos Villarias as the hot-blooded Count. (Courtesy of Ronald V. Borst/Hollywood Movie Posters)

The dramatic possibilities of torchlight greatly enhanced the Spanish film's final sequences. The American version settled for lanterns.

Pablo Alvarez Rubio

creative team. The actors, with the single exception of Carlos Villarias, were not permitted to view the English-language dailies. Villarias was encouraged to be as Lugosi-like as possible. The actor even wore Lugosi's hairpiece, and in several scenes the resemblance is uncanny. There were differences, however. Villarias was notably lacking one of Lugosi's most distinctive physical characteristics: the long, expressive Henry Irving–like hands. Villarias had small hands and short fingers, more like paws than talons.

The casts of both films were introduced. The Americans, Tovar remembered, "were very nice, but condescending. We were the children and they were the grown-ups, you see." And unlike *The Cat Creeps,* Kohner was not welcome as an artistic consultant to Browning. The obvious joint photo opportunities apparently never happened, and the productions proceeded on their separate tracks and levels. The Spanish film was moving so quickly that many of the sets were not completely finished when Kohner was ready for them—Carfax Abbey, for instance, was completely devoid of cobwebs and dust. Nonetheless, Kohner's crew barreled ahead, and compensated with atmospheric lighting. The cast and crew were remarkably free of temperament. "They didn't pay us much, but we didn't complain," said Tovar. "We were happy to have some money—most actors were starving. So it was manna from heaven. We had tremendous respect for George Melford—the director of Valentino was, to us, like a god. We did everything that was required of us, worked twenty-four hours a day, did publicity. We were the most obedient crew. And there was no union then."

Kohner's courtly attentions continued through the production, prompting Tovar's costar Barry Norton to kid her about her weight. "If you keep eating Paul Kohner's candies, Dracula won't be able to carry you up those stairs," he told her. "The head electrician was a Mexican named Tommy Valdez," Tovar remembered. "He used to watch me from the catwalks. Every once in a while when I was sitting between takes, a Hershey bar would drop down." The crew took to signaling Tovar from above when there was something in her performance they liked.

The Spanish *Dracula* finally wrapped on November 8, after only twenty-two nights of shooting (compared to seven weeks for the American version) at a final cost of $66,069.35, almost $2,700 under budget.

Kohner scheduled a preview on the Universal lot for the first week in January 1931, more than a month ahead of the American *Dracula*'s release. Retakes were still being shot by Browning as late as January. The January 10 issue of *Hollywood Filmograph* opined that "If the English version of *Dracula,* directed by Tod Browning, is as good as the Spanish version, why the Big U haven't a thing in the world to worry about." (It did, of course, eventually worry about the *Filmograph*'s less-than-warmhearted review of Browning's effort.)

"The other evening before a capacity theatre on the lot there was a screened preview of the Spanish version which was witnessed by Bela Lugosi ... and to use his own words the Spanish picture was 'beautiful, great, splendid.'" The *Filmograph* complimented all concerned, but saved its best praise for Paul Kohner. The Spanish *Dracula* was "far above anything he has yet turned out on the lot. Kohner knows the foreign picture desires perfectly."

Dracula opened to good business in Mexico City on April 4, where it played throughout the month of April. In contrast to the American pattern of release, it opened first at the Cine Mundial, a *cine de barrio* or neighborhood theatre, building word of mouth for a four-theatre engagement in the *primero circuito* of the Monumental, Teresa, Odeon, and Granat cinemas. The Mexican papers were full of praise for Tovar ("*La Novia de Mexico*") and Villarias. A headline in the Mexico City daily *El Universal* promised that "Dracula Will Amaze Mexico," with the article declaring the film to be a "positive triumph."[8] Another evaluation found *Dracula* to be "disturbing," but admitted it was "unlike anything we've seen before on the screen."[9]

The film migrated north to Los Angeles, and opened with some fanfare in the Spanish press (considerably more than had greeted the American film) on May 8 at the California Theatre. Bela Lugosi made a guest appearance on stage with Tovar and Villarias as part of the festivities. For one week, it was possible to see both the English and Spanish versions of *Dracula* at theatres only a few blocks apart—the Spanish version at the California and the American at the Fox Palace. The Spanish *Dracula* was also well-received in its New York City engagements at Manhattan's San Jose Teatro Hispano and Brooklyn's Teatro Gil for several weeks in April and May.

Lupita Tovar remained in Hollywood, and became Mrs. Paul Kohner a few years later. The couple was married in Berlin, where Paul was trying to handle Universal's affairs just as Hitler's shadow had begun to ominously lengthen. "Hitler will be over in three months," Kohner told her. "Good," Lupita replied, "we'll come back in three months."

Lupita Tovar

Renfield (Pablo Alvarez Rubio) is restrained by the asylum attendant (Manuel Arbo). Rubio has much more screen time than his American counterpart, Dwight Frye, and gives an independent performance. Of the cast, only Carlos Villarias as Dracula was permitted to watch the daily rushes and study the classic Lugosi performance. (Photofest)

Who's scaring whom? Bela Lugosi's hairpiece stands on end as Carlos Villarias makes his move on the luscious Lupita Tovar.

Renfield's death is a more gruesome affair in the Spanish version—not only is he strangled, but afterward is hurled over the side of a 125-step staircase. Filming progressed so quickly on the Spanish film that cobwebbing had not been completed on the Carfax set by the time this scene was shot.

Back in the States, Kohner found himself without a job when Carl Laemmle, Sr., sold the studio in 1935; he had worked for Universal without a formal contract. Unable to secure a steady post at another studio, he turned to free-lance agenting, and eventually established himself as one of the most respected international talent agents in the business. (His fifty-year friendship with the late John Huston would also become the longest client-agent relationship in Hollywood history.) Paul Kohner never retired, and, ironically, just before his death in 1988, he agreed to give an interview to *American Cinematographer* magazine on the making of the Spanish *Dracula*. It was just another of the countless fascinating tales that could be told only by a cultured and gregarious man whose professional life had virtually encompassed the history of motion pictures.

Sadly, the interview never took place. Paul Kohner died March 16, 1988. No doubt he had many other stories to tell besides the one reconstructed here without his recollections, but simply not the time to tell them.

The Spanish *Dracula* would be one of the last foreign-language films produced in Hollywood. The Depression had taken firm hold, and most of the large studios were hemorrhaging money and cutting back even on their domestic productions. Talking pictures were beginning to be produced at home by the countries that had previously looked to Hollywood for entertainment. The age of doppelgänger cinema was at a close. The Spanish *Dracula* was shown theatrically in Spanish-speaking countries until the 1950s (the complete version in Havana is a 1950s show print). For obscure reasons, Universal never registered the copyright on the film, nor did it make preservation prints on safety stock. With the demise of foreign-language talkies, the film was evidently considered to have no commercial future and was simply forgotten. The incomplete negative was rediscovered in a New Jersey warehouse in the late 70s, and archival copies were struck as a preservation project of the Library of Congress. A fascinating artifact that has had only two public screenings since its partial restoration, the film is now deposited with the Motion Picture Division of the Library of Congress, and is available only for study by film scholars on editing equipment. Its full restoration is not beyond the realm of possibility if the necessary agencies and institutions will only exert the needed imagination and energy. Viewed together, the two versions of *Dracula* make a unique and powerful case for the rewards of historic film preservation. The Spanish *Dracula* may be filled with cobwebs, but it shouldn't have to collect them.

In addition to producing the Spanish Dracula, *Paul Kohner dubbed the American version into French and German, and oversaw worldwide promotional efforts. Above, the poster for the French release in 1932.*

Chapter Seven

HOLLYWOOD GOTHIC

———————————◆———————————

*In which fortunes rise and fall, and in which the
picture people will not leave an actor to his grave, and
battle for the possession of an immortal soul.*

——————————— ———————————

IN THE END, FLORENCE STOKER MAY NOT HAVE BEEN A HAPPY
woman, but she had triumphed in one regard. She had wrestled with Count
Dracula, the dark ambiguous spectre of her husband's problematic unconscious, trained him, domesticated him, sent him out into the world to make
money, and she succeeded. The monster was her main asset, and she protected it furiously. And in the end the demon became her own protective
familiar, her guardian angel and salvation. "She was very hard up," confirmed
Stoker biographer Daniel Farson. "The Universal film saved her."[1] The
money from Universal enabled her to make renovations in her mews house in
Knightsbridge, amid the zigzagging alleys in the shadow of grander homes.

Vincent Price, before his career as an actor, was an art student at London's
Courtauld Institute, and one day in 1935 had the chance to meet the woman
who had known nearly all, and inspired several, of the major Victorian artistic
and theatrical personalities. "Mrs. Stoker invited me to tea in her small,
fabulous mews house," Price recalled. "Among her treasures were portraits by
Wilde, Burne-Jones and Rosetti. All her books were signed by the great
literati of her lifetime. She was very petite and almost blind, very dear and still
very beautiful. I felt I'd stepped into a most romantic past."[2]

In 1933 Florence Stoker had sold an option on the film rights to the short
story *Dracula's Guest* to David O. Selznick, who intended to produce from it a
film called *Dracula's Daughter.* Selznick hired John L. Balderston to write a
treatment, but the producer was unable to persuade MGM to produce it. The
studio was concerned about infringing on Universal's title to the original
novel, and regarded their deliberations as so sensitive that they adopted the
code name *Tarantula* for their discussions of the property by cable and letter.
Selznick finally resold the treatment to Universal, who would later produce a

*Near the end of his life, Bela
Lugosi still clutched at the role
which had both made and destroyed
his Hollywood career. (Courtesy
Ronald V. Borst/Hollywood Movie
Posters)*

completely different film called *Dracula's Daughter* (with a screenplay by Garrett Fort) without Florence Stoker's consent or participation.

Research had turned up an astonishing fact: due to a loophole in the copyright law, *Dracula* was—and always had been—in the public domain in the United States. Although Stoker had been issued a copyright certificate in 1897, and his widow a renewal certificate in the 1920s, Stoker had never complied with the requirement that two copies of the work be deposited with the American copyright office.[3]

All of the *Dracula* negotiations, then, the effort to suppress *Nosferatu,* even Horace Liveright's contract for the stage play, had been based on an extraordinary shared delusion. Within the borders of the United States, anyone had been entitled to produce whatever kind of adaptation of *Dracula* they chose, without considering Florence Stoker at all.

But she had won in spite of everything, transforming *Dracula* into a personal allegory of female transformation and empowerment.

The widow's health deteriorated. The end came in May 1937. Her will, published two months later, revealed that she had left £6,913, with net personalty valued at £5,921. She made three specific bequests. To the Victoria and Albert Museum, "All her Nailsea glass, including a window stop in the form of an animal and a blue Bristol glass roller, and also her Sheffield toast-rack in the form of a lyre." To the London Library was left her collection of Maria Edgeworth books, and to the London Museum a statuette of Henry Irving in aluminum and his hand in bronze, both by Onslow Ford, as well as a pastel portrait of Irving by Sir Bernard Partridge (which Bram Stoker had been forced to buy from the Irving estate, Stoker himself having been forgotten in Irving's will).[4]

F. W. Murnau, who had invented the vampire movie with *Nosferatu,* was working in Hollywood at the time *Dracula* was filmed, and gave numerous interviews on his many films, but never commented publicly on *Nosferatu* and its debacle. His opinion of the authorized *Dracula* would never be known; he was killed in an auto accident near Santa Barbara shortly before the film's west coast release.

Director Tod Browning returned to MGM after *Dracula,* but never recovered the standing he had achieved through his professional link to Lon Chaney. His most celebrated film, *Freaks,* proved an embarrassment to Metro, who withdrew the picture from circulation. An anomaly itself, *Freaks* was exhibited by independent exploitation outfits under such titles as *The Monster Show* and *Nature's Mistakes.* (In Great Britain, it was banned outright for thirty years.) It enjoyed a theatrical revival in the 60s and 70s, a cult following in France, and was shown on American television for the first time in 1990. Browning is said to have wanted to direct a film adaptation of Horace

F.W. Murnau in Hollywood. (Collection of the Cinémathèque Française)

McCoy's scathing Depression-era novel *They Shoot Horses, Don't They?* but, lacking political leverage, was unable to interest Metro. Browning made his last film in 1939, and retired comfortably on his real estate investments. Until his death in 1962, he is not known to have given a single substantive interview on his career. The inflated critical mystique surrounding Browning's work is probably fueled by the overwhelming sense of enigma surrounding the man and the private obsessions that drove him.

Karl Freund, the legendary cinematographer, similarly left no accounts of his work on *Dracula,* and in his later years contented himself with supervising photography for television's "I Love Lucy" and pursuing technical research. Freund died in Hollywood in 1969.

Horace Liveright, who understood the enormous money-making potential in both *Dracula* and *Frankenstein,* was cut out of the Hollywood largesse from both properties, the victim of his own demons. His stay in Hollywood had been an unhappy one. At Paramount Publix he had been unable to negotiate the film rights for even a single property, least of all *Dracula.* Returning to New York, with fruitless schemes for books and Broadway plays that would recapture his former celebrity, he found himself in much the same position as Florence Stoker after the passing of the Lyceum's golden age. Bennett Cerf, one of his few loyal former employees, wrote after his death, "A poseur to the last, he could be found tapping his long cigarette holder nervously at a table at the Algonquin, a mere shadow of his former jaunty self, announcing ambitious theatrical projects to all the critics . . . although everybody knew he was playing through a heartbreaking farce."[5] Penniless and alone, he died of pneumonia on September 24, 1933.

Dracula has attracted a number of self-destructive personalities in its career, and has had a destructive effect on the careers of others. Actress Helen Chandler is a case in point. Highly successful as a New York stage performer—from her extravagant press clippings, it would certainly be safe to call her a toast of Broadway in the late twenties—Chandler today is remembered for not much else than her appearance in Universal's *Dracula.* Like Liveright, her onetime employer, Chandler's personal vampire was alcohol, compounded by an affinity for sleeping pills. The shadow of chemical dependency was offset by her wistful, childlike manner; even as a young adult, she told interviewers she dreamed of producing and starring in a film version of *Alice in Wonderland.*[6] By the mid-1930s she was unemployable in films, and returned to the stage, where she often costarred with her second husband, Bramwell Fletcher, the actor who had gone so memorably mad in *The Mummy.* In 1940 she was committed to a sanitarium.[7] In 1950, she was severely burned on the face, arms, and upper body, the result of drinking and smoking in bed. Her third husband, a merchant seaman, had shipped out a few days earlier.

Nosferatu, relaxing at home.

Chandler's father gave the Associated Press a peculiar account of her years in obscurity: Chandler, he said, had been stricken years before by a mysterious fever malady, and had impoverished herself by traveling the world over in search of a cure.[8] She died in 1965, following surgery. Her paid death notice in the *Los Angeles Times*—there was no editorial obituary—listed only a brother as a survivor. Her ashes have never been claimed.

Like Chandler, Dwight Frye had been an enormously popular stage actor in New York before coming to Hollywood and making *Dracula*. Unlike Chandler, it would not be personal problems but his association with the role of Renfield that would cruelly limit his career. Once prized for his range and versatility, Frye was typecast as the prototypical monster's assistant. Wild-eyed, hunchbacked, or zoophagous, Dwight Frye became a subgenre unto himself. (He is the only other performer in the Universal film, besides Bela Lugosi, who would later repeat his role on stage—in Frye's case, a 1941 production in Los Angeles opposite actor Frederick Pymm.) During World War II, Frye supplemented his income by working as a machinist. His first chance at a major mainstream role was tragically cut short—on November 7, 1944, shortly after being cast as the Secretary of War in the biographical drama *Wilson*, Frye was stricken with a heart attack on a hot Los Angeles bus as he was returning from a movie matinee with his young son, Dwight, Jr. He died a few hours later. A devout Christian Scientist, Frye had concealed earlier mild coronaries from his family and had never sought medical treatment. The actor's death certificate, in a final irony, listed his occupation as "tool designer." Nearly sixty years after the release of *Dracula*, Frye's son reported that the name is still frequently recognized when he uses his credit cards, and that waiters and shop clerks can be quite willing to give him an impromptu impression of his father's famous, maniacal laugh from the Universal film.[9]

Among the writers, Garrett Fort's career took a turn into mysticism, depression, and suicide following his work on several Universal horror classics. His death by sleeping pills was reported in *Variety* on Halloween, 1945.

Other *Dracula* alumni fared much better. Actor David Manners appeared in a series of horror and mystery films including *The Mummy* (1932), the stylized deco-expressionist masterpiece *The Black Cat* (1934), and in the title role of *The Mystery of Edwin Drood* (1935). Manners turned his back on Hollywood in the late thirties, the better to maintain a private life away from studio and public scrutiny. He published two well-reviewed novels in the 1940s, ran a desert guest ranch for a time, and eventually dedicated his energies to esoteric philosophy and reflection. A still-vigorous nonagenarian living in coastal California, he occasionally publishes collections of his thoughts on life's deeper meanings and mysteries, the most recent being *Awakening from the Dream of Me* in 1987. He has granted interviews on his film

Helen Chandler: drink, drugs, and professional oblivion. (Free Library of Philadelphia Theatre Collection)

career only rarely in the past, and now turns down all requests, tired of answering questions about old horror movies that he disliked originally, and whose continuing obsessive appeal he finds totally incomprehensible.

John L. Balderston continued to supplement his journalistic and political activities with screenwriting. He collaborated with John Hurlbut on the script of Universal's most extravagant horror exercise, *Bride of Frankenstein,* in 1935. In the early 1950s, he sued Universal, claiming that the conception of Frankenstein's monster he had originated (based on the play by Peggy Webling produced in England by Hamilton Deane) had been unfairly exploited in subsequent Universal films. Balderston and Webling (who died in 1947) had sold *Frankenstein* to Universal in 1931 for $20,000 plus 1 percent of gross earnings. Their earnings were considerably compounded when the case was settled in May 1953; Universal reportedly paid Balderston and the Webling estate more than $100,000 in exchange for all rights to the character.[10] He maintained his good humor about *Dracula,* and in 1944 shared a brainstorm with his agent, Harold Freedman: "Sell *Dracula* as a musical! Get that DeMille girl to do a ballet of the vampires in the middle of the tombs and go to town on the things as the first 'horror musical.' It should of course be played and sung straight," Balderston wrote, adding that "the audience would howl and tear up the chairs and everybody concerned would make a great deal of money."[11] Freedman doesn't seemed to have taken him seriously at the time, but eventually the outlandish-sounding idea came to pass: *Dracula* has been reproduced more than once as both musical and ballet. Balderston, however, never saw them; he died in Beverly Hills in 1954.

Dwight Frye's identification with horror roles was a professional stranglehold he never escaped. The actor is seen here in a 1941 Los Angeles stage revival of Dracula *with Frederick Pymm in the title role. (Courtesy of Ronald V. Borst/Hollywood Movie Posters)*

Following the death of Florence Stoker, Hamilton Deane was finally able to enter into a standard and equitable stage contract with the widow's son, Noel, for the Balderston adaptation (which Stoker had never permitted Deane to play in England). In 1939, Deane finally essayed the title role himself in a London revival, directed by Bernard Jukes. Jukes (who was to Renfield what Yul Brynner was to the King of Siam, having played the role over 4,000 times) was killed later that year in an air raid. Deane continued to play Dracula in stock until 1941, before hanging up the cloak forever. He could never have imagined the degree to which *Dracula,* which had begun as just another play in his traveling repertory, would succeed in dominating his professional life. Hamilton Deane died in 1958.

Carl Laemmle, Jr., remained at Universal's helm over several financially rocky years until the sale of the studio in 1936. Though often criticized for his inexperience and impetuousness, Junior Laemmle managed to keep Universal's losses well below those of other major studios during the Depression.[12] In establishing the American horror film as a distinct genre, Laemmle almost single-handedly inspired one of the most consistently profitable categories in film history. His attempts to set himself up as an independent producer failed, and he withdrew from the Hollywood scene. A legendary hypochondriac who avoided physical contact and feared he might die if he slept in a bed other than his own,[13] Laemmle did, ironically, meet up with serious illness. Crippled by multiple sclerosis in the early 1960s, he lived in seclusion as a wealthy invalid until his death. In an eerie coincidence that underscored the lifelong influence of the father to whom he had relinquished his name, Carl Laemmle, Jr., died of a stroke on September 24, 1979 — precisely forty years to the day after the death of Carl Laemmle, Sr.

But the saddest, most dramatic casualty of all those who crossed the path of *Dracula* is without question Bela Lugosi, whose overwhelming identification with the role blurs meaningful distinctions between illusion and reality, vampire and victim, even between life and death. Lugosi's tragedy is second, perhaps, only to the that of Marilyn Monroe as a story of the complete entrapment of a performer by an archetypal screen persona. (Indeed, curators of research collections across the country reported to the author that Bela Lugosi memorabilia ran a close second only to Monroe's in its probability of being stolen. These twin icons of sex and death have the equal ability, it seems, to incite monomaniacal possessiveness and desire. In Dracula worship, there is death-in-sex; in postmortem Monroe worship there is sex-in-death. In Monroe's case, there is more than metaphor. Her crypt, in a memorial park coincidentally adjacent to the author's hotel in Westwood during a research trip for this book, was observed to be smeared with lipstick bearing the fresh imprint of a human mouth. The vault's marble slab had settled, or been forced, sufficiently to allow, if the visitor desired, the insertion of a finger into the cavity.)

Dracula marked both the beginning and the end of Lugosi's Hollywood career. Carl Laemmle, Jr., had wanted to groom him as "the new Lon Chaney," but his fortunes at Universal began to dwindle after he refused to play the monster in *Frankenstein* (test footage was shot on the *Dracula* set, with Lugosi unrecognizably padded and made-up. He objected to the makeup, and to dialogue which consisted of nothing but grunts). Boris Karloff, a relative unknown, shot to stardom with the role. He was a more versatile actor than Lugosi, who had stepped directly into the trap Conrad Veidt had fled Hollywood to escape. Karloff could affect a range of accents, for instance, while Lugosi had only one: the Dracula voice. Karloff sat still for heavy makeup. Lugosi didn't want his features hidden. And yet he fumed and raged at Karloff's ascending star (according to one account, in the middle of the night a few days before his death, Lugosi's wife would find him awake and confused, convinced that Boris Karloff was outside waiting for him[14]). With the *Dracula* contract, Lugosi had proved he could be had cheaply. One of his next films,

THE SCREEN'S MASTER OF HORROR
IN PERSON! ON THE STAGE

BELA "DRACULA" LUGOSI

in EDGAR ALLAN POE'S *Nightmare of Terror*
"THE TELL-TALE HEART"

*"Most electrifying performance I have ever witnessed
... my spine tingled!"* —WALTER WINCHELL

A DON MARLOWE PRODUCTION

Plus ON THE SCREEN!
BELA LUGOSI FULL-LENGTH CHILLER!

As far as the public was concerned, Bela Lugosi's middle name was "Dracula." (Courtesy of Ronald V. Borst/ Hollywood Movie Posters)

White Zombie, was an independent quickie shot on the Universal lot, making use of some re-dressed *Dracula* sets and properties. The atmospheric film, now regarded as a classic, recreated his *Dracula* contract on a poverty-row level as well. His total payment for a week's work on the film, which made a million dollars for the Halperin Brothers, was reputed to be between $700 and $900—and was possibly even less.

Prestige roles eluded Lugosi. He was rumored to be a contender for the Rasputin role in *Rasputin and the Empress,* but the part went to Lionel Barrymore in a casting coup that brought all three Barrymore children together (John and Ethel were the royals). His appearance in Tod Browning's *Mark of the Vampire* for Metro could hardly have endeared him to Universal, who tried unsuccessfully to block the picture as an infringement of *Dracula.*[15]

Lugosi was an undeniably talented performer, who shone especially in ethnic or lowlife characterizations. His marvelous work as the demented Ygor in *Son of Frankenstein* is a splendid example of the actor at the height of his powers. After the mid-1930s, Lugosi struck less and less of a figure in evening wear, but fish-and-soup was part of the old *Dracula* formula and the look was insisted upon in film after film. Although it may have seemed to the filmgoing public that Lugosi played nothing but Dracula, in reality he only portrayed the part twice on the screen, first in the 1931 film and finally in *Abbott and Costello Meet Frankenstein* in 1948.

Lugosi with an unidentified Lucy in a late 1940s stock engagement of Dracula. *The actor periodically renounced the role, but to no avail: producers would offer him little else.*

Frustrated by studio typecasting, Lugosi looked vainly for a stage role that might undo Dracula curse, but producers resisted offering him anything but the Deane and Balderston script, often on insulting terms. He was once given the chance to play the part in Bermuda, for example, but only if he would pay for his own transportation. He changed agents frequently, frustrating them with his periodic refusals to accept any engagements in *Dracula* at any price. But soon reality would set in and the agents would be sending out their feeler letters. Yes, they would write almost penitent, Mr. Lugosi is available again for *Dracula,* and yes, on almost any terms. . .

Veteran Broadway actress Elaine Stritch played opposite Lugosi in a 1947 stock production of *Dracula* at the John Drew Theatre in East Hampton. (In addition to Stritch's Lucy, the cast included Ray Walston as Renfield.) In a 1990 interview with this author, Stritch recalled Lugosi as an actor who took his work seriously, to the point of wearing full costume from the first day of rehearsals. After work, Stritch related, "he'd take us out to knock back a Scotch, and told some wonderful stories. He was a very good actor, you know, but he wasn't lucky professionally. I remember him telling me, 'You know, Elaine, if it wasn't for Boris Karloff I could have had a corner on the horror market.'" It was not doubt a further irritant to Lugosi that the only other stage part he could successfully tour was the Karloff role in *Arsenic and Old Lace.*

Stritch's most vivid memory of the *Dracula* revival was its opening night. The actor who played Jonathan Harker was having more than a bit of trouble with his climactic line in the crypt: "Let me drive it in deep!" had given him the giggles all through rehearsals and had caused some concern among the company. By the end of the first performance, however, he managed to deliver the line perfectly. He placed the wooden stake over the Dracula dummy's heart while Lugosi crouched behind a curtain, prepared to give a frightening cry. He raised the hammer, swung it down. . . and missed. The rubber hammer bounced off the dummy, Lugosi gave his yell on cue as if nothing was amiss, and the audience and company just froze in silence. Finally the actor who played Van Helsing blurted out an unforgettable, exasperated ad lib:

"Hit him *again,* Harker!"

The audience went to pieces, stopping the show for a full two minutes.

Lugosi's career declined irretrievably after his second film appearance as Dracula—he would never again have a speaking role for a major studio. The nadir came with his three-film involvement with transvestite producer/director Edward D. Wood, Jr., often cited as the worst filmmaker of all time for pictures like *Glen or Glenda,* a cross-dresser's bizarre "plea for tolerance" featuring Wood in the title role with Lugosi providing a demented narration. Next came *Bride of the Atom,* released as *Bride of the Monster,* in which the actor is devoured by a rubber octopus which he jiggles himself to provide a threadbare illusion of animation. As the film's mad scientist, Dr. Eric Vornoff, he delivers a monologue about the inequities that have driven him to the godforsaken hell where he cultivates demonic resentment and plots a mono-maniacal revenge. It is a quintessential Lugosi moment. Like Joan Crawford, whose rags-to-riches roles mirrored her actual life, Lugosi often played roles that offer a thinly veiled commentary on his own circumstances. Lugosi's mad scientists, often double-crossed in business and driven into desperate straits, take on a poignant resonance when viewed as unintentional allegories. The ultimate Bela Lugosi movie would probably center on a blackballed actor who finds a macabre means to wreak his revenge on Hollywood producers.

In April 1955, Lugosi committed himself to a state hospital for the treatment of a decades-long drug addiction that had grown from the use of prescriptive painkillers. He was seventy-two years old. The public was shocked to see the formerly commanding actor now a drained human shell in a hospital gown, the images of vampire and victim now in disturbing and paradoxical juxtaposition. Was Lugosi the bat . . . or the bitten? The image of Dracula had become a picture of Dorian Gray.

Lugosi was successfully treated and released, but public sympathy and goodwill did not translate into work. (The actor was several decades ahead of his time; drug rehabilitation was not the chic, career-reviving Hollywood ritual it has become today.) Lugosi made his last appearance in Edward D. Wood, Jr.'s execrable *Plan Nine from Outer Space.* The silent test footage of the actor that is cut into the finished film looks more like outtakes from a home movie than a professional effort. On August 16, 1956, during the making of *Plan Nine from Outer Space,* Bela Lugosi died in bed while reading the script of a proposed film, *The Final Curtain.* Wood finished *Plan Nine* using his wife's chiropractor as a stand-in, with a cape covering his face.

The final curtain would, however, indeed be a cape. Visitors to the funeral home where Lugosi's corpse was on view were surprised to find him laid out in full Dracula regalia—cape, tuxedo, medallion. Makeup was applied, the eyebrows darkened, and the hair was dyed to an approximation of its 1931 sheen. Like Dracula himself, who grew younger as he drank more blood, so Bela Lugosi was rejuvenated in death. (Stoker: "There lay the Count, but looking as if his youth had been half-renewed, for the white hair and moustache were changed to dark iron-grey; the cheeks were fuller, and the white skin seemed ruby-red underneath; the mouth was redder than ever . . ."[16]) Some souvenir photos were taken of the body, and copies of the bereavement card were later offered for sale by mail order by one of Lugosi's former associates. Interment took place at a Catholic cemetery, which apparently had no objection to the demonic burial vestments.

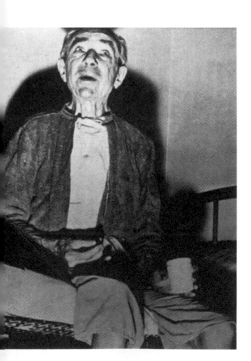

The bat or the bitten? A shockingly emaciated Bela Lugosi was one of the first Hollywood stars to self-publicize his treatment for substance abuse.

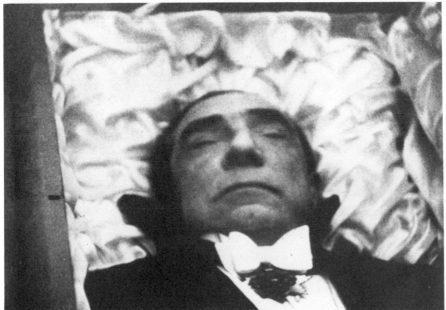

The lid was nearly closed on the actor's career when he opened "The Bela Lugosi Revue" in Los Vegas in 1952. (Courtesy of Ronald V. Borst/Hollywood Movie Posters)

The real thing: 1956.

Questions of taste aside, it was perhaps the only time in theatrical history in which an actor had been so identified with a part that he took it to the grave. (Indeed, next to Hamlet, it is the role most associated with funereal iconography.) The Dracula mystique was one of Lugosi's few remaining, if intangible assets; his estate was reported to have been just $2,900.[17]

Lugosi died just as Hollywood's interest in horror and science fiction films was beginning to enjoy a revival. *Dracula* had already been resurrected a number of times during Lugosi's lifetime. The film was issued again in 1938 on a double bill with *Frankenstein,* rereleased by Universal in 1947, and then again by Realart in the early 50s, and finally to television in 1957 as part of the immensely popular "Shock Theatre" package of vintage horror films.

The late 50s revival was accompanied by the rise of a fascinating subculture or "fandom" of adolescent and preadolescent males, revolving around the television screenings of the classic films by "horror hosts" in major cities (Zacherley in New York, Vampira in Los Angeles, Ghoulardi in Cleveland, etc.) and the rabid consumption of illustrated magazines like *Famous Monsters of Filmland, Castle of Frankenstein,* and many others. Several of today's prominent filmmakers were weaned on these magazines and the activities they generated, including Steven Spielberg, John Landis, and John Carpenter. While no full-length sociological study of this phenomenon ever resulted, monster culture provided a rite of passage recognizable in anthropological terms, a classic initiation into the mysteries of sex, death, and metaphysics. At the center of monster culture were Dracula and Frankenstein, low-calorie Christ substitutes for the Populuxe[18] age. Both creatures could die and be resurrected, and were inextricably linked with Christian iconography and themes. Both characters reflected aspects of adolescent sexual anxiety. Frankenstein's fumbling inability to find a mate found its flip side in Dracula's instantaneous control of women—especially maids, nurses, and mother stand-ins. The sex was symbolic, and, for the moment, safe. (As James Warren, publisher of *Famous Monsters,* told *Look* magazine, "After us, there's nothing but *Playboy.*"[19])

In a suburbanized, plasticized America, monster culture answered a need among male baby boomers for haunted houses instead of tract houses, an ancient, Europeanized structure of meaning. The need would find its most popular apotheosis in two television series, "The Munsters" and "The Addams Family," in which the nightmarish undercurrents of the American nuclear family would be playfully exorcised.

In 1963, Bela Lugosi, Jr., an attorney in Los Angeles, noticed a plastic model kit for sale in toy and drugstores, the package bearing his father's image, eyes blazing, beckoning children to come forward and buy. The model kit, manufactured by Aurora Plastics, contained component parts that could

Dracula toys and model kits became popular pastimes for young baby boomers in the early 1960s.

be assembled into a miniature statue of Count Dracula in a "hypnotic" stance that could be displayed and admired in the bedrooms of young boys. Model planes, then model dinosaurs ... why not, then, model bloodsucking vampires?

Lugosi soon learned that the model kit was not the only place his father was making a postmortem appearance as Dracula. When he discovered a paint-by-number kit on sale at a local drugstore, he requested to see copies of his father's contracts at Universal. After studying the documents, he retained the legal corporation of Irwin O. Spiegel of Los Angeles to represent himself and Hope Lininger Lugosi (the actor's fifth wife and widow) in an action against Universal.[20]

Their complaint alleged that Bela Lugosi's 1930 contract with Universal for *Dracula* had granted the studio the use of the actor's likeness only to advertise and publicize the film, reserving all other commercial uses of the Lugosi's likeness to the actor himself. The rights to his likeness were held by the plaintiffs to be tangible property to which they were entitled as Lugosi's heirs. In entering into commercial licensing arrangements, Universal had, the Lugosis claimed, "damaged, diluted, and impaired" the value of their own implied rights. They sought minimum damages of $25,000.[21]

Universal's licensing activities had been rather extensive. Henry Irving— presumably at Bram Stoker's insistence—had imprinted his likeness as Mephistopheles on crackers to drum up business in the towns he toured. But Irving's character was a pale commercial spectre indeed compared to its descendent, Count Dracula. There was, apparently, almost no kind of consumer product or novelty that could not be enhanced by Lugosi's presence as the vampire. Among the licensed items featuring Lugosi's screen image as Dracula were children's phonograph records, plastic toy pencil sharpeners, greeting cards and talking greeting cards, plastic model figures, tee-shirts, sweatshirts and patches, rings and pins, monster old-maid card games, soap and detergent products, Halloween costumes and masks, enlargograph sets and kits, target games, picture puzzles, mechanical walking toys, ink-on transfers, trading cards, Halloween candy and gum, comic books, self-erasing magic slates, cutout paper dolls and books, "monster mansion" vehicles, wax figurines, candy dispensers, transparencies, kites, calendars and prints, sliding square puzzle games, children's and ladies' jewelry, belts and belt buckles, wall plaques, wallets, juvenile luggage, "bike buddies" (a novelty in the shape of a monster head on a spring device, to be attached to a bicycle handlebar), animated flip books, lapel buttons, photo printing kits, advertising campaigns, stirring rods and spoons and toy horoscope viewers, junior high school English textbooks, five-cent candy, two-for-one-cent taffy candy, hard candy cigarettes, tattoo transfers used on inner wrappers of bubble gum, decals, printed vending-

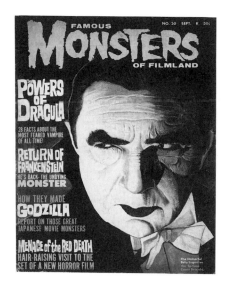

Famous Monsters of Filmland: *the house organ of monster culture.*

machine gumballs, filmstrips, and hors d'oeuvres accessories.[22]

In the initial case heard by the Superior Court of Los Angeles County, the Lugosis argued that Universal had not licensed a generic Dracula character — they had cast other actors of distinctive appearance as Dracula, notably John Carradine and Lon Chaney, Jr., but had made no attempt to merchandise their images. "The essence of the thing that Universal licensed . . . was the uniquely individual likeness and appearance of Bela Lugosi," the suit maintained.[23]

Lugosi's 1930 agreement with Universal had contained the following clause: "The producer shall have the right to photograph and/or otherwise produce, reproduce, transmit, exhibit and exploit in connection with the said photoplay all of the artist's acts, poses, plays and appearances of any and all kinds hereunder. . . . The producer shall likewise have the right to use and give publicity to the artist's name and likeness, photographic or otherwise . . . in connection with the advertising and exploitation of said photoplay."[24]

The Lugosis argued that the clause clearly retained all rights of exploitation except for the direct promotion of the film *Dracula,* and cited the repetition of the phrase "in connection with." Cocktail accessories could hardly be considered advertising "in connection with" a film not even in general release. Universal maintained the opposite: since there had been no specific limitation expressly stated, Universal's right of exploitation was, therefore, limitless. Furthermore, they argued, Lugosi's right of likeness ended upon his death. Likeness was not a transmissable asset.

The issues raised by both sides were compelling, and many without precedent.

The public records of the court proceedings make for interesting reading, both for the legal issues raised, and also for their subtext. Like the actors in the play, wrestling with the empty cape, the legal players were finding the vampire to be, once more, maddeningly elusive. Who — or what — was the essence of Dracula? Where was Dracula? In the costume, in the contract, in the fraction of a millimeter of greasepaint that the actor wore in the role?

Lugosi wore almost no makeup at all in *Dracula,* his stage appearance being naturalized for the film. Nonetheless, one witness for Universal went so far as to state that even though he recognized Bela Lugosi, the actor, he found Lugosi unrecognizable in the role of Dracula (the vampire, one might add, has always had the power to cloud men's minds). Universal's other horror characters — the Frankenstein monster, the Wolf Man, and the Mummy, for instance, were totally original creations of the studio that buried the actors beneath grotesque makeup concocted by their resident makeup artist, Jack Pierce. Dracula was also unique in having originated in another medium. Universal acquired the film rights to *Dracula,* but not the theatrical rights. (The play is still frequently produced, with the character described and

costumed in the same cape, costume, makeup, and accent that Lugosi popularized on stage and screen. When Frank Langella played the role on Broadway in 1977, Universal was not a partner to the production, and when the
studio remade the film with Langella, the stage producers were similarly not
involved in the movie.)

The Lugosi lawsuit was ground-breaking in its claim that, while the late
actor never commercially licensed his likeness during his lifetime, the unused
potential was a form of real property, descendible to his heirs. In a January 31,
1972, memorandum opinion, superior court judge Bernard S. Jefferson con-
curred, and ruled for the plaintiffs. Lugosi's contract, Jefferson wrote, "by
express language, limits the producer's right."[25] The defendant's contention
that "the possibility that the photoplay *might* be exhibited on television"
rendered its merchandising activities a form of advertising was "untenable and
unacceptable."[26] Jefferson made special note of the fact that Universal had
obtained Lugosi's written consent to use a wax dummy of the character in the
1937 film, *Dracula's Daughter,* in which Lugosi himself did not appear. Wrote
Jefferson, "If plaintiff's employment by defendant as Count Dracula in the
movie, *Dracula,* had conveyed to defendant the right to portray Bela Lugosi as
Count Dracula apart from his appearance in the movie, *Dracula,* it would not
have been necessary for defendant to obtain Bela Lugosi's written
consent . . ."[27]

Oddly, in a point never raised in the trial, the wax dummy in *Dracula's
Daughter* was a generic prop bearing no resemblance to Lugosi at all. Universal had, in effect, obtained Lugosi's permission to use the character, and didn't
bother to recreate his likeness.

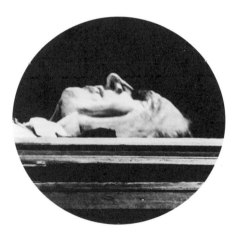

*Not much resemblance: the wax
effigy from* Dracula's Daughter
(Photofest)

Jefferson ruled that the Lugosis were entitled to recover damages arising
out of each of the licensing agreements within two years of February 3, 1966,
due to the applicable statute of limitations.[28] The interlocutory judgment was
filed on April 21, 1972, calling for an accounting of damages. A final
judgment by the superior court came more than two years later, on July 9,
1974. The Lugosis were awarded the sum of $53,023.23, plus accumulated
interest for a total award of $72,993.86.

Lugosi v. Universal Pictures had by that time lasted longer than Florence
Stoker's campaign against *Nosferatu.* And, like all things both legal and
Draculean, the final word had yet to be heard.

Universal appealed the superior court ruling, restating its assertion that
Lugosi had portrayed Dracula only as an actor for hire and retained no rights
in the character as presented to the public by Universal.[29] "It is adroit
juggling indeed to transpose Lugosi from hired actor to exclusive owner-in-
perpetuity of the character portrayed by him in another's copyrighted photoplay," the defendant claimed. Universal also found fault with many of the

trial court's conclusions in regard to its accounting of *Dracula*-related merchandising.

The district court of appeals agreed, and overruled the trial court's decision. Since Lugosi had created no tangible property or merchandising contracts, no rights could be transmitted to his family. Upon his death, his personality entered into the public domain and could be exploited by anyone for any legitimate commercial purpose.[30]

Given the long history of *Dracula* in the courts, preceding even Lugosi, or Universal, the case could not be over. And it wasn't.

The Lugosis petitioned the California Supreme Court, citing the numerous larger issues at stake, in addition to their own claims. The effects of the district court opinion, they held, "unfairly discriminate in favor of the motion picture producers as an entrepreneurial class to the detriment of the surviving families of actors and other creators of artistic and intellectual property."[31] An actor like Bela Lugosi, they maintained, had protectible rights with a clear basis in common law.[32] The plaintiffs noted the disparity between the parties to a contract: the studio's rights were automatic and did not need to be exercised in order to be enforced; an artist was required to actively exploit retained subsidiary rights in order to perpetuate them.[33] The producer's rights were (by metaphorical implication) almost un-dead, "of potentially infinite duration not limited or measured by the life of the actor, whereas the artist's retained subsidiary rights cannot endure beyond his lifetime."

On December 3, 1979, the California Supreme Court upheld the appeals court decision. "Lugosi's right to create a business, product or service of value is embraced in the law of privacy and is protectable during one's lifetime but it does not survive the death of Lugosi," the court ruled.[34]

A concurring opinion was filed by Justice J. Mosk: "Factually, not unlike the horror films that brought him fame, Bela Lugosi rises from the grave 20 years after death to haunt his former employer. Legally: his vehicle is a strained adaptation of a common law cause of action unknown either in a statute or case law in California."[35] It was clear, wrote Mosk, "that Bela Lugosi did not portray himself and did not create Dracula, he merely acted out a popular role that had been garnished with the patina of age . . . his performance gave him no more claim on Dracula than that of countless actors on Hamlet who have portrayed the Dane in a unique matter."[36] Mosk added, rather bizarrely, given the facts in the case, that Lugosi had been paid "handsomely" in 1931 terms, and that any limitations the actor wished to place on his employer needed to be specified in the contract, not interpreted after the fact.[37] He raised the spectre of the descendents of George Washington suing the secretary of the treasury for placing Washington's likeness on the dollar bill, and similar legalistic nightmares.[38]

Chief Justice Rose Bird (who would later lose her position for not being sufficiently bloodthirsty on the issue of capital punishment to suit Californians) filed a lengthy dissenting opinion. She argued that the issue at stake was not solely one of privacy, but publicity,[39] and the fair recognition of an individual's labor and energy in creating a recognizable public persona. "While this product is concededly intangible, it is not illusory."[40]

The majority opinion, Bird reasoned, insisted on a double standard: the actor's right of publicity was fragile and would die with him if not exploited, but the same right, if assigned to the undying corporation, could remain dormant indefinitely until circumstances were favorable for exploitation.[41] (In Dracula's words, from the stage play: "I go to sleep in my box for a hundred years . . ."[42] Time, indeed, was on Dracula's side when he assumed a corporate mantle. This theme would eventually be made explicit in a film called *The Satanic Rites of Dracula,* in which actor Christopher Lee portrayed the count as an undead CEO in a modern office tower.)

Lugosi v. Universal Pictures can be read as a kind of postmodernist gothic text as much as a legal document. The horror themes are implicit . . . but not illusory. We have an actor, his career itself a Faustian parable, his fame dependent on perpetuating a certain contemporary image of the devil. The image drains the actor in a Dracula/Dorian Gray/doppelgänger fashion, he dies and is resurrected, his ghost employed to attract and fascinate children for purposes of economic exploitation. Vampirism and consumerism blur; one begets the other. By the 1970s, the corporate entity that controls the actor's demonic alter ego resides in a black tower risen on the very site that once impersonated Transylvania—a fictive, filmic ritual that both saved and prolonged its corporate life. Conflict arises over the possession and control of the dead actor's valuable essence. Rituals are performed, dealing with themes of identity, materiality, blood ties, possession, and things that survive death. Obsession ensues.

In the Victorian context, *Dracula*'s meanings are distinctly sexual. A century later, the metaphors are economic. But Bram Stoker is already ahead of us. Late in his novel, with the Count trapped in commercial Picadilly, Jonathan Harker takes a literal stab at his peculiar alter ego: "The blow was a powerful one; only the diabolical quickness of the Count's leap back saved him. A second less and the trenchant blade had shorn through his heart. As it was, the point just cut the cloth of his coat, making a wide gap whence a bundle of bank-notes and a stream of gold fell out."[43] Dracula escapes with a handful of money, smashing through a window. And amid the crash and glitter of the falling glass, Dr. Seward discerns an unmistakable sound: gold sovereigns, tinkling musically on the flagstones.

Blood money, if there ever was.

Lugosi was a far more versatile actor than the public suspected, as demonstrated by his early stage role of Christ in The Passion.

The ultimate exploitation of the Dracula image: a tongue-in-cheek advertisement for the Lutheran church. (Courtesy Fallon McElligott, Minneapolis; Dean Hanson, art director; Tom McElligott, copywriter)

Are your kids learning about the power of the cross on the late, late show?

With all due regard to Hollywood, there's more to Christianity than stopping vampires. Come with your children to the Lutheran Church this Sunday as we celebrate the resurrection of Jesus Christ in love and fellowship.
The Lutheran Church

Dracula has become a big business indeed, and one far beyond the purview of Universal Pictures. In England, Hammer Films, which had scored a major hit with its 1958 blood-soaked Technicolor remake (called *Horror of Dracula* in America), had parlayed the Count into a money-spinning series of films featuring Christopher Lee in the title role. By 1970, fans could expect to see Lee gnashing his teeth (possibly in discomfort over the huge red contact lenses he wore) more than once a year. The actor managed to distance himself somewhat from the role, but would rarely be cast as anything but a villain again. One of Lee's appearances was in a badly produced, but nonetheless important Franco-Spanish production called *Count Dracula* (1970), where, for the first time, the original novel was fairly carefully followed, including the physical description of the Count.

In 1972, historians Raymond T. McNalley and Radu R. Florescu published *In Search of Dracula,* the first detailed account of the life and times of Wallachian prince Vlad Tepes, the historical figure who actually bore the name Dracula (Rumanian for "son of the devil"), and displayed behavior to fit. Tepes' favorite method of dispatching his enemies was by impalement, which has an unmistakable resonance for vampire mythology. The Rumanian government soon began to encourage Dracula tourism, which has grown into an important economic segment.

American television turned to the Stoker novel for a 1973 prime-time adaptation starring Jack Palance. The producer was Dan Curtis, whose phenomenally successful soap opera "Dark Shadows" had already proved there to be an enormous market for vampirism among daytime television viewers. At night, it can be assumed, they would be all the more receptive. Andy Warhol had his first fling with the Count the same year, with the imaginatively titled *Andy Warhol's Dracula.* The kitsch market was in full swing by this time, with Count Chockula materializing as a breakfast cereal.

Daytime vampire: Jonathan Frid as the undead Barnabas Collins thrilled jaded soap opera viewers in the 1960s television serial "Dark Shadows." (Photofest)

The Deane and Balderston play was very successfully revived on Broadway in 1977, first with Frank Langella in the lead, succeeded by Raul Julia, Jeremy Brett, Jean Le Clerc, and David Dukes. Terence Stamp played the role in London. The production was conceived as an Edward Gorey cartoon, with Gorey himself designing the sets and the costumes. The play defied the somewhat lukewarm reviews and proved an immense crowd-pleaser. Langella was then tapped for an elaborate remake of *Dracula* by Universal, released in 1979, with an impressive cast including Laurence Olivier as Van Helsing, Kate Nelligan as Lucy (the name was switched yet again), and Donald Pleasance as Seward. Despite brilliant moments, the film was not a box office hit. Langella made a languid, almost Wildean vampire, and the film was marred by some grotesque editing—Van Helsing's daughter, called Mina here, becomes a vampire and is destroyed twice in completely contradictory scenes.

The late 70s vampire revival also saw the BBC's ambitious, elegant miniseries, *Count Dracula,* in which Louis Jourdan essayed the role for what must be the most careful adaptation of the novel to date, and the most successful. It refrains only from reproducing Stoker's vampire as described— Jourdan has buckets of oily charm, and looks like, well, Louis Jourdan. The scene of Dracula scaling the wall of his castle was finally produced in a manner befitting Stoker's chilling original vision. Another scene, also taken directly from the novel, was censored for American television after its first broadcast: the sight of the three vampire wives feasting on a plump baby Dracula has brought them in a bag was evidently antithetical to public television membership drives.

Christopher Lee, the premier film Dracula of the post-Lugosi age, seen here in his little-seen performance in Count Dracula, *a low-budget film that was faithful to Stoker's description of the character.*

In 1979, Werner Herzog produced a wrong-headed and rather pretentious "remake" of *Nosferatu,* with Klaus Kinski as the vampire and Isabelle Adjani as his victim. The film is notable for the use of a plenitude of white rats, though their obvious, lab-sanitary origins makes them less than convincing as harbingers of pestilence.

Just when vampires seemed to be totally co-opted by films and television, there was a totally unexpected literary event: a first-time novelist, Anne Rice, earned a reputed $1,000,000 for her manuscript, *Interview with the Vampire,* which became a best-seller in 1976 and was followed by two sequels, *The Vampire Lestat* (1985) and *Queen of the Damned* (1988). More sequels are slated to follow, in an apparently unending profusion. Rice's brilliant narrative strategy was to present her story sympathetically from the vampire's point of view; "vampirism" in Rice's hands becomes an evocative but never precise metaphor for aspects of the human condition, including the androgynous aspect, which is frequently at the surface of her tales. Rice's vampires are sensuous, sexual renegades; her prose is ripe and lushly readable. It is probably no exaggeration to say that with *Interview with the Vampire,* Rice revived and elevated the vampire story to much the same degree as Stoker did with *Dracula,* and much more craftily. To Rice, who shared her thoughts on the subject with *Psychology Today* magazine, Stoker's vampires are "presented as close to animals, but I always saw them as angels . . . finely tuned imitations of human beings imbued with this evil spirit."[44] In Rice, vampires are presented not as nightmares but as objects of glamorous transcendence and desire.

Dracula continues to exert its influence on writers, artists, and performers, and not all of them genre-based. Actress Glenn Close, whose performance in the blockbuster film *Fatal Attraction* was, in a way, an influential cultural update of Mrs. Patrick Campbell as "The Vampire," told an interviewer that Stoker's novel had been one of her favorite books, exerting a major influence on her life.[45] Les Grand Ballets Canadiens has added to its repertoire a strikingly original ballet version, featuring sex, nudity, and animal skins—and no DeMille girls anywhere. Argentine novelist Manuel Puig, whose work has explored both the politics of sexuality and the cultural tyranny of Hollywood, revealed in a 1979 interview[46] that the opening chapter of his acclaimed novel *Kiss of the Spider Woman*—a dialogue-only tour de force in which two political prisoners dissect the plot and larger implications of Val Lewton's 1942 thriller *The Cat People*—had been *Dracula*-inspired in its first draft. Given Puig's incisive analytical sensibilities, one can only assume his fictional exegesis of *Dracula* would have been nothing if not provocative. And in early 1990, the ultimate cultural validation came to pass: *Dracula* was announced as a syndicated television series, to be produced in Europe, with a large segment of the U.S. television market already sold on the basis of the title.

Is there an end in sight? Apparently not. The story grows stronger with each telling, compelling beyond reason and capable of a thousand transmutations. Mutability, somehow, is its essence.

As one examines even a portion of the enormous outpouring of plays, books, and especially films that have been inspired by *Dracula,* one pattern does become clear. In keeping with the process by which Stoker first arrived at his characters (doubling, splitting, and reassigning identities and relationships), the adaptors and imitators of *Dracula* have continued this process as well, obsessively merging and recombining the core players and situations, almost into infinity. Thus Mina can become Lucy and become Mina again. Harker becomes Renfield. Dracula is an animal. Dracula is a gentleman. In the Langella film, Dracula even becomes Van Helsing in a sense as he turns the tables and drives a stake through the vampire killer himself.

Shadows, it would seem, are chasing shadows.

As Bram Stoker observed in *The Jewel of Seven Stars,* "it is in the arcana of dreams that existences merge and renew themselves, change and yet keep the same—like the soul of a musician in a fugue."[47]

And in the arcana of *Dracula,* a fugue of light and shadow, our century has found and forged some of its most disturbing yet irresistible dreams, urgent visions that must be confronted, assimilated, images of violence and darkness, substance and soul, identity and blood.

The blood is the life, after all. And *Dracula* is the lifeblood of dreams that never end.

DRACULA AT A GLANCE

---◆---

*Being a user-friendly guide to the origins and exploits of the
world's favorite vampire, and un-dead near relations.*

——————— ———————

A complete compendium of every *Dracula* antecedent, adaptation, or deriva-
tion would be a book in itself, but what follows is an attempt to present
highlights of the myth's development in a chronological fashion, against a
background of selected historical and cultural events. (Film titles are American unless otherwise noted.)

PRE-1800

Vampire myths from antiquity.

Vlad "The Impaler" Tepes, prince of Wallachia, 1430(?)–1477(?)

Elizabeth Bathory (1560–1614), Hungarian countess seeking rejuvenation,
slaughters as many as 650 girls to bathe in their blood.

Early 1700s: vampire hysteria sweeps Europe.

1734

The word "vampyre" enters the English language in translations of German
accounts of vampire frenzy.

1797

Goethe's *Bride of Corinth*.

*Isabelle Adjani and Klaus Kinski
in Werner Herzog's* Nosferatu,
the Vampyre *(1979). (Photofest)*

1819

The Vampyre by John Polidori. A story conceived at the Shelleys' celebrated house party that spawned *Frankenstein.*

1820-1830

Vampire craze in Paris theatres.

Der Vampyr, opera by Heinrich Marschner.

1847

Bram Stoker born in Dublin.

Varney the Vampyre, or, The Feast of Blood by James Malcolm Rymer.

Verdi's *Macbeth.*

1852

Adaptation of *Le Vampire* by Dumas and Maquet.

1859

Darwin's *On the Origin of Species* posits evolutionary link between man and lower animals.

1871

Carmilla by J. Sheridan Le Fanu.

1875

Bram Stoker's first published horror fiction, "The Chain of Destiny."

1876

Stoker meets Henry Irving.

1878

Bram Stoker marries Florence Balcombe and simultaneously accepts position as acting manager of Irving's Lyceum Theatre.

1882

Bela Blasko born, Lugos, Hungary.

Bram Stoker publishes macabre collection of children's stories, *Under the Sunset*.

1885

Faust enters Lyceum repertoire; Henry Irving portrays Mephistopheles.

1886

Robert Louis Stevenson publishes *The Strange Case of Dr. Jekyll and Mr. Hyde*.

1890

Oscar Wilde publishes *The Picture of Dorian Gray*.

Stoker begins research on his novel, *The Un-Dead*.

1893

Freud commences publication of *Studies on Hysteria*.

1894

Trilby published; George du Maurier introduces Svengali.

1895

The trial of Oscar Wilde.

The Time Machine by H. G. Wells.

1897

The Un-Dead published as *Dracula.*

Staged reading at the Lyceum Theatre.

Kipling's poem "The Vampire" accompanies exhibition of painting by Philip Burne-Jones.

1901

First British paperback abridgement of *Dracula.*

1902

Burne-Jones' *The Vampire* shown in New York.

1904

Freud publishes *The Interpretation of Dreams.*

Dorothy Peterson and Bela Lugosi in Horace Liveright's 1927 production.

1905

The death of Henry Irving. Stoker suffers stroke and begins memoirs during his recuperation.

1906

Publication of Stoker's *Personal Reminiscences of Henry Irving.*

1910

Stoker's last novel, *The Lair of the White Worm.*

1912

Death of Bram Stoker.

Sinking of the *Titanic.*

1913

Stoker's working notes for *Dracula* sold at auction.

Publication of *Dracula's Guest.*

1919

The Cabinet of Dr. Caligari, prototype horror movie, produced in Germany.

1920

Record of lost Hungarian film entitled *Drakula.*

First French edition of *Dracula.*

1922

Nosferatu: Eine Symphonie des Grauns produced as a pirated film by Prana-Film, Germany. Florence Stoker takes legal action through the British Society of Authors.

1924

Hamilton Deane enters into contract with Stoker for a stage adaptation of *Dracula*.

1925

German court rules in favor of Stoker's claim and orders all prints of *Nosferatu* destroyed.

Florence Stoker prevents a private screening of *Nosferatu* by the Film Society, London.

Deane stage version has preview/premiere at Grand Theatre, Derby.

1926

Deane play successfully tours the provinces.

1927

London production of *Dracula* opens in February at the Little Theatre.

Horace Liveright contracts for American stage rights, hires John L. Balderston to write adaptation.

Florence Stoker privately commissions another stage adaptation of the play, to which she owns all rights. Charles Morrell version is unsuccessfully produced at the Royal Court Theatre, Warrington, in September.

Deane and Balderston version opens at Fulton Theatre, New York, October, with Bela Lugosi as star.

Metro Goldwyn Mayer produces a vampire film, *London After Midnight,* with Lon Chaney as star. Producer Irving Thalberg fears infringement of *Dracula,* instructs director Tod Browning to make story changes.

1928

American stage version closes after successful run; west coast tour mounted.

Universal Pictures leaks false press announcement that it has purchased film rights, mentions Conrad Veidt as possible star. Universal's British agent grants permission to Film Society to screen *Nosferatu* on the grounds that Universal now controls copyright. Stoker and lawyers threaten action.

1929

Film Society turns over their print of *Nosferatu* to Florence Stoker for destruction.

Legitimate negotiations for film rights begin.

Nosferatu surfaces in New York and Detroit. Agent Harold Freedman negotiates with exhibitor to obtain print.

Liveright's gross earnings on stage play said to exceed $2 million.

Stock market crash.

1930

Universal, Pathe, Columbia, and Metro all consider *Dracula*. Carl Laemmle, Sr., opposes production without Lon Chaney, who is under contract to Metro, and terminally ill.

Producer Horace Liveright threatens to block film sale with litigation. Settles for $4,500.

Liveright loses stage rights over $600 in owed royalties.

Universal purchases novel and film for $40,000.

Nosferatu turned over to Universal "for purposes of destruction." Novelist Louis Bromfield hired to write screen adaptation, is replaced by Dudley Murphy and Garrett Fort.

Bela Lugosi cast in film after extended studio indecision. Filming commences in September, finishes in November.

Spanish-language version shot simultaneously.

Edna Tichenor models a diaphanous shroud for Tod Browning's London After Midnight *(1927).*

1931

January: Spanish film previewed to good notices.

February: American film premieres at Roxy Theatre, New York.

Attempt at Broadway revival in wake of the film is unsuccessful; closes after a few performances.

April–May: *Dracula* receives belated West Coast premiere. Spanish and American versions exhibited simultaneously in Los Angeles.

Tod Browning leaves Universal and returns to Metro.

Nosferatu director F. W. Murnau dies in Hollywood.

Swedish director Carl Dreyer produces *Vampyr* as art film in France.

Dracula ends the year as one of Universal's top money-makers, despite mixed notices. Studio has its only profitable year of the decade.

1933

David O. Selznick options *Dracula's Guest,* and hires John L. Balderston to draft a treatment, called *Dracula's Daughter.* Metro fears infringement of Universal film, and negotiates sale of property to Universal.

Due to a loophole in the American copyright law, the novel *Dracula* is judged to have always been in the public domain.

Death of Horace Liveright.

1935

Tod Browning remakes *London After Midnight* as *The Vampires of Prague* for Metro, with Lugosi as a caped count. Universal unsuccessfully seeks a restraining order. Film released as *Mark of the Vampire.*

1936

Dracula's Daughter released by Universal.

1937

Death of Florence Stoker.

U.S. horror film cycle comes to a temporary halt due to British embargo on monster films.

1938

Dracula successfully rereleased on double bill with *Frankenstein*. Some prints tinted green.

Orson Welles dramatizes novel for radio; *Mercury Theatre on the Air* production features Welles as Dracula and Agnes Moorehead as Mina.

1939

Hamilton Deane secures rights to Balderston adaptation and finally acts the role of Dracula on the London stage.

Actor Bernard Jukes, who played Renfield over 4,000 times, killed in an air raid.

Tod Browning directs his last film, *Miracles for Sale*.

1943

Son of Dracula, with the remarkably miscast Lon Chaney, Jr. Lugosi appears as a thinly disguised Count for Columbia in *Return of the Vampire*.

Lugosi tours eastern seaboard in revival of Deane and Balderston play.

1944

Dracula teamed with other Universal monsters in *House of Frankenstein*.

1945

House of Dracula. Another monster festival from Universal.

1947

Theatrical rerelease of *Dracula* by Universal.

1948

Lugosi plays Dracula on film for the second and last time in *Abbott and Costello meet Frankenstein* (U.K. title *Abbott and Costello meet the Ghosts*).

1952

Lugosi appears in stage revival of *Dracula* in Brighton, England, and films *Old Mother Riley Meets the Vampire*. Takes "The Bela Lugosi Revue" to Las Vegas.

1953

First non-Western adaptation: *Drakula Istanbulda* produced in Turkey.

1954

John L. Balderston dies.

Mexican actor German Robles has a prominent dilemma in The Vampire's Coffin *(1959). (Photofest)*

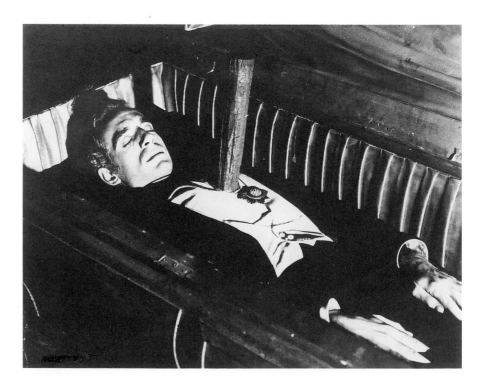

1955

Lugosi commits himself for well-publicized treatment of drug addiction.

1956

Bela Lugosi dies of a heart attack August 16; is buried in Dracula costume and makeup.

John Carradine plays the Count in first television adaptation of *Dracula* on "Matinee Theatre."

1957

United Artists produces the first non-Universal *Dracula* title, *The Return of Dracula* (later titled *The Curse of Dracula*), starring Francis Lederer.

1958

Hammer Films (U.K.) produces *Dracula* (called *Horror of Dracula* in the U.S.). Christopher Lee is established as the cinema's new king of vampires.

American International Pictures capitalizes on the title, though not the character or story, in *Blood of Dracula*.

El Vampiro (Mexico) with German Robles as the first Spanish vampire since Carlos Villarias.

Universal's horror film series, *Shock Theatre,* released to television. Regional TV "horror hosts" such as Zacherley and Vampira promote monsters to an impressionable new generation.

Famous Monsters of Filmland magazine is established as the bible of monster culture. Readership will include future film mega-director Steven Spielberg.

The death of Hamilton Deane.

1959

Eminent Shakespearean actor Sir Donald Wolfitt wears Bela Lugosi makeup for *Blood of the Vampire* (U.K.).

Maurice Richardson publishes influential article, "The Psychoanalysis of Ghost Stories," placing *Dracula* in an overtly Freudian context for the first time.

1960

Brides of Dracula (U.K.). First Hammer follow-up to Christopher Lee remake, this one heavily Oedipal and with no Count in sight, despite the title.

Black Sunday (Italy). One of the most evocative and frightening vampire films ever made, an homage to the entire genre by director Mario Bava.

Blood and Roses (France). Roger Vadim's atmospheric foray into *Carmilla,* titled *To Die of Pleasure* in Europe.

1961

The Bad Flower. First Korean adaptation.

1962

Harry Ludlam publishes *A Biography of Dracula: The Life Story of Bram Stoker.*

Tod Browning dies.

1963

Universal's commercial licensing of monster toys and games reaches a fever pitch. Lugosi heirs commence legal action, charging unjust exploitation of his father's likeness.

Christopher Lee, the leading post-Lugosi screen Dracula, seen here in a classic pose from Horror of Dracula *(1958). (Photofest)*

1964

Dracula is revived as a tired Jewish grandfather in the CBS television series "The Munsters." Transylvania and suburbia blur.

1965

Christopher Lee returns in Hammer's *Dracula, Prince of Darkness* (U.K.).

1966

John Carradine travels west for *Billy the Kid vs. Dracula.*

Il imperio de Dracula (Mexico).

"Dark Shadows," ABC daytime television serial, brings Dracula trappings to New England.

1967

The Count makes a brief appearance in Conrad Rooks' *Chappaqua.*

1968

Limited theatrical rerelease of *Dracula* and *Frankenstein* to revival house and college circuits.

Dracula Has Risen from the Grave (U.K.), bringing with him once again the actor Christopher Lee.

Dracula Meets the Outer Space Chicks.

1969

The Fearless Vampire Killers (U.K.). Roman Polanski's extravagant spoof, featuring Polanski, Sharon Tate, and elaborate references to earlier films.

Blood of Dracula's Castle.

Men of Action Meet Women of Dracula (Phillipines).

Dracula Sucks (first version).

Dracula (The Dirty Old Man).

1970

Guess What Happened to Count Dracula?

Dracula (U.K.). BBC-TV production, with Denholm Elliot.

Dracula vs. Frankenstein (Spain).

Count Dracula. A low-budget, though faithful multinational adaptation of Stoker's novel, notable for Christopher Lee's close resemblance to Stoker's physical description. With Klaus Kinski as Renfield.

The Scars of Dracula (U.K.). Christopher Lee again. This time he stabs as well as bites.

Taste the Blood of Dracula (U.K.). In which hypocritical Victorian men looking for kicks dabble in demonism. Stylish, witty, and gruesome. Christopher Lee sets an all-time record for film portrayals of Dracula in a single year.

Dracula vs. Frankenstein. Yet another version, this one American, in a bumper-crop year.

Jonathan (West Germany). A Dracula-like premise in a parable of fascism.

Lake of Death (Japan), also known as *The Lake of Dracula* and *Japula*.

1971

Count Dracula by Ted Tiller becomes a popular vehicle in regional, community, and college theatres.

1972

Blacula. A Caribbean Count.

Dracula A.D. 1972 (U.K.). You can't keep a good vampire down. Christopher Lee proves his durability, as England swings.

El gran amor de Conde Dracula (Spain).

Raymond T. McNalley and Radu R. Florescu publish *In Search of Dracula*, the first modern account of the "historical Dracula," Vlad Tepes.

California court rules in favor of Bela Lugosi's son and widow in lawsuit against Universal Pictures; plaintiffs awarded $72,000. Universal appeals decision.

Louis Jourdan as Dracula in the
BBC's elegant 1978 mini-series.
(Photofest)

1973

La saga de los Draculas (Spain).

The Satanic Rites of Dracula (U.K.). Christopher Lee, round eight, this time as a CEO in a corporate office tower, plotting world domination via germ warfare.

Dracula. TV film with Jack Palance.

Andy Warhol's Dracula (Italy/France).

1974

The Seven Brothers Meet Dracula (U.K./Hong Kong coproduction).

Tender Dracula, or the Confessions of a Blood Drinker (France).

Old Dracula (U.K.). With David Niven.

1975

Spermula.

Alucarda (Mexico).

Daniel Farson publishes second full-length Stoker biography, *The Man Who Wrote Dracula.*

Carmilla, in a musical stage adaptation by Wilford Leach.

Deafula. In sign language, for the hearing-impaired.

1976

Dracula, père et fils. Christopher Lee, on vacation in France.

Author Anne Rice receives a $1 million advance for her first novel, *Interview with the Vampire.*

1977

Zoltan—Hound of Dracula (U.K.; American title: *Dracula's Dog*).

Deane and Balderston play revived on Broadway in a tongue-in-cheek production designed by Edward Gorey, with Frank Langella in the title role.

California Supreme Court reverses lower court decision on *Lugosi vs. Universal Pictures;* studio's Dracula merchandising found not to be in violation of Lugosi's film contract. Actor's claim on likeness held not to survive death.

The Hardy Boys and Nancy Drew Meet Dracula (television film).

1978

Count Dracula. British television adaptation with Louis Jourdan; perhaps the most ambitious attempt to faithfully reproduce the novel.

1979

Dracula. Universal's stylish $40 million remake on the heels of the Broadway revival, with Frank Langella repeating his role opposite Laurence Olivier as Van Helsing. Kate Nelligan costars.

Nosferatu: Phantom der Nacht (West Germany). Werner Herzog's idiosyncratic homage to Murnau, filmed in two versions, German and English (the latter considered unreleasable). With Klaus Kinski and Isabelle Adjani.

Love at First Bite. George Hamilton stars in one of the best spoofs of the genre.
The True Life of Dracula (Rumania).
Dracula Sucks. Yet again, this time with porno star Jamie Gillis.
Vampire Dracula Comes to Kobe: Evil Makes Women Beautiful (Japanese TV movie).
The Passion of Dracula by Bob Hall and David Richmond is an off-Broadway hit.

1980

Dracula's Last Rites (France).

1982

Phyllis A. Roth publishes first full-length critical survey of Bram Stoker.

1983

Cliff's Notes published for *Dracula.*

1984

Restored version of *Nosferatu* screened at the Berlin Film Festival, with live orchestral accompaniment.

1985

Anne Rice's *The Vampire Lestat* published; reaches best-seller lists as the second novel in her "Vampire Chronicles."

1986

Dracula image used to advertise the Lutheran and Episcopal churches.

1988

1931 *Dracula* poster sells to collector for a rumored $9,000, over three times what Bela Lugosi received to appear in the film. Lugosi autographs will soon ask as much as $1,000, original-release stills from *Dracula* up to $250 each.

Mama Dracula (France).

Dracula's Widow.

Restored archival print of Universal's *Dracula* released on videodisc.

The Queen of the Damned, Anne Rice's third best-seller of blood-drinking.

1989

Rumania overthrows and executes its dictator, Nikolai Ceauçescu, widely referred to in the news media as "Dracula." Dracula tours and historical sites an important part of the Rumanian tourism economy.

1990

Dracula announced as a syndicated television series.

Hollywood Gothic.

Don't Dream Of DRACULA

Keep This Magic Wolfbane
Under Your Pillow!
It Will Keep "DRACULA" Away
Don't give away the secret of this picture to your
friends. Tell them to see it—and let "Dracula"
surpirse and thrill them as it did you!

STANLEY
Theatre   19th & Market Sts.

STARTING
FRI. FEB. 27

NOTES

INTRODUCTION

1. The quotation was used, significantly, as an epigraph to one of *Dracula's* penny-dreadful precursors, *Varney the Vampyre,* in 1847.
2. *New Theatre,* March 1937, p. 11.

CHAPTER ONE

1. The Rosenbach Museum & Library, Philadelphia.
2. Bram Stoker, *Dracula* (Oxford and New York: Oxford University Press, World's Classics paperback edition, 1983), p. 306.
3. Ernest Jones, *On the Nightmare* (New York: Liveright, 1951).
4. *Ibid.,* p. 84.
5. *Ibid.,* p. 117.
6. *Ibid.,* p. 127. "The incest complex, which underlies the Incubus belief, shows itself equally in the Vampire one . . . the whole superstition is shot through with the theme of guilt . . ."
7. Mario Praz, *The Romantic Agony* (London/New York/Toronto: Oxford University Press, 1933), p. 76.
8. *Ibid.*
9. Montague Summers, *The Vampire: His Kith and Kin* (Hyde Park, NY: University Books, 1960), p. 290.
10. *Ibid.* The spelling of the name varies among adaptations and translations and in accounts of the same—Ruthven, Ruthwen, Rutwen, etc.
11. *Ibid.,* p. 293–94.
12. *Ibid.,* p. 303.
13. *Ibid.,* p. 305.
14. Anne Rice, *The Vampire Lestat* (New York: Alfred A. Knopf, 1985).
15. Herbert Gorman, *The Incredible Marquis: Alexandre Dumas* (New York: Farrar & Rinehart, 1929), p. 71.
16. *Ibid.,* p. 78–80.
17. *Ibid.,* p. 356.
18. Summers, *op. cit.,* p. 807.
19. *Ibid.,* p. 311.
20. *Ibid.,* p. 313.
21. *Ibid.,* p. 314.
22. Bram Stoker, *Personal Reminiscences of Henry Irving,* in 2 vols. (New York: The Macmillan Company, 1906), vol. 1, p. 31.
23. *Ibid.*
24. Sheridan Le Fanu, "Carmilla," in Leslie Shepherd, ed., *The Dracula Book of Great Vampire Stories* (Seacaucus, N.J.: The Citadel Press, 1977), p. 36.

25. Bram Stoker's correspondence with Walt Whitman, quoted in Horace Traubel, *With Walt Whitman in Camden*, vol. 4 (Philadelphia: University of Pennsylvania Press, 1953), p. 181–85.

26. Stoker, *Personal Reminiscences*, vol. 2, pp. 96–108

27. Stoker, *Personal Reminiscences*, vol. 1, p. 31.

28. *Ibid.*

29. *Ibid*, p. 33.

30. Daniel Farson, *The Man Who Wrote Dracula* (New York: St. Martin's Press, 1975), p. 42.

31. Horace Wyndham, *The Nineteen Hundreds* (New York: Thomas Seltzer, 1923), p. 118–19.

32. Records of Henry Irving's 1893–94 American tour, manuscript collection of the Folger Shakespeare Library, Washington, D.C.

33. *Ibid.*, p. 117–18.

34. Farson, *op. cit.*, p. 87.

35. Bram Stoker, "The Dualitists; or, the Death Doom of the Double Born," *The Theatre Annual* (London: Carson and Comerford, 1887), p. 23–24.

36. *Ibid.*, p. 22.

37. *Ibid.*, p. 27.

38. Summers, *op. cit.*, p. 335.

39. Leonard Wolf, ed., *The Annotated Dracula* (New York: Ballantine Books, 1976), p. xvi–xvii.

40. *Ibid.*, p. 164.

41. Nina Auerbach, *Ellen Terry: Player in Her Time* (New York and London: W. W. Norton & Company, 1987), p. 199.

42. *Ibid.*, p. 200–01.

43. Stoker, *Personal Reminiscences*, vol. 1, p. 29–30.

44. Auerbach, *op. cit.*, p. 199.

45. *Ibid.*

46. Farson, *op. cit.*, p. 164–65.

47. Mark Muro, "Dusting off Dracula's Creator," *Boston Globe*, April 1, 1983.

48. Traubel, *op. cit.*, p. 183–84.

49. Clive Leatherdale, *Dracula: The Novel and the Legend* (Wellingborough, Northamptonshire: The Aquarian Press, 1985), p. 210–11. Leatherdale's book is one of the most intelligent and comprehensive surveys of the various critical approaches to *Dracula*.

50. Bram Dijkstra, *Idols of Perversity: Fantasies of Feminine Evil in Fin-de-Siècle Culture* (New York, Oxford: Oxford University Press, 1986), p. 343.

51. For an extended discussion of Pan's relation to demonic dreams, see Wilhgelm Heinrich Roscher and James Hillman, *Pan and the Nightmare* (Dallas: Spring Publications, Inc., 1988).

52. Peter Gay, *The Bourgeois Experience: Victoria to Freud, Vol. 1: Education of the Senses* (New York/Oxford: Oxford University Press, 1984), p. 169.

53. *Ibid.*, p. 197.

54. Acton, quoted by Gay, p. 153.

55. Steven Marcus, *The Other Victorians: A Study of Sexuality and Pornography in Mid-Nineteenth Century England* (New York: Basic Books, 1966), p. 28.

56. *Ibid.*, p. 27.

57. Dijkstra, *op. cit.*, p. 342.

58. Andrea Dworkin, *Intercourse* (New York: The Free Press, 1987), p. 119.

59. Nina Auerbach, *Woman and the Demon: The Life of a Victorian Myth* (Cambridge, MA, and London: Harvard University Press, 1982), p. 22, 24.

60. Gay, *op. cit.,* p. 212.

61. Wyndham, *op. cit.,* p. 119.

62. *Ibid.,* p. 213.

63. *Punch,* September 11, 1886, p. 126.

64. Farson, *op. cit.,* p. 213–14.

65. Phyllis A. Roth, *Bram Stoker* (Boston: Twayne Publishers, 1982), p. 127–28.

66. Stoker, *Dracula,* p. 53.

67. Christopher Craft, "Kiss Me with Those Red Lips: Gender and Inversion in *Dracula,*" *Representations* 8 (Fall 1984), p. 109–10.

68. *Ibid.,* p. 110.

69. Stoker, *Dracula,* p. 281–82.

70. *Ibid.,* p. 25.

71. Joseph S. Bierman, "Dracula: Prolonged Childhood Illness and the Oral Triad," *American Image,* vol. 29, no. 2 (Summer 1972), p. 186–98.

72. Rupert Hart-Davis, ed., *The Letters of Oscar Wilde* (New York: Harcourt, Brace & World, Inc., 1962), p. 24.

73. *Evening Telegraph,* undated clipping, Robinson Locke dramatic scrapbooks of Henry Irving, New York Public Library.

74. Rupert Hart-Davis, ed., *More Letters of Oscar Wilde* (New York: Vanguard Press, 1985), p. 75. The editor notes that the autographed book and accompanying letter fetched $8,500 at Christie's, New York, in 1984.

75. Emmanuel Cooper, *The Sexual Perspective: Homosexuality and Art in the Last 100 Years in the West* (London and New York: Routledge & Kegan Paul, 1986), p. 80.

76. Quoted by Farson, p. 209.

77. C. F. Bentley, "The Monster in the Bedroom: Sexual Symbolism in Bram Stoker's *Dracula,*" *Literature and Psychology,* vol. 22, no. 1 (1972), p. 33.

78. *Athanaeum,* No. 3635, June 26, 1897, p. 835.

79. Ellic Howe, *The Magicians of the Golden Dawn: A Documentary History of a Magical Order 1887–1923* (London: Routledge & Kegan Paul, 1972), p. 50.

80. *Ibid.,* p. 285; see also Farson, p. 207.

81. Cleveland Moffett, "How I Interviewed Irving," *The Theatre,* January 1, 1902.

82. Quoted by Farson, p. 223–24.

83. Carol F. Senf, *The Vampire in Nineteenth Century English Literature* (Bowling Green State University Popular Press, 1988), p. 67.

84. "Hommy," of course, sounds remarkably like an amalgam of "Tommy" and "Harry," the fast friends of "The Dualitists."

85. Hall Caine, "Bram Stoker: The Story of a Great Friendship," the *Telegraph,* April 24, 1912.

CHAPTER TWO

1. Thring to Stoker, April 27, 1922, Society of Authors Archives, British Library, London.

2. Eve Paul Margueritte to Society of Authors, June 30, 1933.

3. H. Montgomery Hyde, *Oscar Wilde* (New York: Da Capo, 1983), p. 136.

4. M. Bouvier and J.-L. Leutrat, *Nosferatu* (Paris: Cahiers du Cinema/Gallimard, 1981), p. 230.

5. *Ibid.,* p. 234.
6. *Ibid.,* p. 230.
7. Lotte H. Eisner, *Murnau* (Berkeley and Los Angeles: University of California Press, 1973), p. 109.
8. John D. Barlow, *German Expressionist Film* (Boston: Twayne Publishers, 1982), p. 15.
9. Lotte H. Eisner, *The Haunted Screen* (Berkeley and Los Angeles: University of California Press, 1973), p. 56–58.
10. *Ibid.,* p. 41.
11. Enno Patalas, "*Propos sur la reconstruction du Nosferatu,*" *La Cinémathèque Française* no. 15 (November 1986).
12. Berndt Heller, "*La musique de la 'fete de Nosferatu,'*" *La Cinémathèque Française* no. 15 (November 1986).
13. This scene is one of the first instances on record in which a vampire is actually destroyed by sunlight. Previously, vampires avoided sun and enjoyed their greatest powers at night. But even Stoker's Dracula stalked London at midday.
14. Bouvier and Leutrat, *op. cit.,* p. 26.
15. See Siegfried Kracauer, *From Caligari to Hitler: A Psychological History of the German Film* (Princeton: Princeton University Press, 1947).
16. Bouvier and Leutrat, *op. cit.,* p. 224.
17. Roger Dadoun, "Fetishism in the Horror Film," in James Donald, ed., *Fantasy and the Cinema* (London: British Film Institute, 1989), p. 55.
18. Stan Brakhage, "F. W. Murnau," *Film Biographies* (Berkeley: Turtle Island Press, 1977), p. 245–70.
19. Sylvain Exertier, "*La lettre oubliée de nosferatu,*" *Positif,* March 1980, p. 47–51.
20. Bouvier and Leutrat, *op. cit.,* p. 231.
21. Eisner, *Murnau,* p. 108.
22. Thring to Stoker, May 9, 1922.
23. Thring to Stoker, May 15, 1922.
24. Thring to Stoker, July 10, 1922.
25. Thring to Stoker, January 23, 1923.
26. Thring to Stoker, March 13, 1923.
27. Thring to Stoker, June 5, 1923.
28. Thring to Stoker, August 8, 1924.
29. Stoker to Thring, May 12, 1925.
30. Stoker to Thring, October 12, 1925.
31. Thring to Stoker, October 14, 1925.
32. Stoker to American Dramatists and Composers, October 12, 1925.
33. Montagu to Bang, October 10, 1925.
34. Bang to Stoker, October 15, 1925.
35. Bang to Stoker, October 20, 1925.
36. Thring to Stoker, January 6, 1926.

CHAPTER THREE

1. Harry Ludlam, *A Biography of Dracula: The Life Story of Bram Stoker* (London: Fireside Press/W. Foulsham & Co. Ltd., 1962), p. 154.
2. Correspondence, John L. Balderston to Harold Freedman, November 28, 1927.
3. Hamilton Deane, *Dracula* (London: Lord Chamberlain's Manuscript Collection, British Library).

4. Ivan Butler, interviewed by author, October 1989, London.

5. Deane, *op. cit.*

6. Interviewed by author, October 1989, London.

7. *The Times* (London), February 15, 1927.

8. Unidentified newspaper clipping, February 20, 1927, collection of the Theatre Museum, London.

9. *Evening Standard,* February 19, 1927.

10. Ludlam, *op. cit.,* p. 161–62.

11. *Ibid.,* p. 161.

12. Undated clipping, *Westminister Gazette,* Society of Authors Archives, British Library.

13. Thring to Stoker, June 11, 1928.

14. Charles Morrell, *Dracula* (London: Lord Chamberlain's Manuscript Collection, British Library).

15. Ludlam, *op. cit.,* p. 163.

16. Anonymous, burlesque version of *Dracula* in verse, performed at the New Recreation Hall, Penbeth, February 1930. (London: Lord Chamberlain's Manuscript Collection, British Library).

17. Unidentified clipping, December 10, 1927, Theatre Research Collection, New York Public Library.

18. *Ibid.*

19. Walker Gilmer, *Horace Liveright: Publisher of the Twenties* (New York: David Lewis, 1970), p. 154–55.

20. Balderston to Freedman, January 15, 1929: "She refused to have anything to do with him and said she didn't like him and would only deal with me . . ."

21. Draft contract between Florence Stoker and Horace Liveright, undated, Brandt and Brandt Dramatic Department, Inc., New York.

22. Deane, *op. cit.*

23. Hamilton Deane and John L. Balderston, *Dracula, the Vampire Play* (New York: Samuel French, Inc., 1933), p. 38.

24. Clipping, undated, in scrapbook of actor Dwight Frye.

25. Robert Cremer, *Lugosi: The Man Behind the Cape* (Chicago: Henry Regnery, 1977), p. 100–01.

26. Thring to Stoker, March 5, 1925.

27. Cremer, *op. cit.,* p. 101.

28. Cremer, *op. cit.,* p. 102.

29. *New York World,* October 6, 1927.

30. "A Mystery Play Took to the Road," *The New York Times,* March 2, 1930.

31. Memorandum, Freedman to Carl Brandt, December 8, 1927.

32. Balderston to Freedman, November 28, 1927.

33. Undated earnings sheet, Brandt and Brandt Dramatic Department, Inc., New York.

34. *Ibid.*

35. "Dracula Provides Thrilling Entertainment at Lobero," *Daily News,* Santa Barbara, CA, June 14, 1929.

36. Undated clipping, Philadelphia newspaper, 1930.

37. "A Mystery Play Took to the Road," *op. cit.*

38. Balderston to Freedman, January 8, 1929.

39. *To-Day's Cinema* (London), October 6, 1928.

CHAPTER FOUR

1. Stoker to Thring, December 16, 1928.
2. Thring to Stoker, December 17, 1928.
3. C. D. Medley to Thring, January 22, 1929.
4. Medley to Thring, February 7, 1929.
5. Stoker to Medley, February 21, 1929.
6. Medley to Thring, March 25, 1929.
7. Balderston to Louis Cline, December 27, 1928.
8. Dorothea Fassett to Carl Brandt, August 30, 1930.
9. Interviewed by author, October 1989, London.
10. Balderston to Freedman, November 6, 1928.
11. Balderston to Cline, December 27, 1928.
12. Balderston to Freedman, January 8, 1929.
13. Balderston to Freedman, January 15, 1929.
14. For a detailed photographic look at the Film Guild Cinema, see Lisa Phillips, *Frederick Kiesler* (New York: Whitney Museum of American Art in association with W. W. Norton & Company, New York, London, 1989.) pp. 16–18, 91, 144, 162.
15. Cline, memorandum to Horace Liveright, June 4, 1929.
16. *The New York Times,* June 4, 1929.
17. *Herald Tribune,* June 4, 1929.
18. *New York Post,* undated clipping, June 1929.
19. M. Bouvier and J.-L. Leutrat, *Nosferatu* (Paris: Cahiers du Cinema/Gallimard, 1981), p. 261.
20. Thring to Stoker, July 1, 1929.
21. Balderston to Stoker, December 16, 1929.
22. Balderston to Stoker, December 17, 1929.
23. Cline to Balderston, November 30, 1929.
24. Freedman to Balderston, January 31, 1930.
25. Fassett to Freedman, November 14, 1929.
26. Telegram, Fassett to Freedman, November 27, 1929.
27. Telegram, Fassett to Freedman, November 28, 1929.
28. Freedman to Balderston, January 31, 1930.
29. Freedman to Balderston, February 14, 1930.
30. Fassett to Freedman, March 4, 1930.
31. Thomas Schatz, *The Genius of the System: Hollywood Filmmaking in the Studio Era* (New York: Pantheon Books, 1988), p. 89.
32. Freedman to Balderston, August 13, 1930.
33. Freedman to Fassett, August 13, 1930.
34. Gladys Hall, "Uncle Carl and Junior Laemmle Have Made Movie History," *Motion Picture* magazine, undated clipping.
35. See Schatz for a positive revisionist assessment.
36. Freedman to Balderston, August 13, 1930.
37. Freedman to Balderston, August 5, 1930.
38. Freedman telegram to E. M. Asher, July 31, 1930.
39. Freedman to David C. Werner, August 15, 1930.

CHAPTER FIVE

1. Damon Runyon, "Damon Runyan Says" column, Rochester *Democrat-Chronicle,* December 13, 1938. Cited by Morrison Brown, *Louis Bromfield and His Books* (Fair Lawn, N.J.: Essential Books, Inc., 1957), p. 77.
2. David D. Anderson, *Louis Bromfield* (New York: Twayne Publishers, Inc., 1963), p. 12.
3. Thomas Schatz, *The Genius of the System: Hollywood Filmmaking in the Studio Era* (New York: Pantheon Books, 1988), p. 85–90.
4. *Screenland,* March 1931, p. 31.
5. Fred Pasley, "What a Life! Directing Freaks Is a Man's Job in the 'Talkies,'" *The Evening Bulletin* (Philadelphia), February 11, 1932, p. 16.
6. Philip J. Riley, *London After Midnight* (New York/London/Toronto: Cornwall Books, 1985), p. 28–29.
7. Freedman to Verne Porter, Universal Pictures, March 13, 1930.
8. Wood Soanes, "Jane Fooshee Will Open Special Fulton Season Following Lugosi Week," *Oakland Tribune,* July 6, 1930, p. 8. "As the vessel comes on to the rock-bound coast Dracula is at the wheel of the charnal vessel but the countryside had been aroused. The Britons are awaiting him, prepared to drive the stake through his heart. . . . Dracula runs the ship onto the rocks, wrecks it and turns himself into a wolf. As they shoot at him, he changes to a bat, flies away and escapes. It should make a most stirring picture." The interview suggests that Lugosi may have read other, speculative treatments of *Dracula,* perhaps in connection with his efforts to interest studios other than Universal.
9. Scott MacQueen, "Roland West," in Frank Thompson, ed., *Between Action and Cut* (Metuchen, N.J.: Scarecrow Press, 1985), p. 146.
10. *Life,* October 11, 1948.
11. Marguerite Tazelaar, "Film Personalities," *New York Herald Tribune,* April 2, 1933.
12. Ruth Rankin, "A Child of the Theater," *The New Movie Magazine,* January 1932, p. 109.
13. Lew Ayres, in conversation with Ronald V. Borst, 1988.
14. *New York Daily News,* October 17, 1930.
15. Gregory Mank, "David Manners: Surrendered Stardom for Privacy and Peace of Mind," *Films in Review* (December 1977), p. 599.
16. John Norris, unpublished interview with David Manners, 1975.
17. David Manners, correspondence with John Norris, 1972.
18. Philip J. Riley, ed., Universal Filmscripts Series: *Dracula* (Abescon, N.J.: Magic-image Filmbooks, 1990).
19. Arthur Lennig, *The Count: The Life and Times of Bela "Dracula" Lugosi* (New York: G. P. Putnam's Sons, 1974), p. 100.
20. John Norris, unpublished interview with David Manners, 1974.
21. Bela Lugosi, quoted in Tom Hutchinson and Roy Pickard, *Horrors: A History of Horror Movies* (Seacaucus, N.J.: Chartwell Books, 1984), p. 15–16.
22. Schatz, *op. cit.,* p. 90.
23. *San Francisco Chronicle,* September 11, 1927.
24. Raymond Lee, "Hollywood in Miniature," *Classic Film Collector* (Fall 1972), p. 53.
25. Gregory William Mank, *It's Alive!: The Classic Cinema Sage of Frankenstein* (San Diego and New York: A.S. Barnes & Company, Inc., 1981), p. 14.
26. Norris, *op. cit.,* 1974.
27. *Ibid.*

28. William H. Rosar, "Music for the Monsters: Universal Pictures' Horror Film Scores of the Thirties," *The Quarterly Journal of the Library of Congress,* Fall 1983, p. 393.

29. Hamilton Deane and John L. Balderston, *Dracula, the Vampire Play* (New York: Samuel French, Inc., 1933), p. 74. The epilogue was cut from the film after its first release, and its negative was in such poor condition that it was deemed impossible to resurrect for MCA's videodisc restoration of the film. For frame enlargements of this rare footage, see the May 1988 issue of *American Cinematographer.*

30. George Turner, "The Two Faces of *Dracula,*" *American Cinematographer,* vol. 69, no. 5 (May 1988), p. 37.

31. Marcella Burke, "Hollywood's Youngest Genius," *Hollywood Magazine* (undated, circa 1932), p. 62.

32. Schatz, *op. cit.,* p. 90.

33.. Riley, *op. cit.,* p. 72.

34. *Hollywood Filmograph,* April 4, 1931.

35. March 11, 1931.

36. *Ibid.*

37. Rosar, *op. cit.*

38. Gregory Mank, *Karloff and Lugosi* (Jefferson, N.C.: McFarland & Company, 1990), p. 15.

39. *Los Angeles Times,* March 30, 1931.

40. Contract between Stoker, Deane, Balderston, and Alfred Wallerstein, October 7, 1931.

41. From documents submitted as evidence in the antitrust case *U.S. v. 20th Century Fox Film Corporation,* December 5, 1955.

42.. Riley, *op. cit.*

CHAPTER SIX

1. Lupita Tovar, interviewed by author, April 1989, Los Angeles.

2. Frederick Kohner, *The Magician of Sunset Boulevard: The Improbable Life of Paul Kohner, Hollywood Agent* (Palos Verdes, CA: Morgan Press, 1977), p. 54.

3. Director Gregory La Cava, quoted in Neal Gabler, *An Empire of Their Own: How the Jews Invented Hollywood* (New York: Crown Publishers, Inc., 1988), p. 75.

4. Kohner, *op. cit.,* p. 56.

5. Thomas Schatz, *The Genius of the System: Hollywood Filmmaking in the Studio Era* (New York: Pantheon Books, 1988), p. 87.

6. Lupita Tovar, *op. cit.*

7. Bram Stoker, *Dracula* (Oxford and New York: Oxford University Press, World's Classics paperback edition, 1983), p. 37.

8. *El Universal* (Mexico City), April 9, 1931, p. 6.

9. *Excelsior* (Mexico City), April 4, 1931, p. 9.

CHAPTER SEVEN

1. Daniel Farson, correspondence with author, September 1989.

2. Vincent Price, correspondence with author, October 1989.

3. *California Reporter,* Sup. 160 (*Lugosi v. Universal Pictures*), p. 325.

4. Harry Ludlam, *A Biography of Dracula: The Life Story of Bram Stoker* (London: The Fireside Press, 1962), p. 135–36.

5. Walker Gilmer, *Horace Liveright: Publisher of the Twenties* (New York: David Lewis, 1970), p. 236.
6. Nancy North Vine, "Cute," *The New Movie Magazine,* January 1932, p. 62.
7. *The New York Times,* January 25, 1940.
8. *The New York Times,* November 10, 1950.
9. Dwight D. Frye, interviewed by author, August 1989.
10. Donald F. Glut, *The Frankenstein Legend* (Metuchen, N.J.: The Scarecrow Press, Inc., 1973), p. 45.
11. Balderston to Freedman, March 31, 1944.
12. Thomas Schatz, *The Genius of the System: Hollywood Filmmaking in the Studio Era* (New York: Pantheon Books, 1988), p. 97.
13. Neal Gabler, *An Empire of Their Own: How the Jews Invented Hollywood* (New York: Crown Publishers, Inc., 1988), p. 418.
14. Gregory Mank, *It's Alive!,* p. 167.
15. Philip J. Riley, *London After Midnight* (New York/London/Toronto: Cornwall Books, 1985), p. 29.
16. Bram Stoker, *Dracula* (Oxford and New York: Oxford University Press, World's Classics paperback edition, 1983), p. 51.
17. Arthur Lennig, *The Count: The Life and Films of Bela "Dracula" Lugosi* (New York: G. P. Putnam's Sons, 1974), p. 317.
18. A term coined by Thomas Hine for his book *Populuxe* (New York: Alfred A. Knopf, 1986), a study of American culture in the 1950s and early 60s.
19. Ira Mothner, "Those Clean-Living All American Monsters," *Look,* September 8, 1964, p. 50.
20. *Lugosi v. Universal Pictures,* plaintiff's replies to defendant's interrogatories, Los Angeles County Superior Court, July 19, 1971.
21. *Ibid.,* plaintiff's complaint for declatory relief, etc., February 3, 1966.
22. *Ibid.,* court transcript, p. 155–85; see also plaintiff's petition for hearing before the California Supreme Court, p. 11.
23. *California Reporter, op. cit.*
24. Employment contract between Universal Pictures and Bela Lugosi, September 11, 1930.
25. Hon. Bernard S. Jefferson, memorandum opinion, January 31, 1972, p. 7.
26. *Ibid.*
27. *Ibid.,* p. 24.
28. *Ibid.*
29. Appellant's reply brief, Court of Appeals, Second Appellate District, State of California, January 24, 1977, p. 8.
30. District court of appeals opinion, p. 12.
31. Plaintiff's petition, p. 4.
32. *Ibid.,* p. 5.
33. *Ibid.,* p. 24.
34. *California Reporter, op. cit.,* p. 326.
35. *Ibid.,* p. 329.
36. *Ibid.,* p. 330.
37. *Ibid.,* p. 331.
38. *Ibid.*
39. *Ibid.,* p. 335.
40. *Ibid.,* p. 336.
41. *Ibid.,* p. 345, note 33.

42. Hamilton Deane and John L. Balderston, *Dracula, the Vampire Play* (New York: Samuel French, Inc., 1933), p. 69.

43. Stoker, *Dracula,* p. 306.

44. Katherine Ramsland, "Hunger for the Marvelous: The Vampire Craze in the Computer Age," *Psychology Today* (November 1989), p. 35.

45. *The Cable Guide,* January 1990.

46. Ronald Christ, "Interview with Manuel Puig," *Christopher Street,* April 1979, p. 26.

47. Bram Stoker, *The Jewel of Seven Stars* (New York: Carroll & Graf Publishers, Inc., 1989 reprint), p. 10.

ACKNOWLEDGEMENTS

◆

Grateful acknowledgment is made to the many people and institutions who shared their collections, memories, and special expertise during the lengthy period of research for this book.

First and foremost, thanks are due my agent, Malaga Baldi, and my editor at Norton, Hilary Hinzmann, without whose determination and enthusiasm this volume would never have been realized. I made several new friends during the course of the project, including film historian Scott MacQueen, who offered me his moral support, criticism, and prodigious knowledge of Hollywood history on an almost daily basis; Ronald V. Borst, who allowed me privileged access to one of the most extraordinary private collections of fantasy film memorabilia in existence; and Philip J. Riley, whose indefatigable work in documenting the history of horror films has produced the Universal Filmscripts Series of classic screenplays; readers should find his own recent and very different study of *Dracula* utilizing unpublished studio files a fascinating and essential complement to *Hollywood Gothic*. I wish to express my gratitude also to Ron and Howard Mandelbaum of Photofest for their tireless assistance in locating the many vintage publicity photos used as illustrations, and to the memory or their late partner Carlos Clarens, from whose extensive collection many of the best images were drawn.

Primary among research collections, I wish to thank the British Library Department of Manuscripts for granting me access to its Society of Authors Archives and the Lord Chamberlain's Manuscript Collection. Its staff was most helpful, both during preliminary transatlantic correspondence and during my stay in London.

· Invaluable research assistance was provided by John Balderston and Ann Burton, heirs to the Deane and Balderston estates, who granted me access to agency files on the original stage and film negotiations. A special thank-you is due Robert A. Freedman, who shared mementos and memories of his father, the legendary literary agent Harold Freedman.

The two most memorable interviews of this project were the wonderful afternoons I spent in 1989 with Raymond Huntley, who originated the role of Dracula in the 1927 London production, and with Lupita Tovar, who starred in Universal's 1931 Spanish-language version. Tovar's son, the producer Pancho Kohner, graciously made available for study his family's private print of the film. Although he died shortly before I began work on this book, Paul Kohner's legendary energy and enthusiasm as both the producer of the Spanish *Dracula* and later as an international film agent whose career encompassed virtually the entire history of motion pictures, was a source of fascination and inspiration.

Major research facilities and sources consulted included the New York Public Library's many divisions, especially the Billy Rose Theatre Collection at Lincoln Center; the Library of Congress, the British Film Institute, the Royal Academy of Arts, the Victoria and Albert Museum, the Cinémathèque Française, the Museum of Modern Art, the Elmer Holmes Bobst Library at New York University, the Free Library of Philadelphia's Theatre Collection, the Academy of Motion Picture Arts and Sciences Library, the Rosenbach Museum & Library, the University of Southern California Performing Arts Library, the New York State Archives, the Hampden-Booth Memorial Library, the Folger Shakespeare Library, the Harvard Theatre Collection, the Cinemateca de Cuba, Anthology Film Archives, the Theatre Museum, the Raymond Mander and Joe Mitchenson Theatre Collection, the New York University School of Law Library, the Huntington Library, the San Francisco Museum of Performing Arts, the Lobero Theatre Foundation, the Harry Ransom Humanities Research Center, the Watson Library of the Metropolitan Museum of Art, and the American Film Institute.

I am most grateful to the U.S. Treasury Department for extending me a visa to visit Havana in order to study the only complete print of the Spanish *Dracula* in existence, and to Hector Garcia Mesa and Maria Eulalia Douglas of the Cinemateca de Cuba, who extended every courtesy in my documentation of this fascinating, forgotten film. Thanks are owed to Bob Guild of Marazul Tours, who made my Cuban travel arrangements as painless as possible. International thanks are also due to John Mraz, who conducted extensive archival research in Mexico City.

Special thanks are due Bernard Davies and Robert James Leake of the Dracula Society, London, and Jeanne Youngson of the Count Dracula Fan Club, New York, for making available some of the rarest visual documents in this book. Individuals who extended courtesies, photographs, memories, and who generally shared their enthusiasm include Richard Bojarski, Carroll Borland, Julianne Burton, Ivan Butler, Dr. Jose M. Caparrós-Lera, Stephen Cloud, John Cocchi, Ned Comstock, Mary Corliss, Samuel R. Crowl, William Cumiford, James Curtis, Bob Dahdah, Ian Dejardin, Norine Dresser, Geraldine Duclow, the estate of Kenn Duncan, William K. Everson, Daniel Farson, Todd Feiertag, Laurence Fitch, Jan Frazier, Dwight D. Frye, Barbara R. Geisler, Walker Gilmer, David O. Glazer, Richard Haigh, Eric Held, Irene Heymann, William Horrigan, Michael Isador, Susan Jenkins, the late Stephen Jochsberger, Mrs. Frederick Kiesler, James Kotsilibas-Davis, Richard Koszarski, Miles Kruger, Carla Laemmle, Emily Laskin, Arthur Lennig, Elizabeth A. LeServiget, Julian Bud Lesser, Bill Littman, Greg Lukow, John

McLaughlin, Ken Mandelbaum, Elizabeth Ireland McCann, Gary Miller, Norman Miller, Leslie A. Morris, Mrs. J. William Morrison, Glenn Myrent, Donna Nardo, Susan Naulty, Jeanne T. Newlin, John Norris, William G. Obbagy, Jerry Ohlinger, Bill Pence, David Pierce, Vincent Price, Harold Reeves, Robert J. Reicher, Laura Ross, Andrew Sarris, Eli Savada, Misha Schutt, Carlton Sedgeley, Nicholas Scheetz, Anne Schlosser, Rose Schwartz, Nadia Shtendera, Elliott Stein, Patrick Stoker, George Stover, Elaine Stritch, Gary Svehda, George Turner, Lisa Tuttle, Marc Wanamaker, Tom Weaver, Patricia Wilks-Battle, and Lee Wise.

Additional thanks to Donal F. Holway, Gerry Goodstein and Steven Speliotis for their photographic expertise, advice, and assistance, to Arthur J. Walsh for working miracles with an airbrush; to Joe Marc Freedman of Sarabande Press and Dan Solo of Solotype for superb typesetting; to Heriberto Quinones, Loraine Machlin, Jason Cunliffe and Arlene Lee for production; Lisa Pliscou for perceptive copyediting and editorial suggestions; and to Sandra Skal-Gerlock and Kimberly Fronek who provided invaluable assistance in duplicating court records in Los Angeles.

A special credit is due Forrest J. Ackerman, whom I have never met in my adult life, but whose magazine *Famous Monsters of Filmland* and its April 1963 feature story on *Dracula* was an undeniable inspiration for the book you hold today.

And a final acknowledgment should go to my parents, Mr. and Mrs. John Skal, who initially disapproved of my interest in horror movies, but who eventually came to see things my way.

INDEX

Dr. Jeanne Youngson, president of the Count Dracula Fan Club, on a pilgrimage to the grave of Bela Lugosi. (Courtesy of Jeanne Youngson)